ZOLA

Also by Harry Harris

Ruud Gullit – The Chelsea Diary
Ruud Gullit – Portrait of a Genius
Glenn Hoddle's Autobiography Spurred to Success
Terry Venables' The Inside Story

ZOLA

The Thrilling Inside Story of Football's Numero Uno

HARRY HARRIS

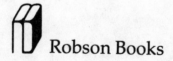 Robson Books

First published in Great Britain in 1998 by Robson Books Ltd,
Bolsover House, 5–6 Clipstone Street, London W1P 8LE

British Library Cataloguing in Publication Data
A catalogue record for this title is available from the British Library

ISBN 1 86105 169 7

Set in Times by Derek Doyle & Associates, Mold, Flintshire, North
Wales.
Printed in Great Britain by Butler & Tanner Ltd, London and
Frome.

To Linda,
a true Blue

Contents

Acknowledgements

My thanks go to Chelsea chairman Ken Bates, chief executive Colin Hutchinson, former player-manager Ruud Gullit and of course to Franco Zola himself for the insights into his career at Stamford Bridge.

My gratitude goes to the following for the exceptional catalogue of photographs:

Giancarlo Galavotti for the early Zola pictures from the *Gazzetta dello Sport*'s library in Italy.

Gerrard Farrell, the only man to get aboard the celebration bus after the FA Cup triumph and for his portfolio of Zola pictures throughout the season.

A long time friend and colleague Tommy Hindley of Professional Sport International for his portfolio of pictures of the Zola family at home in Parma.

Kelly Murphy in Tesco's press office for the Zola pizza pictures. The Carling Premiership sponsorship press office for use of the pictures when Zola won the Player of the Month award.

The use of excellent photographs from the *Mirror* Syndication Department, where Phil Le Blanc provided expert photo selection.

Special thanks to Dennis Signy, the doyen of football writers, for his insights into Zola's Footballer of the Year award and for extracts from his book with Norman Giller celebrating the fifty years of the award.

Of course, I'd like to thank Kate, Charlotte and Jeremy at Robson Books.

Introduction

Trust the irascible Chelsea chairman Ken Bates to come up with an original: 'If Zola played cricket, England would win the Ashes.'

The white-bearded emperor of the Bridge made one of his usual irreverent remarks as he took immense personal pleasure in detailing how he anticipated selling £1 million worth of new blue Autoglass Zola shirts. As the Chelsea Megastore ran out of Zs just a few weeks after opening its doors and had to send out urgently for more, it was anticipated that the club would sell 40,000 shirts in the first season, worth almost £1.5 million – and at least 14,000 would be with the name of Zola on the back. Zola might even eventually outstrip the number of Eric Cantona shirts sold by Manchester United when the Frenchman was their inspirational talisman. With Cantona gone, Zola was becoming the fastest-selling commercial property in football. Bates told me that the Zola shirt would be at least as popular as Cantona's, saying: 'It would appear so, the rate they are selling at the moment.' Within just three weeks of opening the store, the club had sold 14,000 shirts, 4,000 of which carried Zola's name.

Bates had waited patiently and frustratedly for fifteen years, ever since he bought the club in 1982 for £1, for the moment of FA Cup triumph at Wembley. The decision to appoint play-manager Ruud Gullit as Glenn Hoddle's successor, and Gullit's subsequent decision to recruit Gianfranco Zola to the Bridge, had been the catalyst for the Cup triumph and laid foundations for Chelsea to be considered realistic championship challengers.

Not satisfied with the success of his Italian imports – Zola and Roberto Di Matteo, at least – Gullit remained one of the country's

biggest importers of overseas stars. Five of his six close-season signings were from abroad, as Chelsea prepared for their assault on the
title, and a European campaign in the Cup-Winners' Cup. The ever-
multiplying expectancy levels meant that money was pouring into
Stamford Bridge, which was undergoing an incredible transformation
both on and off the pitch.

Bates's brainchild, the club Megastore, is, as he proudly boasted,
'twice the size of the one at Old Trafford'. In its first ten days of business, Chelsea took an astonishing £500,000. At that rate it would take
well over £10 million in its first season.

And of course, little Zola shirts are the biggest seller.

Zola had been instantly elevated to every Chelsea fan's all-time
'Dream Team' – Gullit's included. Finally, the names from the glory
days of the seventies were fading from the supporters' memories.
Now there were new trendsetters, and in most Chelsea fans' eyes, a
superior version.

Chelsea were threatening to climb the Premier League table in
terms of income, second only to Manchester United, and Bates knew
what that commercial revenue would bring: more investment in players to go along with the £65 million spent redeveloping the stadium
and its adjacent block of flats and hotel.

Bates used to be King of the Bridge. Now, with his office oversee-
ing the stadium development and a new media set-up, he would soon
be Emperor Bates, installed in his penthouse flat, worth £770,000,
high above the Bridge.

The Chelsea Website, Chelsea Radio, an internal TV station, a
glossy club magazine, newspaper, and their own travel agency . . .
Bates had even bought the prototype and oldest soccer magazine,
Football Monthly. A media empire was taking shape alongside the
magnificent development at the old Shed End.

Where once there was a breeding ground for the National Front,
there was now a team of foreign superstars led by English football's
lone black boss, with a team inspired by the mesmerizing skills of an
Italian striker who was once the understudy to Diego Maradona.

Tony Banks suggested that English-based foreign stars, such as
Zola, ought to qualify to play for England. The Chelsea-loving Minister
of Sport's idea was given short shrift, but those who witnessed the

magical skills of Zola knew what he meant. Banks, as a regular at the Bridge, marvelled at the contribution of players like Zola to the club landing their first major trophy for more than a quarter of a century.

Such was Zola's impact in English football that Tesco's marketed a pizza dedicated to his name, and the popular Chelsea star was enjoying his renaissance in English football to such a degree that he was considering opening a restaurant – Italian, of course.

Not that he didn't get good pasta at Sainsbury's, where his wife shops, but there were few places offering his favourite local Sardinian food, apart from the one in the Old Fulham Road. He longed for the authentic cuisine of his home town, and would import the right chef for the job.

So the new football season kicked off in the kitchen, with the launch of the pizza named after Zola. He unveiled it at a football skills event for local youngsters in Hammersmith, west London. Zola's Italian Pizza was available at Tesco's during August before being distributed more widely to other supermarkets. It came in two varieties, a ham and pepperoni and traditional margarita (cheese and tomato). As Zola smiled enchantingly as ever for the cameras to record the event, he said: 'I really enjoy playing football in England but I must admit I miss a real Italian pizza, so I have created my own. It's just the job for any budding footballers. Pizza is a good meal for sportsmen. I don't want to offend English pizza, but I was in a restaurant the other day and, well, let's say it's just not the same. I loved my four years playing in Naples – that's where pizza was born. So I decided to make my own here. My favourite is the traditional margarita. I love these pizzas; I hope you do, too.'

A group of six fifteen-year-olds from the Chelsea FC Community Scheme, who turned out to have their football skills judged by their hero, certainly seemed to endorse his pizzas. Ten-year-old Ebony Browne, from Putney, said with her mouth full: 'It's really good – honest.' Andrew Palmer of Bourne, Lincolnshire, said: 'I liked it, too.' Tamara Brown, also ten, of Putney, agreed: 'It's excellent.' Wonderful public relations – and the picture of Zola dressed as a chef had the desired effect; acres of space on the back pages.

The off-the-field spin-offs were the result of the tiniest player in the Premiership, with the broadest smile, having made perhaps the biggest impact of all time in the shortest number of games.

Zola was crowned with the most prestigious individual award in English football after just twenty-nine appearances in his first season. He was the Football Writers' Association's fiftieth Player of the Year, attracting the vast majority of the votes from the country's 200-plus soccer writers.

My vote included.

I voted for Zola because of his marvellous goals and wonderful skills, coupled with his refreshingly humble attitude to life: no super-star primadonna ego, just a disarmingly warm smile. When I saw him at the training ground mixing with his young fans, signing virtually every autograph and still maintaining that little-boy smile, it was the clincher. He fulfilled all the original criteria of the oldest individual football award – dignity, sportsmanship and extraordinary talent.

His reaction to the award was typical of the man: 'It's a great pleasure, it's a triumph, it's wonderful news. In Italy there is nothing like this. It's unbelievable that I've managed to win it in so few months.'

When asked whether he had expected to be Footballer of the Year, Zola said: 'Honestly, I did not. There must have been an attack of collective folly!' His Italian way of joking that they must have been mad to have voted for him. He added, more seriously: 'The fact that I win in a league with so many excellent players is a great compliment and makes this award even more worthy. To have come out on top of so many stars ... let's not forget Alan Shearer came third in the Golden Ball [the World Footballer of the Year award].'

Zola became the first Italian and the first ever Chelsea player to become Footballer of the Year. The first recipient of the oldest such award, Sir Stanley Matthews, presented it to him, with his father Ignazio present at the glittering evening at the Royal Lancaster Hotel two days before the FA Cup Final.

History was rewritten at a muggy Wembley on 17 May 1997 with Zola playing a pivotal role.

Gullit, the first foreign coach to reach the FA Cup Final, master-minded a Chelsea victory to claim the most traditional of English trophies, on the day sixteen foreigners paraded their talents in the showpiece game. Zola, Di Matteo and Gianluca Vialli became the first Italians to win FA Cup medals.

Mark Hughes became the first player this century to win four FA Cup winner's medals, and the fastest Wembley Cup Final goal by Roberto Di Matteo came after just 42.4 seconds.

Chelsea's first major trophy for more than a quarter of a century was achieved by a man in only his first season in management. In his first six months in charge, Gullit bought and sold twelve players for a transfer turnover of more than £18 million. He imported Vialli, Zola, Di Matteo and Frank Leboeuf for a cost of £12 million and sold off old favourites like John Spencer, Terry Phelan and Gavin Peacock. Ruthless Ruud also sold Paul Furlong and youngsters like Anthony Barness and Muzzy Izzett, with Mark Stein and David Rocastle loaned out. The reconstruction on the field went apace with the hotel, flats and new stands off it. More arrivals and departures were planned the following season as the Chelsea quest for silverware did not end with the FA Cup; it was just the platform to launch the club towards becoming a European superpower, with the Champions' League Gullit's long-term goal – the cup 'with the big ears', as he put it, was his ultimate prize.

Zola, Gullit's best purchase, fulfilled his destiny on Cup Final day, returning to Wembley, after scoring the winner there for Italy against England, to guide Chelsea to the trophy. It was the climax of a whirlwind start to his Stamford Bridge career, but Zola felt settled and very much at home, with his Italian pals as neighbours and Harrods and Harvey Nichols, his wife's favourite shops, close by.

The FA Cup adventure all began when Zola and Hughes chalked up the goals as West Brom were put to the sword in the third round 3–0; then it was the most memorable game of all, the 4–2 win over Liverpool, followed by the controversy against Leicester, the testing quarter-final in the fog at Portsmouth, the semi-final tussle with Wimbledon at Highbury and finally Middlesbrough at Wembley. The final itself was the customary let-down, hardly fulfilling its billing and virtually over before it had hardly begun when Di Matteo's thirty-yard dipper beat Ben Roberts. It was a long wait until one of the few home-grown talents on view, Eddie Newton, sealed matters with a late goal courtesy of a wonderful back-flick by Zola.

Reflecting on Chelsea's epic cup run, the Liverpool encounter will always be the highlight. Gullit outwitted them at their own game of possession football. Two-down at half time, Chelsea brought on Hughes to overwhelm Liverpool by playing all three attacking players – Zola, Vialli, and Hughes – for the first time. It was a devastating second-half transformation, Liverpool losing a two-goal lead for the first time in thirty-three years.

It could not have been achieved without hugely talented players. Gullit said midway through the season: 'We now have the players that the fans want to see, and more and more people want to buy season tickets. At our away games as well, supporters are piling in to see us play football. Then, as the new stand goes up, companies want to be involved and there is a waiting list for that as well. I want to know how the club is developing as a whole. I have no practical involvement on the business side, but we just like to keep in touch.'

A formidable triumph at Manchester United at the start of November failed to disguise the boardroom rumblings of the time that were eventually sorted out. But all the question marks over the future of the club after Matthew Harding's death were answered by the signing of Zola.

When Zola arrived, the club had to hurriedly find a shirt small enough for his debut! The Little Italian, though, could not have been happier: 'Ruud has given me the opportunity to complete my football life. All players should go abroad to complete their football education. It's a united Europe, so Englishmen should try for Italy, Germany or Spain. Don't be afraid to try something new. But some things are the same – the jokers. Here, it is Gianluca Vialli, and I thank Roberto Di Matteo for the best advice anyone has given me in England. He said: "Always taste your coffee carefully; you never know if Vialli has put salt in it." That's the sort of problem I have!'

Zola had become unsettled at his previous club Parma, in conflict with coach Carlo Ancelotti who played him out of position. When Chelsea had first enquired about Zola, they were quoted £10 million. He turned out to be the bargain of the season at £4.5 million.

On his home debut against Newcastle, a trademark Zola free-kick ended up in the back of the net, but Vialli claimed the goal, having got what could only have been the faintest of touches with his head. Did it come off one of his hairs? How could it? He's bald! But Zola said: 'It doesn't matter, he can have it. The important thing is for the team to score.'

Zola built his reputation at Napoli alongside Diego Maradona: 'I had the possibility to see the best football player in the world. I improved. I was young. I wanted to learn. He was important, very, very strong. In my first year we won the championship. Napoli was a big team in Europe, not only in Italy.' From 1989 to 1991, Zola played in the same team as the now disgraced Argentinian and led the southern side to the 1990 title. A year later, when Maradona left, Zola flourished in his own right as the wearer of the No. 10 shirt.

Financial difficulties, debts, and allegations of corruption forced Napoli to sell their best players, and Zola was off loaded to Parma in 1993, joining a team that had forced its way up from the Italian Third Division. In his first season, Parma lost the European Cup-Winners' Cup Final to Arsenal: 'We were favourites, but we didn't play good, so we lose.' The following year, with Faustino Asprilla and Tomas Brolin alongside him, Parma won the UEFA Cup – against Vialli and Juventus: 'We won in Parma one-zero, and it was 1–1 in Milan – there were problems with Juventus in their stadium, so we played there. Vialli scored, a very, very good goal in the top corner. Then Dino Baggio scored for us.'

Zola was sent off in the 1994 World Cup against Nigeria just minutes after coming on as a substitute; it was the beginning and end of his tournament. But he recovered to establish his place in the national team and such was his form that Roberto Baggio, the star of World Cup '94, was often overlooked as Zola became the team's most creative influence.

Zola, who played alongside Vialli in his first international, came to the Bridge with twenty-six caps, still a regular in the side despite nursing bitter memories of his penalty miss against Germany that sent the Italians home early from Euro 96: 'It was a bad experience. But I don't think of it anymore. If needed, I kick the penalty for Chelsea. I don't have problems.'

He arrived in England with his wife Franca, five-year-old son Andrea and daughter Martina, aged four. Gianfranco spoke only a little English, but there were always Italian journalists on hand to help. 'I am lucky to be able to complete my education here, both as a footballer and a person. My family have the chance to learn new things. When our English is better, we can't wait to try out all the cinemas and theatres.' He took his English lessons seriously, and even strolled around the Bridge with the largest dictionary under his arm, intent on mastering the language, with the club's interpreter never far behind.

The Italian connection brought a new dimension to the fan-base of Chelsea Football Club. Jason West, director of the Leicester Square School of English, pointed out: 'Many of our students are asking me to arrange trips to Chelsea. It's definitely the club they're all interested in.'

Language problems in team talks? Not at all. Gullit had always kept them to the point, upbeat, eminently sensible and, most of all, simple. Captain Dennis Wise explained: 'First, you have to point out that he is always very relaxed. That is his nature. He just says, "This is the way they play and this is the way we play . . . let's make lots of good passes and score lots of good goals, enjoy having the ball." He tells us who is marking who and puts the responsibility very much on the individual. He says if we don't do our job then we are letting the others down in the team. "We are one, we are a team," is one of his favourite expressions.'

One of England's finest ever imported players, Ossie Ardiles, who arrived from Argentina in 1978 and still has a home north of London, told me: 'I think coming to London is a big advantage for Gullit and his Italian signings. It is a big, big difference living in the capital than living in the north of England. There was a big Argentinian community in London that helped me to settle, and there is similarly a large Brazilian and Italian community in the capital. Klinsmann is the ultimate professional and when I signed him he would have been okay irrespective of where he lived. But London, and the Chelsea area in particular, is definitely more conducive to keeping star overseas players happy. If Juninho was in London, it would be different. Middlesbrough! Well, that's different.

'Would you want to live in Middlesbrough?'

Another big advantage for Chelsea's foreign stars was that Gullit, a world renowned traveller, had experienced the same settling-in difficulties himself. And few people in world football were better equipped in handling big-name stars than the Dutchman.

That was true on the pitch as well as off it. Gullit explained: 'It is to do with controlling games our way and letting the players play without feeling too inhibited. Most of the time now during games we are in control. That is a big difference between now and when I joined. Although we will always make mistakes, we have the confidence to continue. We are building towards something better, and part of that building process inevitably involves losing matches along the way – and part of what I then have to do is raise the team up and boost them when they are deflated. The next step is to eliminate the results that cause teams to dip in confidence and form, and always build up self-belief.

'Something else I do is build up trust with my players. A player must feel that he is allowed to try to do things on the park. If he makes mistakes, he needs to know I won't be harsh on him. If he makes those same mistakes over and over again, then I take a different attitude, but he must know it is okay to get it wrong when he tries something new. Now I am the boss I have to give advice, and I want to help with my experience to make the lads improve. We often need to react to situations on the pitch during a game, but when they come in at half-time I tell them that things are going exactly as we predicted. When we realise at the end of a game that it worked out how we thought, then that gives the players a real boost. The lads like it when tactics and the game all work out in our favour, and they respond to that.'

Zola became an instant hit with the fans. Even when he scored a stunning winning goal for Italy in the vital World Cup tie at Wembley and attracted a few boos in his next couple of games from rival fans, he never lost his popularity with the Chelsea faithful. And his spectacular goals that earned him a Carling Player of the Month award, two Goals of the Month on BBC TV and endless column inches of praise finally led to him receiving the coveted Footballer of the Year award, a memory he will carry with him forever.

Zola was truly moved by the 'fair play' nature of English football and his new adopted home.

When asked for the best moment he would treasure from his first season in the Premiership, he said thoughtfully: 'Actually, there are two. One was to score against England at Wembley, and isn't it wonderful that they voted for me in spite of that. The second, without any question, was my goal against Liverpool which steered Chelsea to the FA Cup Final.'

Chelsea's trio of Italian internationals became known as 'The Three Englishmen' back in Italy because they were thought to have developed an even greater steel in their play as a result of participating in the more rugged world of the Premiership. Zola said: 'Yes, but it's not so much a matter of commitment, because every player is committed when he plays for his country. But what I have got from playing in England is a healthy mental preparation which makes us get onto the pitch in the best frame of mind. So, when you play like that, you can really express your potential to its best. So, playing in England has given me total freedom of mind to express my best football.'

Zola already had a reputation as a world-class striker before his surprise move from Parma. His arrival was the catalyst for a new, lethal partnership with Mark Hughes, coinciding with the Welshman's upward curve in form. Zola, too, managed to rise another notch, something he hadn't thought possible moving from the more sophisticated *Serie A* to a league with a reputation for being more brutal than beautiful. Now he had a vastly different perception of life in the Premiership. He said: 'This experience has given me a lot and helped me to improve a lot, most of all because of the attitude, the maturity that I've acquired and the ability to go into a football match in perfect tranquillity. Since I've come to England, I've got this perfect feeling with English football, the fans, London and the press – even if they've just written that I'll be leaving Chelsea!' While in Naples on Italian World Cup duty, Zola had talked affectionately about the team where he built his reputation in the same side as Diego Maradona. But with only one year gone of a four-year contract, Zola was committed to Chelsea and, unlike Fabrizio Ravanelli, was not looking to the skies and an Alitalia flight back to Italy.

Zola had not only been sensational on the pitch, he'd also been the perfect ambassador for Italy off it; open, approachable and honest. He played a hectic schedule of games, carrying injuries without complaint or loss of form, while others whinged about virtually everything they found in English football (no prizes for guessing who).

The more success Gullit could bring to the Bridge, the greater the chances were of attracting more of the world's best. Gullit said: 'It's now very easy for us to get these sort of players and attract them. World-class players want to be a part of Chelsea. They like what we're doing here and enjoy themselves. That's something I've always wanted to create here, and by changing a few things, we are now more professional in every department. We have our own doctor and our own surgeon and well-organized travel arrangements. That's what I was used to and I've never been more content. I want us to feel we are one of the big clubs and to think like one. I don't know how far down the road we are to getting there, but we will see. Life's an adventure and you have to see what brings you joy. This job does, and gives me great pleasure. It makes you find out your limits and what you can achieve. So here we just take it week by week and see what happens. But I have ambitions for myself, and want to win things to be really happy.'

The debate raged about the virtues of bringing in such large quantities of overseas stars. Would the home-grown players be squeezed out? At Chelsea, concern mingled with respect when the Italians first appeared, but young Jody Morris felt he had improved as a player since their arrival: 'You must be if you spend every day that you do training with the first team. You've got to learn off people like Zola. It's unbelievable what he does in training.' While the youngsters learned from mingling with players with vastly different outlooks, off the field the club once again had the swagger of the old days. The Blues were big box-office again.

Chelsea were the original fashionable club of the swinging sixties, when Raquel Welch sat alongside Dickie Attenborough at the Bridge and there was no trendier place to be seen. Now the buzz was back. Alan Hudson, the all-time crowd favourite, and trendsetter, spoke passionately about the new sensation sweeping the famous borough of Kensington and Chelsea. He felt it was 'the nearest we've ever got to the atmosphere of the seventies. I've been over there without there even being a game on and you can still sense it. I do know one thing, the club has been very dour for a long time; but Stamford Bridge now is alight.' Everyone wishes 'Huddie' a full recovery after a terrible road accident late in 1997.

The successful integration of the foreign stars by Gullit at the

Bridge was perhaps best illustrated by their integration behind the scenes. Gullit refused to allow a star system, tried to avoid players gathering in cliques, and encouraged the continuation of some of the traditional English 'peculiarities'.

The overseas' stars first experience of a typical English Christmas was not restricted to the notoriously crowded fixture list. The players' Christmas lunch at the training ground was a surprise for the big name foreign stars as well – they had to sing for their lunch! The staff act and dress as waiters in their wing-collared white shirts and bow ties. Ruud claimed he was still a player and sat at the back enjoying the hilarious proceedings, as the youth team and all the new players sang for their meal.

Leboeuf was the star turn with a rendition of 'My Way' in French. There were cheers for the Italian trio, Vialli and Di Matteo on lead vocals and Zola doing some sort of soft-shoe song-and-dance routine. Frode Grodes performed a Norwegian folk song which included jumping on a table. Leboeuf said: 'The new players must sing, that's what we were told. But it was a lie. It was just the young players who have to do that. But they wanted us to perform. I only knew two hours beforehand. Yes, I enjoyed it. I liked our three tenors, Pavarotti, Domingo and Carreras!'

With such behind-the-scenes insights and anecdotes, this is the story of how Gianfranco Zola took English football by storm. It plots his first year, from the moment he joined Chelsea in November 1996 through to January 1998 when packed houses at Stamford Bridge were witnessing, for the first time in the living memory of many of them, a genuine Chelsea championship challenge.

It includes full details of Zola's part in Chelsea's FA Cup triumph, Italy's rollercoaster World Cup campaign, and above all, Zola's own goals, contributions and inspirational performances for club and country.

Zola has established himself as one of the world's great players and this is the first time an Italian's career, his impact on the English game, has warranted such a biography. It has been my great pleasure to have followed Zola and Chelsea's fortunes from the instant he arrived here, with unhindered access within Stamford Bridge from the boardroom to the dressing room.

1

Little Zola

Born on 5 July 1966, in the remote Sardinian village of Oliena, the month England won the World Cup, it was perhaps Franco Zola's destiny to make an immense impact in English football.

The Zolas are a small but fiercely loyal family. His mother Giovanna, father Ignazio and sister Silvia live a simple, rural life. 'All in all, I had a very happy childhood,' recalls Franco. 'My family have always been very supportive of my career, especially my father Ignazio, who loves football just as much as me. My mother and sister also like to watch me, and my sister was upset at not being able to come over for the Cup Final because of work commitments.

'My family all still live in Sardinia, and I have two cousins, Dario and Massimo, who play for the same team that I played for as a youngster.'

Franco passed his exams but never really enjoyed study: 'No, I wasn't a naughty boy. I was good at school. I wasn't a big student, but I studied a little bit, enough to pass my exams.'

Oliena was the equivalent of being brought up in Guernsey; precious little scope for football. Zola says: 'You know it was my dream as a boy to become the best footballer I could be. No-one else in my family played football but my father was the chairman of the local team, Corrasi, for many years. He was mad for football. Yes. Mad. So from the first time when I was four years old and he took me to see the team, football came into my blood. I liked it. I loved it. From

13

that time, all my thoughts were with football. Nothing else. Not at all.

'Sometimes journalists ask me what else I wanted to do – I cannot remember that there was ever any interest for me. You can call me a little bit crazy, but that is it. My first experience with football was with the local boys' team Corrasi. I started at the age of eleven and played up to the age of seventeen. It was a good standard but we all played for enjoyment and I had some very good friends that I played with for many years.'

Like all little boys, he had his heroes and dreamed of football stardom, especially as the golden boy of the Italian team at that time, the revered Gigi Riva, was also from Sardinia. 'As a boy, my favourite team was Cagliari, who are the biggest team in Sardinia. All my friends supported the club and we all dreamed of playing for them. Their greatest player was Gigi Riva, who is the all-time top goalscorer for the national team. He played when I was very young so I didn't see that much of him, but he was a natural striker and scored many wonderful goals.'

Like any kid from the backstreets of London, Liverpool or the North East, nothing gave football-loving Zola more pleasure than kicking a ball around on any spot of green he could find: 'I had many friends as a child and we all shared the same love of football. Sometimes I go back to Sardinia and still see the people who were my friends from years ago. It is very important for me to stay close to my family, and I love going back to Oliena when I can.

'I went to a village school as a boy – it is not the same as in England. We didn't have a school football team. I learned to play by myself and with my first team Corrasi.'

His proud father, sixty-six-year-old Ignazio, travelled to London for the first time in his life to watch Gianfranco receive the prestigious Footballer of the Year award and go on to star in the FA Cup Final. It was the sort of occasion the Zolas had been told to expect when their son was only seven, playing with other youngsters from their village. Ignazio, a retired truck driver and bar owner, recalled: 'One of the local football heroes saw Gianfranco playing and told us he was going to be a great player. That was the first time we realized his talent for the game. It was a former Italian player who watched him control a ball and told us he would go right to the top.

'Back home in Cagliari the people are very proud of him. It is the first time I have been to England and I cannot tell you what it feels like to watch your son collect an award as the best player in a foreign country. I am so proud of him.'

From his modest upbringing as the son of a bartender in a hostile area renowned for bandits and kidnappers, the little Zola was soon an emerging talent in Italian football. But living in such a remote area was a distinct handicap in trying to catch the eye of the big clubs. Zola recalled: 'It didn't make it very easy to get on as a footballer. Living on an island has disadvantages. Many young people just don't get the chance to prove themselves.'

Zola's big breakthrough came when he played for *Serie C2* side Nuorese: 'When I was eighteen, I went to play for my first professional team, called Nuorese, who were based in a town near my village. They were a *Serie C2* team then, which is the equivalent of the Third Division in England, but they have had a lot of problems since then and are now out of the league.'

It was during his time with Nuorese that he met and married Franca: 'I met my wife when I was very young. I was playing for Nuorese and I met her at my cousin's house, who she went to college with. We married in a town near Oliena, where Franca lived. She wasn't a football fan then, but of course, she is now.'

After making thirty-one league appearances for Nuorese, scoring ten goals, Zola's next step was a move up to *Serie C1*'s Torres, where he played for three years, making eighty-eight league appearances with twenty-one goals. He finally made it to the mainland when he joined Napoli in 1989.

Spotted by Luciano Moggi, general manager of Napoli at that time, Zola signed for the club for £170,000 and was soon being hailed as the new Diego Maradona. On 13 December, he unleashed a wicked thirty-yarder to embellish a 3–1 win over Atalanta and the next morning *Gazzetta dello Sport* made the Maradona connection: 'Zola, so good, he looked like Maradona.'

Zola was playing in place of the Argentinian captain that day, and even his appearance – small and stocky – mirrored that of Maradona. Near the end of the match, he was given a rousing reception by the Napoli fans as he was replaced by Maradona himself, the world's most outrageous footballer giving Zola a congratulatory pat on the back. The fans dubbed Zola 'Marazola'.

Zola recalls: 'The coach at the time was Bigon, who is now coaching in Switzerland. It was a very good time for me at Napoli. It was my first time in *Serie A* and I was playing with Maradona, which was a dream. I was young and I learned so much from him. It was just a joy to watch some of the things he did.'

Zola is now remembered for his winning strike against England at Wembley in the vital World Cup tie, but his first game against England saw him on the end of a 7–0 thrashing when he was a virtual unknown. Zola says: 'I remember it well. England were in my homeland of Sardinia preparing to play under Bobby Robson for the 1990 World Cup. Gary Lineker and Peter Beardsley scored goals against us. It was so easy for them because we were just a village team. I had just signed for Napoli and was the only professional in the side. None of the England players knew who I was, and there was nothing I could do to stop them doing what they liked.'

John Barnes, however, was impressed even then: 'We heard that Diego Maradona's understudy at Napoli was going to play. They lost 7–0 but he still showed a few good touches.' Zola was watched at the game in nearby Oristano by a crowd of friends and relatives. 'I think I won my revenge for that day by scoring a World Cup goal against England at Wembley,' he says.

Now Barnes names Zola as the best foreign player to arrive in the Premiership in 1996–97: 'Zola's been one of my favourite players for years, and I think he has given Chelsea a new dimension. He would be the first name on any nation's team sheet, in my opinion. His movement, his sharpness, his brain and his awareness are all exceptional. I am not surprised how quickly he's settled in England. People said he was too small, but if you play the ball to his feet, well . . . We are not used to his type of player in this country.'

Zola scored twice in eighteen appearances – thirteen of them as substitute – as a Maradona-inspired Napoli won the *Scudetto* for only the second time in their history. Maradona had a profound influence on Zola; the master of the free-kick gave Zola an insight into the power and efficiency of his dead-ball technique. Franco's favourite goal is still his first in *Serie A* with Napoli.

That championship-winning season was the last time Maradona was to have such an influence in Naples, and his hasty departure from Italy brought inevitable repercussions for Zola and the team. Zola was described as 'modestly wearing the Maradona shirt' and in the first season without him they finished fourth, with twelve goals from the by now newly-capped Zola.

Napoli were third from bottom by October 1992, Brazilian striker Antonio Careca, a friend of Maradona, wanted to leave, the coach was sacked, and Zola was accused of hitting an irate fan who had broken into the training ground to protest against the team's demise – an act that seems totally out of character for the little man. Since arriving in England with his broad smile he has been gentle, warm, approachable and accommodating off the field, and devastating on it. Apart from a touch of dissent at times, and a faint hint of retaliation in the face of the persistent attention of the hatchet men, there has been absolutely no sign of violence. So yes, striking a fan would be totally out of character – Zola is no Eric Cantona. But there are few more volatile fans than those in Naples. Rioting and objects being thrown onto the pitch are hardly rare occurrences and the Napoli Ultras can be quite intimidating.

'Yes,' agreed Zola, 'but they throw only fruit, honestly!' He has a wicked, quick sense of humour. He admitted: 'I'm glad they are on my side, because they scare the f*** out of me. It was good for me to play those fans, and it is like that in England every week; the atmosphere in England is very exciting to play in. There are games like English games with loud fans, but they happen less often in Italy. In England it happens every week. The games are very intense, very tiring here.'

Zola went through a traumatic period in Naples, in stark contrast to his lifestyle now in London. He stresses that his home life and his surroundings here are much more tranquil and settled, providing the perfect platform for the best form of his career culminating in the Footballer of the Year award and the FA Cup success.

But the second half of that tumultuous 1992–93 season with Napoli did see an improvement, with Zola in superlative form and the team recovering to finish mid-table. Zola recalls: 'The crowd liked my performances on the field and supported me a great deal. They were amazing times for me. I had come from Sardinia, where I was living with my father and mother who run a bar, but when I moved to Naples, a huge city with many people and a lot of fans, then it could not have been more difficult for me. Sometimes I felt a bit lost at the beginning, but after a while it became so good for me. The fans helped me a lot.'

Napoli president Corrado Ferlaino refused to discuss the renewal of Zola's contract, and with finances tight because of the renovation of the San Paolo stadium, problems off the pitch transmitted themselves to the team on it. Zola's form dipped, while Roberto Baggio of Juventus was the golden boy of Italian football. Zola was little more than on the periphery of the Italian squad. He recalls: 'At Napoli, the club was having difficult times; there were a lot of things happening off the pitch which the team could not control. Our form was affected and Baggio was playing superbly; it was hard to get into the *Azzurri*. Only when I went to Parma did things begin to change.' Giuseppe Giannini, Roberto Mancini and Gigi Casiraghi were also ahead of Zola in the Italian pecking order. 'I found it hard to get into the squad for some years,' he admitted. But his philosophical attitude helped him: 'Even when things were going badly at Napoli, I tried not to let it affect me. The club was in big financial difficulties, they had to sell me. Then Nevio Scala [Parma coach] came in for me, and at Parma things were easier.'

Zola was sold off to Parma for £4.5 million in July 1993 and his fortunes would change, notably on the international scene. There were a profusion of clubs chasing Zola but he chose Parma, teaming up with Colombian World Cup star Faustino Asprilla and Swedish international forward Tomas Brolin.

Zola rang Maradona, who told him he had made the right choice. Zola said: 'He told me Parma is a side that can battle all the way with Juventus and Milan.

'I've learned everything from Diego. I used to spy on him every time he trained and learnt to curl a free-kick just like him.'

In England at the time, Zola was known only to those *cognoscenti* of Italian football addicted to Channel 4's *Football Italia*. Glenn Hoddle, then managing Chelsea, knew his worth, but when Chelsea first enquired on Hoddle's behalf about Zola they were told he would cost them £10 million.

It was worth the wait for Zola to arrive at the Bridge, and among his most immediately noticeable contributions were the wicked, whiplash free-kicks he had perfected on the training field alongside Maradona.

Zola charmed and amazed the Chelsea fans with his variety of wicked dead-ball tricks. 'Usually I train at free-kicks once a week for thirty minutes, or maybe twenty minutes now. Before, when I played in Naples, I used to train more, maybe for an hour. I have some quality, but I have to train my quality. When you train yourself you improve a lot. The important thing is to believe in it. Nothing is impossible. Everybody can do it. It is most important to try, try, try. You have to understand yourself. I'm very happy to have a free-kick. It is important when I have the ball in a game that I believe I can do it. Very important.'

There were others who fired his imagination besides Maradona: 'I always liked to play football when I was young, always liked it. I watched television and could see great players shooting free-kicks. For me this was very important – I had an example to follow. Yes, Maradona, Platini, Zico and others. I am sure there are others I don't know of. Maradona was my favourite because I played with him and I think he was the best player of all time. Every day I saw him kicking; so I could learn other things to improve my technique.

'I am always happy when I score. My best was in a very important game against Juventus four years ago. They were champions and we were 0–0. Five minutes before the end, I scored from a free-kick. It was the same position as against Everton, maybe even a little nearer.'

In his first season with Parma Zola guided them to their second European Cup-Winners' Cup final, which they lost to Arsenal in Copenhagen. He earned a place in the Italian World Cup squad but played just twelve minutes in the finals in the United States, coming on as a substitute in the second-round tie against Nigeria only to be promptly sent off.

But he made a storming comeback the following season with his best ever haul of nineteen goals in thirty-two league matches and five more in the UEFA Cup as Parma beat Juventus in the final. Parma also finished third in *Serie A*, their highest ever position.

Not only had he taken over the famous Maradona No. 10 shirt with

Napoli, he superseded the 'Divine Ponytail' Baggio in the Italian national team. Zola had made his debut for Italy in a European Championship qualifier against Norway in Genoa on 13 November 1991 – the first match of Arrigo Sacchi's five-year reign as manager. He scored in three consecutive European Championship qualifiers as Italy reached the 1996 finals, but it all went horribly wrong once he got to England, Old Trafford to be precise. Zola missed the crucial penalty against Germany in Euro 96 and Italy went home in disgrace.

Forced to play on the wing for Parma after the arrival of £10 million Enrico Chiesa from Sampdoria, he joined Chelsea for £4.5 million in November 1996. 'Parma wanted to change the way they played, and I felt it was a good time to move,' Zola explained. He believed the turning point was the penalty miss against Germany: 'I got the impression that the people at Parma started to have doubts about me.' Parma started with three strikers, but crashed out of two cups and were on the slide in the league when Chelsea made their timely move and he was sold off. The fee had plummeted to less than half of what Glenn Hoddle had been quoted a year earlier.

Zola says: 'I had three great years with Parma. Nevio Scala was the boss and I enjoyed myself tremendously. The football was great and my only disappointment was that we didn't win the title while I was there. I was sad to leave Italy but I was looking forward to joining Chelsea, and after only a short while, I realized the massive differences between the two countries when it comes to football. The main difference is the media side of things. In Italy, the press are asking questions when the final whistle is blown and they don't stop talking about the game until the next one comes around. In England, you play the game, then forget about it and go home to relax. I know which approach I prefer, and it is one of the reasons I love England. The actual football is also different in both countries. The game in Italy is more tactical and defensive, whereas things are more attacking and faster in England. I am proud that I have settled into the style of play in England so quickly and that I have been able to perform well for Chelsea. I am very happy here, as I was in Italy.'

Luciano Moggi, now the Juventus sporting director, who discovered Zola, plucking him from the obscurity of the lower Italian leagues, and then took him to Napoli, helped him make up his mind to sign for Chelsea. It was Moggi who had effectively sent Gianluca Vialli to Stamford Bridge by letting him know he was surplus to Juventus' requirements despite helping them win the European Cup. After the two Italians had starred in Chelsea's epic cup win over Liverpool, Moggi recalled: 'I bought Zola for £170,000 and eventually I sold him to Parma for £5 million, so we made quite an interesting profit! When the chance of the move to Chelsea came up for Gianfranco, I persuaded him to go for it. I had moved to Juventus by then but remained friends with his advisers. So I was able to tell Zola that Chelsea were a great club with serious intentions. They should also remember at Stamford Bridge that, as Juventus sporting director, I was the one who brought about Gianluca Vialli's departure for London, too. I'm delighted to hear what happened against Liverpool, particularly for the sake of Gianfranco and Gianluca.'

At the Bridge, even Zola's glittering career took on new dimensions. He went on to exorcise the agony of the penalty miss in Euro 96 by scoring the winner against England at Wembley in a World Cup qualifier. Initially booed by rival supporters as a result, he was soon as popular as ever with English fans for his sheer genius on the field, and his likeable demeanour off it. While some foreign stars struggled with the language, or didn't even bother, Zola was anxious to learn as quickly as possible. While some of his Italian colleagues came to this country dripping in Armani and Valentino, he wore English-style woolly cardigans and jumpers – much to the amusement of his team-mates.

But he had earned the players' instant respect – and admiration for his ability, if not his dress sense.

In Zola's first training session, he made the sort of impact that surprised team-mates and coaching staff alike. Graham Rix, the Chelsea coach, said: 'When Franco arrived, we did a keep-ball session. We have players who are very good at this, such as Dan Petrescu and Roberto Di Matteo, so the standard was quite high. On his first morning, Franco joined in and was head-and-shoulders above everyone else. No-one could get the ball off him or even get near him. The other lads responded to this in a positive manner and everything went up a notch. His attitude is very professional, on and off the field. I'm not sure if I can really teach him anything new. I try to keep him confident, and the last thing I say to Franco when he goes onto the pitch is, "Play with a smile on your face." He does, all the time. He's a great footballer, wonderful lad and signs all the autographs. Franco hasn't come here just for the money. He wants to show people what he can do.

'His first touch is amazing. He has such a positive approach and has the ability to go forward while changing direction that others can only dream about. He can beat a player on both sides and if a defender dives in, boomph, he's away. Frightens them to death. All this and he plays with a smile on his face. I wish I'd played with him.'

A teetotaller and a family man, Zola's lifestyle couldn't be more diametrically opposed to that of Maradona. Franco and Franca are so proud of their little Zolas in their new school uniforms as they go to school in Chelsea. Six-year-old Andrea and five-year-old Martina are the centre of the Zolas' new life in the Royal Borough of Hammersmith and Chelsea. Gianfranco explained: 'My children are the most important thing in the world to me and I was worried about them when we first moved to England. They were a bit upset in the first week, but they settled in very well and they love it in England. They go to a very good school called Hillhouse and they are very happy. My wife also loves life in England and has settled in well. We live in Lowndes Square, which is near Hyde Park Corner and it is fantastic, a very lovely area. Luca Vialli lives nearby and he also loves it. I never imagined how well I would settle into life in England, and I am enjoying everything about it at the moment.'

Franco is so down-to-earth and modest that his weather-beaten father Ignazio was not even aware of his son's Footballer of the Year award until he read about it in an Italian newspaper. He said: 'Gianfranco is so modest. He did not even tell me he had won this prize. When I saw him, I asked him why he had not told me and he simply shrugged his shoulders and said, "I forgot." That is typical – he has always been the same. But I am overjoyed for him. I did not play football myself, but I supported Cagliari when I was younger. Then I became a fan of Napoli, Parma, and now Chelsea, to follow Gianfranco's career. He has made me a very proud man.'

Zola was embarrassed by his father's tribute. He said: 'I'm not really modest. My father is just trying to hide my real personality. If I told you what that was, I'd end up in prison. It gives me a lot of satisfaction to have him here alongside me at the award dinner and also watching at Wembley.'

The Cup Final also became a family affair for one of Zola's Italian team-mates, Roberto Di Matteo. His blind sister Concetta stayed at the midfielder's flat along with their father, who kept her informed of her brother's record-breaking goal at Wembley.

Middlesbrough defender Gianluca Festa confronted Zola in the Final – they had been together as small boys on the island of Sardinia, living just round the corner from each other in Cagliari. Festa said, 'I know him very well. We come from the same part of Cagliari and we played against one another as kids.'

He might now live close to Luca Vialli, in the grandest part of Belgravia, but for Zola there are no pretensions. He enjoys 'doing the shopping' and goes to his local Sainsbury's. In a fascinating profile in *Goal* magazine, he said: 'You can buy good pasta everywhere here, it would be silly to bring it over, especially from Italy.'

Jurgen Klinsmann's mastery of the language and the way he integrated into London life was mirrored by Zola. As his English improved, he took in more of the nightlife. But not the clubs, pubs and discos: 'I feel like a little boy who is always looking around to see new things and make new discoveries. I go to the theatre quite often. We particularly enjoy musicals and I thought *The Blues Brothers* was fantastic. Now we are hoping to go and see *The Phantom of the Opera* before long. London is a very beautiful city, but it is more expensive than Italy. I'll have to explain that to my wife!' he laughed.

Zola describes himself as a proud, stubborn man. 'Sardinians,' he explains, 'achieve with heart, body and soul. When we have our minds on something, we have to achieve. In football, that attitude is not uncommon.'

Music and computers are his weakness. For at least one hour every evening he plays on his computer: 'I can stop when I want. I have not developed a chronic phobia.' With his wife and children he enjoys a trip to the Trocadero and Sega World in Piccadilly 'to play on the computer games, and then out for a meal'. He has been determined to learn English fluently, with nightly lessons from a man Chelsea recommended: 'I thought I was getting on well – and then I try to listen to Dennis Wise and do not understand a word.'

He quickly mastered the English sense of humour. He was surfing the Internet when he discovered a list of the ten ugliest footballers in England; he was in second place. 'I hope,' he said, 'it is the only thing I do not win this season.' Ian Wright topped the list: 'I would like him to stay there.' But at Chelsea, it's the beautiful game that counts, and Zola's beauty emanates from his feet.

He has a beauty in his smile and his attitude to life. His love of children shone through when he surrounded himself with them when Leicester came to the Bridge on Saturday 19 April 1997.

Zola stayed behind at the end of the 2–1 win to sign autographs and personally shake the hands of the thirty-six excited seven-year-olds from Form 2T from the Warren Park Primary School in Leigh Park, Havant, who had made a record about him; a remake of the Kinks' sixties hit 'Lola', renamed 'Zola'. The song echoes around the Bridge as Zola's exploits won the hearts of the west London crowd.

Zola said at the time: 'When I received a cassette of the song, I was surprised and amazed. To have a song written about you, especially by children, is one of the most satisfying things for any player. My grandfather always told me to listen to what children say,' he smiled. 'He said that's because they always tell the truth. Me too. Perhaps that is why they like me and I like them. That's why I say that what has happened to me in the five months since I came here is something I could only dream about.'

Zola paid for all the kids and their two teachers to be his guests. Les Terry, teacher, composer, and guitarist, strummed away as the children sang long and loud; Zola smiled and hummed along. 'We wrote the words, sent off a tape and were amazed when the club wrote back and said Gianfranco liked it,' said Terry. 'The kids weren't expecting anything – he must be swamped by things like this – but we're now here. We've had £500 worth of free tickets, we've all got pictures and autographs and are hoping to get a signed jersey. What a day, it's been brilliant.' Terry and Colin Harris, the Warren Park head, couldn't thank Zola enough. His reply: 'It's my pleasure and I hope I will see you again.'

Zola and his new team-mates were soon in a west London recording studio to do their own FA Cup Final song 'Blue Day'. He was more nervous about his part in the song than playing at Wembley! 'I am very worried about the record, but at least it will be something we can remember forever,' he said.

Zola learned the piano as a boy and can still play Beethoven, but his favourite is Elton John.

When the players were relaxed during a trip to Milan for a friendly, in the hotel foyer, he was persuaded to play some Elton John at the piano:'I was able to play the piano, but now I lost a lot because I don't play for a long time. I played just a little bit, but I forgot the ... I'm not sure how you call it, the scales. I had lessons when I was in Naples for three years, but when I went to Parma I stopped having lessons. I didn't have a lot of time to do it. I haven't played a piano at home in London yet. I will have to buy one. Sometimes I like to play, because I find it very relaxing. I love classical music, it is very nice. And pop music I try hard to play, but I have not been able to play pop music. I like Elton John, he's a great singer. I'd like to be able to play all his songs, but it's not possible. It is just a dream.'

The most memorable game at the Bridge for many years was the Cup tie that made it all possible, a phenomenal 4–2 win over Liverpool after being two goals down by half-time. Zola scored one and made two more, all the time keeping a family secret. Only days before, he had heard that his father had been partially blinded by a burst bloodvessel in one eye. 'Gianfranco has been phoning every day to find out how his father is,' said his mother Giovanna from their Sardinian village. 'I had to reassure him that we are okay and told him to concentrate on his job. Ignazio suffered a haemorrhage or thrombosis, call it what you will, in one eye. It has covered half the eye and it means he can only see fully out of the other one. Hopefully, he is starting to recover now. But in all honesty, it is quite a serious thing to happen and has caused the whole family concern. So you can imagine what a boost it was to us when we heard what Gianfranco had been able to achieve with Chelsea. A friend of the family called from London to tell us that my son had equalized after Liverpool had been two goals ahead. I screamed with joy. Then he called again to say Gianfranco had been involved when Gianluca Vialli had put Chelsea ahead. Minutes later, the phone rang yet again and it was this same Sardinian man, named Mario, to tell us that our son's free-kick had set up Vialli for the fourth. The last call came on the final whistle and by then I was in tears. We are so proud of our son. In fact, the tears are starting to flow again now when I speak to you about it all.'

Giovanna wasn't surprised her son showed such character: 'We have suffered in the past as a family, for example when Gianfranco was sent off against Nigeria in the World Cup in America. That was absurd. Then we suffered again when he missed that penalty against Germany during Euro 96 in England. If he hadn't reacted in the right way to that disappointment, he could have been finished. But Gianfranco has learned to suffer and to fight, and I hope you saw that on Sunday. I am so pleased for Chelsea and the fans in England. I'm delighted for Ruud Gullit, too. When Gullit was at AC Milan, I was one of his biggest fans.'

Zola's mum was so happy about his relationship with the fans: 'It is enough to know my son is already adored over there almost as much as we adore him here. He has made his mother and father so proud and happy. Best wishes to the English. But I hope you understand we must support our son against England in the World Cup match. After all, we are Italian.'

To ensure Zola felt at home, the club assigned Gary Staker to his side as his interpreter. As Zola strolled the corridors of the Bridge in the early days with a huge Italian-English dictionary tucked under his arm, Gary was never far from his side. Whenever Franco searched for the right phrase, Gary would provide it.

Gullit's assistant Gwyn Williams knew of 38-year-old Gary Staker's linguistic ability, if not that he had an Italian mother, Mafalda, from Trieste. A devoted fan as a boy, he later became a season ticket holder and eventually a club steward. 'Gwyn asked me if I could stand in as an interpreter when Luca signed. Gianfranco and Roberto followed. They really are three genuine blokes with a great sense of humour. They call me Gazza. Well, look at me!'

Gianfranco gives credit for Staker in helping him settle in quickly. Staker recalls: 'Three three of them were used to the club doing everything. I had to sort out bills, telephones and plumbers. For Roberto it's always parking tickets.

'Luca taught Gianfranco golf. Now he beats him. That causes a bit of banter.'

Vialli smiles when he sees Gary. 'I will not kiss you, Gianfranco will be jealous!'

Franco enjoys doing all his interviews with the English media in English – with Gary's help. Gary is Chelsea's chief steward and his mother is Italian. A familiar face around the club, Gary's sphere of importance widened dramatically with his new-found fame as the Italians' language minder, supplementing their formal lessons and ensuring they are not misinterpreted in the papers – at least, not too often.

Zola's status increased with his move to the Premiership. With Chelsea in vogue, Zola appeared in *Loaded* magazine and the interviewer kissed Zola's shoes; Gary followed suit and boasts about tackling the great Italian master. 'If you tackle me, Gary, then I break your f***ing face' – Zola's smile breaks into a huge grin. Zola clearly has deep affection for Gary, who has become such a vital ingredient in the settling-in process of the Italian contingent.

Zola's love of children and willingness to put his name to good causes persuaded him to join players like Eric Cantona, Ian Wright, and John Barnes in a video aimed at schoolchildren throughout Europe to campaign against racism.

Franco said: 'We have some problems of racism in Italy in some cities, but it is not a big problem and I think the main reason for racism is lack of education and ignorance, because I think all the children must know there is no difference between people. It's very important to teach them to respect all the people around you and to have an opinion about the other people – not to the colour of their skin. Their behaviour is the main important thing.'

When asked what advice he would give to kids hearing racism, Franco felt more comfortable answering in his native tongue – he felt it was too important to risk his message being misinterpreted. The organizers of the anti-racism in football campaign kept rigidly to Zola's words in their translation. He said: 'I think what I can say to the young children is that it is a great thing to have conversations with people different to you without any bad idea about them. It's good for yourself because you can be a better man, more complete;

you can compare your ideas with other ideas. It's different from your normal thoughts. It's very important, you can be better because of it. So I think that in the world, there are many people who have different ideas and if you get more things in your brain, it is good for you, because you have more experience. I think the best thing to do for yourself is to talk with everybody thinking they are the same person, without, as I said before, preconceived ideas.

'I think it is the same thing in football. I read many newspapers who suggest that it is no good that many footballers are playing here, it's no good for our footballers. I think it is not correct, because we had the same thing in Italy many years ago when many players came to play in our championship. The Italian player grew. Now we have many talents. If you want to learn, the foreign players can give you some new things. If you are interested in football and you want to grow in football, you can get ideas and you can use your ideas with the ideas of others so you are a better player. This is what I think. I had good help when many players came to Italy, when Maradona came to Italy, when Platini came to Italy. I could get some ideas from them, and I could improve my football. This is the same thing here. It is not a bad thing for youngsters! I think in the next years we will have many, many good young players in England. I really think that.'

2

The Zola Deal

Tragedy struck Chelsea Football Club when Matthew Harding died in a helicopter crash on the way back from watching their Coca-Cola Cup defeat at Bolton.

The floral tributes on the gates of Stamford Bridge were evidence that Matthew was a footballing icon of the boardroom; the fans still sing his name in homage to an individual's love affair with his club.

His untimely death caused shock waves at the club at the time, uncertainty about the team's future, the purchasing power within the boardroom.

Gullit's first season in charge of the team, 1996–97, began with huge expectations, and as the side climbed to second in the Premiership by the end of August, the summer's arrivals of Luca Vialli, Frank Leboeuf and Roberto Di Matteo were hailed as inspired signings.

Gullit's new team touched the heights at times at Highbury, but the frailties began to emerge as they were eventually held to a 3–3 draw. A crushing, demoralizing 5–1 defeat at Anfield confirmed Gullit's suspicions that there was a long haul ahead before the team would find the right balance, spirit and effectiveness. Chelsea slipped down to seventh and it was a struggle to regain the momentum for a title challenge.

The Coca-Cola Cup exit at Bolton was still being digested by the fans when they were struck down by the thunderbolt of tragedy. In the eyes of the fans, Matthew Harding was a saviour. Within the corridors of power, there had been a conflict between Harding and chairman Ken Bates, culminating in a battle for control of the Bridge, but the facts became submerged under a barrage of rhetoric and acrimony. The fans were baffled and angered by the internal politics that threatened to rip the club apart, but that was nothing compared to their feelings of grief when Harding was killed. If the outpouring of grief over Diana, Princess of Wales, touched the entire nation, then Harding's death was a local version of how an individual galvanized a community, united in grief.

As Gullit, the team and the club emerged from the aftermath of Harding's death, the realities began to set in: that while it was obvious there were weaknesses at the back, the team was also not functioning as well as it might in attack. Would Chelsea be in a position to continue their team re-building plans without Harding?

Gullit had believed that the goals would be shared right the way through the team, and while that had become a reality, the strike pairing of Vialli and Hughes had not produced goals in sufficient quantity.

Harding's death in October temporarily postponed the inevitable move into the transfer market. The first post-Harding match, against Spurs at the Bridge, was an emotional affair. It was followed by a remarkable 2–1 win at Old Trafford.

But Gullit wasn't blinded by the glory of a win over Manchester United, and still knew he had to act – but finding the right player at such a stage of the season seemed an unlikely proposition. When he captured Zola, it was a complete surprise. With a pedigree that included replacing Diego Maradona at Napoli and Roberto Baggio in the Italian national side, there were few players with a more impressive CV. The move for Zola instantly dispelled the fans' uncertainty created by Harding's death.

The first public inkling of Gullit's moves for Zola emerged at the beginning of November.

At the age of thirty, Zola wanted to quit Parma after a series of rows with new coach Carlo Ancelotti. He was unhappy about being played out of position and had been assured by Gullit that at Chelsea he would either be used in attack or directly behind the front two.

Gullit conducted his transfer deals on strictly Continental lines. He selected the targets and Chelsea's managing director Colin Hutchinson conducted negotiations with the selling club on the fee, and with the player and his representatives on personal terms. The transfer budgets were worked out by Hutchinson and club chairman Ken Bates. Gullit was uninterested in how much a player earned so long as he wanted to play for him and the club. All he did was make an initial call on his mobile phone – and normally when Gullit rang, a player was interested.

Once Gullit had established that Zola wanted to play in the Premiership with a London club and would come to Stamford Bridge, Hutchinson spent the evening with Parma's sports director and general manager Riccardo Sogliano in London. Talks finished at 1am. A fee of £4.5 million was agreed by president Giorgio Pedranaschi.

In fact, Gullit had wanted Zola as his first Chelsea signing, but Parma refused to sell at the time. His persistence paid off after getting the go-ahead to spend big again, with Bates determined to prove to his fans that there would be no loss of financial stability after Harding. It took Gullit's spending to over £12 million, but the club were planning to balance the books with a number of departures. Parma coach Ancelotti hardly seemed about to break into tears at the expected loss of Zola at the time, when he said: 'If he has been able to get a good deal, that's good for us. We're both happy.'

With another high-profile new foreign acquisition made, the arguments intensified about the development of young talent at clubs like Chelsea. But at the same time as Zola's arrival, Jody Morris signed a new two-year contract, reflecting his growing stature within the club after having emerged through the YTS scheme. Morris made the breakthrough to the first team under Hoddle and had also become part of the England Under-21 set-up under Gullit. His progress caught the imagination of everyone at Stamford Bridge, and counterbalanced the debate about the takeover of foreign players.

Hutchinson flew to Italy and spent two hours with the Parma president. Zola finally sealed the deal with Hutchinson at 3.30am after all-day negotiations. He agreed a four-year contract worth

£25,000 a week. He would get a basic £16,000 a week, but with
bonuses and signing-on fees that figure soared to £1.25 million a year.

The first signing since the death of Harding was proof that the
dramatic rise of Chelsea continued unabated.

Zola was grateful for an escape route from his Parma misery. He
said: 'I will be able to play in my proper role in England, whereas
Parma could no longer find a place for me. At the start of the season
I was shattered after my penalty miss against Germany. I tried to
recapture my best form, but the atmosphere at the club had changed.
I kept reading claims that I was an egotist, or that I had failed to work
with the other strikers Parma had signed and later sold – such as
Faustino Asprilla or Hristo Stoichkov. I was being made scapegoat
for all the team's problems and I couldn't face staying to put up with
all those lies.'

He had become totally disillusioned: 'During the last few months,
I hated it, I didn't want to play football anymore. I was expected to
play wide on the right. I was very unhappy and my football suffered.
I decided to join Chelsea because I wanted to be happy at my club.'
Vialli immediately predicted that Zola's arrival would improve
Chelsea's disappointing strike-rate: 'Zola is one of those players who
bring strikers good fortune. He is a great character and a winner.'

Zola's arrival inevitably placed a huge question-mark over the
futures of Mark Hughes, Dennis Wise and John Spencer, with almost
weekly speculation in the tabloid press. After lavish spending, surely
Gullit would begin to claw some of the money back – and in the case
of Spencer, that is how it turned out.

Bates had no doubts that his manager had made another first-rate
signing, despite the sniping about Zola's age. Bates said: 'Ruud said
that Zola was the best striker in the world and that he wanted him. A
lot has been made of his age, but as Ruud pointed out, Ian Wright was
going to play for England again at the age of thirty-three. That was
good enough. Colin was due to fly over on Wednesday morning, but
there was a strike in Milan so he flew from Stansted on Thursday and
got to Milan at 9pm. We had to act fast as we knew that Arsenal were
interested. He finally agreed the deal at 3.30am on Friday morning
and got home late on Friday afternoon.

'I know everyone is thinking, "How can they afford it?" Well, we are up to 35,000 capacity next year, that's 3,000 extra. If we are sold out every game, that is worth £2.8 million and playing in Europe is worth £1 million. I feel we have to start qualifying for Europe, and don't forget every place up the Premiership ladder is worth another £100,000.

'Also, buying players from Italy we can spread the money over three years. We are taking advantage of the big TV money that kicks in from next season and that we will have over the next few years. I suppose we are taking a risk, but it's a risk worth taking.' Bates also felt that, as the season progressed, clubs would be in difficulties and come to Chelsea to make realistic bids for their surplus players.

TV pundit Andy Gray, a big fan of Gullit's, praised him for bringing another Italian superstar to the Premiership. In his *Sunday Express* column, he wrote: 'Zola's arrival from Italy tells me that manager Ruud Gullit is here to stay and that can only be good for Chelsea, the Premiership and the rest of English football. I'm not surprised that Gullit's return to the transfer market should take him to Italy. That is the market he knows best, having spent most of his career in *Serie A* with AC Milan and Sampdoria. At Milan they had three Dutchmen, Gullit, Marco van Basten and Frank Rijkaard, as the core of the side and that formula is repeating itself at Stamford Bridge with Zola, Gianluca Vialli and Roberto Di Matteo . . . Zola is the latest piece in the jigsaw for Gullit, who is gradually introducing a more flexible, European system to the English game. But he ought to know that his place in the side is not just a matter of turning up. Gullit has shown with his treatment of Vialli that he is quite prepared to make difficult decisions and leave out star names for the benefit of the team. There are a lot of other managers who would not have had the courage to do that.'

Zola also had the option to sign for Spurs. Initially, it was suspected that their chairman Alan Sugar had refused to break the club's wage structure; top players like Teddy Sheringham at that time earned £12,000 a week, the level at which they recruited John Scales, Steffen Iversen and Ramon Vega. But it appeared that their manager at the time, Gerry Francis, wasn't that convinced.

Sports lawyer Mel Goldberg contacted Spurs about Zola three weeks before he signed for Chelsea. Goldberg insisted: 'We offered him to Spurs. They could have had him for the same price and same wages. I was told by Sugar's people, "We are not paying that sort of money for a player." Zola wanted to come to London because he saw that the other Italians had settled well. It is their [Tottenham's] choice and they missed out.'

Although Zola was on a huge salary, he was not the biggest wage-earner in the Premiership. His compatriot Fabrizio Ravanelli was paid £42,0000 a week by Middlesbrough, that included a deal to pay him an image contract. Chelsea were concerned about such contracts being deemed 'side deals' by the Inland Revenue. But at Boro, the club paid Ravanelli £13,000 a week for his image rights in addition to his £29,000-a-week salary as a player. Image contracts are under review by the Revenue.

Chelsea were never in the past known as being among the game's big spenders, but suddenly their perception in the industry had changed. It was boom time off the field, and the club were spending big to attract the top names.

Zola flew into Heathrow Airport from Milan with his wife Franca on Monday 11 November 1996. As soon as he stepped from the plane onto English soil, one of the Chelsea officials' mobile phone rang. It was for Gianfranco – Vialli was on the line. They spoke in English! Vialli invited him to his favourite restaurant, San Lorenzo, that evening for a more detailed rundown on English football and his new team-mates.

Wearing a blue baseball cap and black leather jacket, Zola was confronted with the first of his many interviews of the day at the airport. He said: 'I decided to come here because I wanted another experience in football. This will be a good experience for my life and for my career.' But it had been a tough decision: 'It was not easy to leave Italy and Italian football, which is very important in the world and important for me. But I decided to have another experience and I hope to have many satisfactory seasons here.' He said the fact that two of his close Italian friends, Vialli and Di Matteo, were playing for Chelsea was an important factor in his choice: 'To have two friends in the same team is important, so that you can learn things the right way. I hope to settle in quickly and I'm sure I can adapt, and I plan to stay here until my contract expires in 2000.'

Zola was taken straight to central London for a medical, then Gullit welcomed him to Chelsea at a packed news conference in Drake's restaurant within Stanford Bridge. Gullit felt that Zola would be the piece in the jigsaw to make Matthew Harding's dreams come true, saying: 'This is what Matthew would have wanted. He had a dream for Chelsea and now we can help deliver that dream. Matthew's hope was that we could keep on improving as a club. This is another big step along that trail and I know he would have enjoyed today; he would have been very happy.'

Gullit was delighted to have persuaded Zola to join the Italian exodus into the Premiership. 'I think with Gianfranco that his qualities are obvious,' he said. 'He has great technical ability and he sees the game very well. I think it's vital for us that he is the sort of player who can decide a game with his vision, technique and ability, to open it up from even ordinary situations. At Parma this season he has been a victim of a change in the playing style. If Parma didn't want to use his quality, I knew I'd like to have it. You don't get an opportunity like this every day and when I heard he might be available, I knew that I wanted him to come to Chelsea.'

Zola in turn paid tribute to Gullit's influence as a player in Italy with both Milan and Sampdoria: 'I came to Chelsea because they believed in me. This is a great opportunity for my career and I decided I wanted to play in this team and play in this country. It was important for me to have this opportunity. Conditions at Parma haven't been ideal for me. I've had a lot of problems, but now I want to do the best I can for Chelsea. I have spoken to Roberto and to Fabrizio Ravanelli and they told me that English football is good. They say it's hard and strong but that the football is good, that I can play well and live well here. Perhaps there will be some problems in adapting at the start, but I think I can overcome them. The thing I love about English football is the atmosphere in the grounds and I want to be part of that.

'It made a difference that Ruud wanted me. I played against him in Italy, knew what he could do, and have strong memories of him as a player.' Zola laughed when he recalled one encounter with Gullit in an Italian Cup semi-final 'when he played us a trick; he scored against us just when we were playing well'. Zola insisted in conducting a cheerful interview in English, to give him practice for his new life ahead. He thought long and hard before answering each question.

Zola had played just once more with Vialli, for Italy against Cyprus on 21 December 1991 in a 2–0 when Vialli scored, but he believed the pair could hit it off: 'I think we can play well together and we won't have any problems. I believe I can help him to score goals and that with him I can help the team to reach our aims. If Chelsea want to win the league then I want to be part of that. I certainly think that this team will be in Europe next season and perhaps even better than that. We are fifth now and I am sure we can progress from there.'

Zola spoke to Vialli about life on and off the pitch: 'Gianluca appreciates things in England that he could not appreciate in Italy. He is very pleased to have chosen Chelsea and to play in England. In Italian football there are many good things but also several bad things. For example, the build-up to matches and the need to win lead to tension, exasperation and stress. Gianluca has described situations to me in the Premiership that I find incredible, such as when Frank Leboeuf scored Chelsea's only goal in their 5–1 defeat at Liverpool – the fans wanted him to score again with only minutes to go. Also, after each game the two teams meet up for half an hour at the bar and every nasty tackle gets forgotten. In Italy people look at me very strangely if I go up to congratulate an opponent. Hopefully, I can win the league with Chelsea and help them achieve their goals.'

Vialli intimately knew Zola's pedigree, and knew Zola would click in the new-look attack: 'He is one of those players who can make the fortune of any striker. The way he puts the ball onto your feet is unbelievable. And he can change the course of a game with just one touch of invention. Skill. He makes me look ordinary. He also has another reason for doing well over here: to show Parma what a mistake they made in selling him. It was not his fault that he was made to feel uncomfortable by being played out of position. Sure, Parma made a mistake. So it is a fantastic deal not only for the players but for the fans as well. You will see, and quickly. He will emerge as a revelation in this country. I have a feeling he will prove himself the best Italian player to come here.' Prophetic words from Lucky Luca!

Yet Zola had doubted in the previous summer that his 5ft 5in frame would be sufficient to withstand the rigours and physical demands of the Premiership. Five months on, Gullit had no doubt that the little man would be able to cope: 'Look at Nick Barmby and Dennis Wise, they are not so big.' And Zola showed he had a sense of humour: 'I may have said that in the summer,' he said, 'but I have grown a lot since then!'

As for life in the capital, he said: 'I have only been to London once before and all I saw was Big Ben, so there is a lot to be happy about. I understand that Chelsea is a very beautiful area and I've just learnt that there are some excellent Sardinian restaurants.' He had a lot to learn about the restaurants.

While a debate raged about the motives of the big-name foreign stars, Zola's attractive wife Franca insisted that, unlike Mrs Andrea Emerson, who was homesick or just simply sick of the North East, her husband was not making a fleeting visit to England: 'We are here to stay. I come from Sardinia and compared to that, London is a great and wonderful city, one of the best in the world to live in. It is very exciting for the whole family to be here and there is a big Italian community for us, and that will help us to settle in. I don't know anyone here yet, but I understand that the other wives are friendly, too. We will be here for four years, so it is important to be happy, but it is an exciting experience. The children will join us shortly and we will try to find a house to live in as soon as possible.'

Gullit was equally convinced that Zola would prove a runaway success: 'It's important for Gianfranco that he tries to cope with the different situation here in England. You have to adapt yourself to a new environment and everybody knows that. I'm sure Gianfranco will adapt, but we'll see later in the week if he can play at Blackburn.' Zola was sure to run out in his new No. 25 shirt at Ewood Park, although Gullit was giving nothing away. Gullit added: 'I believe that he can take us up a level from where we are now. Things are getting better all the time, but we know there is more to come and I think he can give us that. I knew he was the player I wanted, and when the opportunity came up I had to take it. I knew other clubs would want him, but we were first when we had to be. I told Luca and Roberto about the signing and they were happy. I think he will give us something extra, and they will make it easier for him to settle here.'

Gullit's spending was temporarily on hold, but he refused to rule out further signings in the future – and he indicated that those signings were again most likely to come from the other side of the Channel: 'Everything over here has gone out of proportion, and class foreign players cost less than class English ones. We would love to have some English players, but when you have to pay £15 million for players like Alan Shearer, that takes them out of the reach of even most of the top clubs. But it's not for me to say it's ridiculous.'

No-one would worry about the overload of foreign stars at the Bridge if they were successful. Gullit joked: 'We had a foreign legion before I arrived. . . . There were Scots, Welsh and Irish.'

Zola certainly had the credentials; an Italian championship with Napoli in 1990, European Cup-Winners' Cup finalist with Parma in 1994 and UEFA Cup winner the following year. At Napoli he scored thirty-four goals in 131 appearances and added sixty-three in 136 games for Parma.

His arrival inevitably intensified speculation about players being sold off. But Gullit promised: 'Nobody has to go. If you look at our last few games, Mark Hughes has been outstanding, a great help to the team. What's been better for him is that he's been playing with better players and finding that fun, and we've now got even more better players with Gianfranco here.' Bolton had expressed an interest in Hughes, but the Welshman wanted Zola to enhance his career at the Bridge, not end it. He argued: 'I don't know what this means for my future. Nothing stops in football and you expect a club like Chelsea to be in the market whenever big-name players become available. It shows how far the club has come in a short space of time. I just hope my situation does not change. Hopefully, it will not; this is a great place for me at the moment.' Spencer's future was always the more likely to be on the line; he needed first-team football to keep his place in the Scotland squad.

Zola made an immediate impression, scoring FIVE goals in his first practice match for the Blues. The bookies slashed Chelsea's title odds from 14–1 to 10–1. William Hill spokesman Graham Sharpe said: 'Chelsea are now the most heavily backed team in the

Premiership. It could cost us £400,000 if they win the championship.'

Zola's first day on the training pitch was an eye-opener even for the seasoned professionals, as they marvelled at his exceptional gifts and were mesmerized by his first touch.

Zola entertained half a dozen Italian journalists, escorted to the large white-walled canteen on the second floor of the clubhouse for an audience with the new signing. After the interviews, Jody Morris was called over. Zola and Morris lined up side by side. Yes, Zola was the new shortest player at the club. Only by half an inch. There was wicked mickey-taking as Wise called Zola the 'fairground freak'. Quite a cheek coming from Wise!

Juventus striker Alessandro Del Piero joined the queue of Italian stars wanting to play in the Premiership, as Zola became the fifth major Italian import of the season. Del Piero, regarded as one of Italian football's hottest properties, declared: 'I wouldn't be at all surprised if an English club was to make a bid for me right now. Their league is currently the richest in Europe. It has undergone vast expansion both in terms of finance and skill levels. What's more, it is far less stressful to play in than *Serie A*. I wish Zola all the best – he is a fantastic player and a great guy.' Del Piero's Juventus team-mate Attilio Lombardo, meanwhile, turned down Sheffield Wednesday. Interestingly, he said at the time: 'I wasn't interested in going to England, despite all the money on offer. I would not have gained anything from it, either as a person or as a player. Had I been in Zola's shoes, I would have stayed put in Italy.' I cannot imagine what prompted him to sign for Crystal Palace before the start of the following season – it must have been either Ron Noades' aftershave, or maybe his money!

Now, when Zola reflects on his move to English football, he appreciates how much he was helped by the friendly reception he received from within the club. The initial period at a new club can often be the most important. Denise Summers, the club's personnel and payroll manager, sorted out the Zolas' home and schools for their children, Martina and Andrea, while Gary Staker translated and still does. Zola pays tribute to them for their help in making his arrival so smooth. 'We have to thank Denise and Gary so much. In that first week there was so much to do and we were unsure, uncertain.

Everything was new and different. If your family is okay – your wife, your children are happy – then you can give your mind to your football properly. And for me this happened very quickly. I was so lucky. It's like when you build a house, the most important thing to build is the basement ... no ... foundation. If the foundation is ... is ... secure, then you have a strong house, a healthy house. The same thing in a football team, yes.'

3

Gullit Predicts Zola Power

Ruud Gullit was a whirlwind success in the Premiership. I remember his first game in English football, a masterly performance in the sweeper's role against Everton at the Bridge. I forecast after that one game that he would be a candidate for Footballer of the Year. I voted for him at the end of a magnificent first season, but he came second to Eric Cantona.

Players with worldwide reputations like Gullit and Jurgen Klinsmann before him, put their status and stature on the line when they go to a foreign country. There have been too many notable flops, but Zola was a recognized Italian international and it was inconceivable that he was coming to England for the ride.

Gullit instinctively knew Zola would take the English game by storm and become a major influence. He predicted just that, as the team travelled north the day before Zola's debut at Blackburn. Gullit forecast: 'Gianfranco was a vital man for Napoli and Parma and now he will be just as important to us. His quality is obvious. He has great technical ability, vision, and the skill to change a match which is so desperately needed today.'

Vialli felt Zola would love the easy-going camaraderie within the Gullit camp, compared with the more rigid regimes in Italian football: 'There is a problem in Italy now because it is getting more difficult for the good players to perform well. It seems there is a negative atmosphere in the Italian game and that is not helping. I have settled

41

in very well at this club and I'm sure Zola will do the same. The atmosphere is tremendous here, better than in Italy where players are more independent.'

There was not a hint of the trouble to come as Vialli ironically expressed his approval at the formidable squad assembled by Gullit and the willingness to utilize it to the full – even if Vialli himself was to become the victim: 'Things are changing in this country. No longer is it a question of selecting eleven players from fifteen. Now there are twenty good players at a manager's disposal. While this is fine for Ruud Gullit, it is not so good for the players. Sure, they get angry when they are out of the team, but it is a bad mentality. If you want to win something, you have to have more than just eleven players. You must accept it. If you want to play every week then it may be better to join another team. Milan is a tremendous example. For the first time, an Italian side had something like twenty-two great players. From that moment they won everything. That is what Ruud is trying to do at Chelsea. He wants the best and he wants lots of them.'

Gullit moved Craig Burley from midfield to sweeper to accommodate Zola. Frode Grodas joined Zola in making his Premiership debut at Ewood Park on Saturday 16 November 1996.

All Zola needed was a goal to have made his debut perfection itself. It almost came, spectacularly, deep in the second half when he volleyed Gullit's cross into the side-netting. To appreciate the skill involved, it should be pointed out that many decent players, presented with a ball at a comparable angle and height, would have propelled it into row Z. 'It was always my intention to play him from the start,' Gullit said, dismissing the notion of a more gentle introduction. 'It is important that he gets to know us and we get to know him as quickly as possible. There is no point in leaving him on the bench. And as you can see, he is very fit and has no problems with the pace. He told me he enjoyed the game.

'He made a very nice debut and will get even better. It was nice to see how he played. He got better and better as the game went on, and ended up playing very well. He is tired, but physically he will have no problems with the Premiership.'

Gullit, on the bench after recovering from a pre-season knee operation, took the field for the final thirty minutes and under his guidance, Chelsea subjected Blackburn's goal to sustained attack. Zola was thwarted in the box by Henning Berg's last-ditch tackle and was then felled by Billy McKinlay on the edge of the area. Two saves by Grodas denied first McKinlay and then Kevin Gallacher in the home side's quest for a late winner.

Zola struck a hefty blow for foreign football, providing the perfect response to the growing army of Little Englanders questioning the motives of the Premiership's overseas recruits. Emerson's disappearing act and the constant jibes of Alan Sugar had called into question the character of the international stars. But on a wet weekend in Blackburn, Zola showed character and bottle to match his undoubted skill. Even when his first game in England was threatening to completely pass him by, the little man with a big heart refused to hide. Blackburn acting-manager Tony Parkes admitted: 'I didn't even mention Zola in my team talk. He scared me to death and I knew he'd do the same to my players. What can you say about Zola, Vialli and Gullit except sing their praises? I'd rather not talk about them at all. I was hoping they'd stick with the side which won their last game at Manchester United. When I saw Zola was playing, I weren't right happy. So I told my team to hound them, to put the pressure on and see how they reacted to that. It was possible they just might not fancy it. But we never got a chance to test them, because they hit it all along to Vialli and made it difficult to crowd them out in midfield.'

Zola gradually grew more influential in a hard, muscular, unmistakably English match. His willingness to learn impressed his new player-manager, who wanted Zola to acclimatize before the encounter with Newcastle. By the later stages, Zola was linking promisingly with Vialli and Di Matteo – and with Gullit. It must have helped to receive instructions in his own language, but footballing intelligence also played a part.

Gullit acknowledged that it was not until he came on to replace Dennis Wise for the last half-hour that his team dominated. He intended to resume his playing role as more than just as a bit-part player.

So how could you assemble a large squad and keep all the players, imported and home-grown, happy? 'You can't,' Gullit said. 'But I have been there and the most important thing I learned from Milan was that you have to create a situation in which, no matter what they think of the coach's decisions, all the players have only one goal, which is for the team to achieve something. I don't mind if they don't like me sometimes, as long as they have a common goal. At Milan, I hated the coach's guts when he left me out, but in the end I realized what he did was right for the team.

'As for myself, I feel that I am now nearly 100 per cent fit and now I just need to find my rhythm.'

Parkes believed Chelsea enjoyed the advantage of playing their foreigners because they were in the top half of the table. He relied on more domestic virtues to ease his struggling side's problems, having already axed Georgios Donis and Lars Bohinen: 'In our position, we need battlers to get us a result. Foreign players are the icing on the cake when things are going well. We can't afford the luxury of guys who are only interested in attacking. We've got to tackle, get close and get a foot in. It's what the crowd expect of us, because they know it's the only way we're going to get off the bottom of the table. We never used to have trouble attracting the biggest stars in the game to Ewood Park when Kenny Dalglish was in charge. But things have changed now and someone like Zola would have taken one look at our league position and gone somewhere else.'

At least Rovers had the consolation of climbing off the foot of the table for the first time in two months thanks to Kevin Gallacher's well-worked goal in the fifty-fifth minute. Yet Chelsea, who finished the game with just two Englishmen, still showed enough commitment to deserve Dan Petrescu's deflected equalizer off McKinlay.

Vialli produced one of his best all-round performances. Grodas was warned after just four minutes and booked in the twelfth for time-wasting – as he waited for his manager to get across his messages from the touchline! Burley's tackle and pass to Vialli, who worked his way round the back to set up Hughes for a shooting chance which he should have buried in the thirty-first minute, was the move of the match and deserved a goal.

Scott Minto, one of those rare Englishmen in the Chelsea camp that day, laughed: 'I've got to learn Italian to get on with everyone now! But there isn't really a communication problem, even if Ruud has to speak a bit slowly at times. All the foreign lads understand English and that's very important. They've come over here and are getting paid a lot of money. But they've realized the English league is very hard physically and are prepared to put the effort in. Luca and Dennis Wise are always playing little pranks on each other and there's a good banter in the camp. No-one says, "I'm on twenty-five grand a week so I'm not talking to you." There was a lot of pressure on Zola today and this was probably a bit of a culture shock for him after living in Parma. But I've already seen a great deal to suggest he'll be a big success. He's only tiny, but he's very strong and his low sense of gravity means he can twist and turn past big defenders. All the Italians are bringing great technique and tactical awareness. But they're also prepared to dig in the English way.'

Norwegian stopper Berg claimed: 'Chelsea are great going forward, but not too many of their players want to defend. It was very difficult for Zola, because it was his first game and he was playing in a position he's not used to. But he wasn't a big threat.'

Zola said: 'It was a physical game, very tiring, but I like that incredible aggression in the English game. For a first match, I was pleased; but I know I will have to get better. I've never felt so tired in my life, yet I'm already looking forward to playing Newcastle; I wish it were tomorrow – that's how exciting it is to play in English football. The atmosphere is simply unbelievable. I've never enjoyed a match so much in my life. It took me a while to adjust, but I think in the second half I started to get going. Vialli was simply magnificent. We only played twice together for Italy but I'm looking forward to a great partnership. I'm pleased and satisfied with my performance because I've only been here for barely five days. Parma is a chapter in my life that is closed for good. I can only say it is exhilarating to play football like this.

'I'm not a novice, I know something about English football. But I still have a lot to learn. I've started on the right foot and for the first match I'm quite satisfied. You play from the first to the very last minute. The aggression was incredible, there were a lot of tackles, but none that were cruel. One of the things that struck me was the intensity and the amazing public all around the pitch. The game was hard. They scored when we were playing our best. But Dan scored an important goal for us. I kick just one free-kick for goal but I kicked too high. Next time, okay. I hope.'

Zola was asked what he should 'call' if he wanted the ball: 'I only know "hello!" '

'I can tell you I felt knackered.' No, it wasn't Wise. It was Vialli. 'We had to fight for a result but in the end we got it and I'm told Chelsea haven't won in Blackburn for several years, so it was even more important that we came away with a point,' said Luca. 'I can see good things coming from myself playing with Zola.'

The coach sped away from Ewood Park as the team caught the last shuttle from Manchester to Heathrow. In the airport departure lounge was Glenn Hoddle, on a mission to watch his England players at Old Trafford, Manchester United against Arsenal. It was the perfect chance for Ruud and Glenn to chat as they queued to board the shuttle. Zola and Di Matteo, who had shared rooms, were joined by *Gazzetta dello Sport* correspondent Giancarlo Galavotti, who translated their conversation . . .

Di Matteo: What would you like?
Zola: No, it's okay, I'll pay.
Di Matteo: You'd better, if I have to listen to certain figures in the press you are being paid.
Zola: Well, actually these figures are not exactly true.

Next was Zola's home debut against Newcastle and the inevitable confrontation with Alan Shearer.

Shearer had been given the green light to make his Newcastle comeback after coming through a training session and was set to return just one month after his groin operation. The England skipper relished his head-to-head with Zola, saying: 'I know what he's all about after watching him on TV several times. He's another example of the exciting players Gullit has brought into the club. Ruud's done extremely well, and if we are to get anything out of the game, we're going to have to be at our best.'

Zola, already nicknamed 'Gorgon' (not exactly original), prepared for his home debut with an unusual problem. It concerned his No. 25 shirt: 'I need a "M", not "XL". I told them that at Blackpool.' He meant, of course, Blackburn, venue for his debut. He mockingly rolled up his sleeves. It brought hoots of laughter during the press conference, and was screened on *Football Focus* where Newcastle's Les Ferdinand was the guest with Gary Lineker. The dry-cleaners opposite the Bridge completed the necessary shortening alterations to Zola's shirt, and kit suppliers Umbro promised one that fitted in time for the next game at Elland Road.

Gullit hailed Zola's debut match at the Bridge on Saturday 23 November as 'a good promotion for English football' despite another 1–1 draw. Less than twenty-four hours after the new Arsenal manager Arsene Wenger foresaw Premiership sides containing seven or eight foreigners, Zola raised Chelsea's Continental complement to six. Gullit, anticipating that a third Italian would attract sceptical comment, drew the parallel in his programme notes with the arrival of himself and two fellow Dutchmen at Milan: 'It looks here now a bit like Milan was when I was there. Milan suddenly had three foreigners, three Dutchmen. Nobody called it in that moment Milan-Dutch. Or called the training ground Hollandello instead of Milanello. Or Milamsterdamo! Everything does need some time to get used to. But everybody will not be talking Italian here. The team is now under more pressure with Zola coming. Players have to perform. There is more competition. Players are aware they have to perform every week. And you supporters will be demanding it of them. It's a new situation for everyone. I know you supporters don't accept complaints from players. We all have one goal, the same goal: winning something. I think you feel something good is coming, and players aren't expected to act for themselves. I want everyone acting professionally and trying to get into the team.'

While the aforementioned Dutchmen, Frank Rikjaard and Marco van Basten, lent moral support from the stand, was it stretching the symbolic point to expect Chelsea's Italian contingent to make a comparable impact? After all, when Gullit and his compatriots exploded on *Serie A*, they were still approaching the peak of their powers, the catalyst for a team already brimming with world-class talent before they arrived, but underachieving.

Gullit received the Cork branch of the supporters' club's Player of the Year award, took it back to the dressing-rooms and then resumed his place on the bench. Vialli and Asprilla exchanged kisses on the cheek and David Ginola, then at Newcastle, shook the Italians' hands before the kick-off.

Zola made an instant impact on his home debut. Newcastle boss Kevin Keegan joked: 'I liked him better in their half than our half! He was a bundle of tricks and he's always going to be dangerous from any free-kick.' It was to Zola's free-kick in the twenty-third minute that Vialli claimed the deftest of touches. Even after watching the replays half a dozen times, it was hard to tell whether he actually had got a touch. 'Maybe it went in off his hair!' said Gullit. 'He has got one?' Zola had whipped in one of his famous free-kicks and Vialli insisted: 'I definitely headed the ball. I would never deprive my old friend of a goal on his debut unless I was sure about it.' It was suggested that Vialli's motive might be a clause in his contract worth £3,000 a goal. Not so, said Colin Hutchinson. Zola was happy to accept Vialli's word for it: 'If Gianluca says he touched it, I believe him. It's no problem, even though I was actually trying to score, as I have done so many times from similar situations in Italy.'

Vialli answered the burning question in English football – were the foreigners good for our game? He delivered an emphatic 'yes', but with a very essential proviso: 'It is important when you buy foreign players that they are the best; they must be very clever, strong mentally as well as physically, and they have to be a teacher. If you choose well, England can improve; if you don't choose well, English football will go down.'

On view at Stamford Bridge that day was £30 million worth of some of the most glamorous of the foreign imports, intriguing confrontations; the French Connection of Leboeuf and Ginola, the Parma Connection between Zola and Asprilla, and the Italian Job lot acquired by the Dutch boss.

The occasion was spoilt somewhat by the sending-off of David Batty, forcing Keegan's hand in withdrawing his flair players Ginola and Asprilla. Keegan explained: 'There is no great magic to this game, it would just have been crazy to carry on with ten men as if it was Roy of the Rovers when real life is not like that. There was still a lot to be written in this game. People think I'm a bit cavalier, and perhaps I am, but it would have been suicide to have left on Ginola and

Asprilla when we were one man short.' Keegan threw a consoling arm around Ginola when he brought him off soon after Batty's dismissal, and there was also a cuddle for the Colombian later in the game as Keegan opted to send on first Steve Watson and then Lee Clark. Keegan moaned that the spectators were the losers by his pragmatic approach of putting ten men behind the ball to protect the point, keeping Newcastle at the top of the Premiership: 'Sadly, the game was spoilt, but I had to take the flair players off. Ruud had a very good side here and they gave us a lot of problems, but I felt at half-time that if we kept possession we could win the match. When you see this result on Teletext, 1–1, you would think it was not very interesting. The truth was both sides wanted to entertain. Please God, we do better than them.'

Batty had swung his elbow and caught Hughes full in the face. He was full of remorse, Keegan full of recriminations. Batty couldn't apologize enough: 'I went over to Mark on the floor to tell him that I was sorry, I didn't mean to catch him. I just felt his presence behind me and I've caught him but not meant to do it. So I deserve to go. I felt bad, I'd let everyone down and said so. It was the first time I've been sent off in my career but there was no intent to harm Mark Hughes at all.' Keegan had no complaint about the referee's decision but felt Hughes should also have been punished, if only with a yellow card: 'Obviously something happened to make David Batty react in that way. One guy is sent off but the other guy goes scot-free.' Needless to say, Hughes was not impressed with that view: 'Mr Keegan's player accepted that he should have done what he did, so I don't know why the manager can't as well. If I don't challenge for every ball, I get stick off *my* manager.'

When asked for his view of the incident, Gullit sounded like a typical English manager when he professed that he didn't see it! 'I was warming up. But I saw his nose. I saw a little bit of blood coming out, and Mark is not a guy who moans a lot!'

At times Shearer was the last man in defence for Newcastle in a backs-to-the-wall display that gave Keegan more satisfaction than some of his glorious attacking successes. Goalkeeper Pavel Srnicek had given Keegan nightmares at times; on this occasion he was outstanding. Keegan declared: 'The keeper answered some of his critics with great saves.'

Arsene Wenger had predicted that Hoddle would be deprived of international talent as foreign stars swamped the top Premiership sides, so it was appropriate that the England coach should be at the Bridge as Keegan delivered his verdict: 'I'm not one of these Englishmen out to protect jobs because they believe that is to the benefit of English football. I've no qualms about the top foreign players coming to these shores and I believe it will make English players better. We should not be scared to learn, and our game will benefit by having top quality stars to learn from.'

Shearer – who else? – grabbed the equalizer in the forty-second minute with persistence, concentration and calmness that marked him down as world-class. He was thwarted first by Grodas but kept his composure to weave backwards past Michael Duberry and shoot into the corner before Wise could tackle, Steve Clarke getting his head to the ball but only helping it into the corner. Shearer was one of the few English players on the same level as Gullit's recruits from *Serie A* and Vialli had nothing but admiration for him: 'He's a great player, very strong. Our keeper was very good to stop him but then he showed unbelievable ability in the middle of three or four of our defenders to score. Congratulations to him.' Asked about Shearer's amazing heart, Vialli added: 'I know, you know, that's Shearer.'

No-one questioned Shearer's long-term commitment – those sorts of accusations tended to be reserved for the Italians. But Vialli didn't plan to be a 'Herr today, gone tomorrow' Klinsmann! 'I am working to put Chelsea on top,' he insisted. 'I want to become an important player for the club. I don't know if I can, but I want to become a Chelsea legend. I am staying here three years to do that. I plan to enjoy myself here and win something with Chelsea, and I think it's looking good. Chelsea played better than Newcastle, we had eight to ten chances in front of goal and we were unlucky. Newcastle are a very good team, Liverpool the same. I'm happy and Mark is happy; we may not score like Ferdinand and Shearer or Ravanelli, but we work hard for the team and as a result sometimes our team-mates score maybe because of us.'

Vialli's verdict on Zola's home debut: 'He's a great player, the best player in the world to deliver to you a pass.' Gullit agreed: 'Everyone is very happy with him. He created so many things, he improved our team performance. Overall, I'm happy about everyone's performance. It was a good game tactically and technically, an open game with a little excitement. I was disappointed when we drew against Nottingham Forest, especially the way we played, but this was a really good game with both sides wanting to play exciting football, so I'm quite happy about the way we played. Of course it was always difficult against ten men, very difficult. But everyone worked very hard, I have nothing to complain about – only the result.'

Gullit made his entry in the sixty-first minute, Di Matteo's turn to be substituted for the first time. Again, no favouritism. Di Matteo said: 'Okay, we have now good players in this team and it can happen that you go substituted, yes? And I hope to play the next game and I hope to play maybe better than this game, or maybe he choose somebody else!' Gullit gave no guarantees that the three Italians would all play every game together, and Di Matteo wasn't sure it was such an advantage being all of the same nationality: 'I don't know; I don't know. We can help each other if we are three Italians. Maybe Franco can help Luca and Luca can help me. But I don't know if we can bring a new style to the Premier League. It depends on the whole team. Because you play with eleven players, not three. So if everybody does what he has to do, I think we can have a good season.'

In the final frenzy when Chelsea might easily have grabbed the winner against the ten men on the retreat, Wise struck a marvellous long-range shot that whacked against the bar, bringing the fans to their feet. Wise recalled: 'I said to Alan Shearer at one point, "In a minute I'll hit a thirty-yarder in the top corner." He said, "If you do it I'll give you a hundred quid." So what happened? I hit the flippin' crossbar from thirty yards. He turned round and muttered, "Unlucky, I nearly had to pay up there." I bet he couldn't have afforded it anyway!'

Gullit was delighted with the extra development of his team with the arrival of Zola: 'He's made a big impact on the crowd at Blackburn and against Newcastle. It's not easy to adapt yourself quickly, but he has. He can play midfield or up front, he has freedom during a game to do what he wants as long as he remembers the responsibilities he must carry out tactically. His arrival was followed by John Spencer leaving. We had a whole lot of players who I didn't want to leave. The policy of this club is that we want them to stay and battle for a place. But if someone only wants to play, if he says, "I don't want to stay if I'm not in the team," then the coach cannot motivate him. If he wants to go somewhere else then he must go, and I truly hope that he finds that luck. Good luck, Spenny! It is the same for Gavin [Peacock] and Steino [Mark Stein]. With Steino, perhaps it is a little different. He's had a lot of injuries for some time, he was having difficulties getting in the squad last year and maybe it is best for him after nearly two years of that and of training with the reserves to go on loan. Gavin is another who didn't want to wait for his chance, who wanted to get away. I regret it, but we can't have people to stay here if they don't want to. Again, I hope he finds his luck. Wisey played very well in his 250th Chelsea game at Manchester United. He's played very well for the last few games. It has been up to him to adapt to the new situation, and he is handling it very well. That's because he is a good professional. He is playing well, better than before. He understands now that we can't assure him or anyone of a place. You have to play well every week. I see players playing better than before, now. Of course, this brings pressure. Good! It makes it easier for the staff. It is difficult with the crowd, too, now. The crowd now demands that you do everything in order to win, and if they can see that the team is doing everything in their power, then it doesn't matter so much if sometimes it doesn't go for you. Like against Newcastle – we didn't win but the crowd was very happy with the performance. The team gave what everybody expected. The staff was happy, too.'

Graham Rix was annoyed at the suggestion that the import of foreign stars would hold back the youngsters at the club: 'It's untrue and I think we have disproved it. Even with all the foreign players who have come in, we have had Jody Morris and Mark Nicholls, at seventeen and nineteen, making their full debuts this season. By bringing in the best, we have set our standards high. Young lads are thinking, "I've got to be a bit special to get in this team," and that's how it should be. We shouldn't settle for mediocrity. On the Tuesday after Zola signed, we were playing an eight-a-side possession game and his technique and the zip in his passing just took your breath away. The next day we did it again and all the home-grown players were trying things as well, to show him what they could do.'

Rix accepted that there was still a problem at Chelsea – the capacity for defeat by the lower orders, as Bolton in the Coca-Cola Cup had illustrated: 'We are trying to instil it into them that if you do not have the right mental approach in the Premiership, you can get beaten by anybody. It's as simple as that.' So how close were Chelsea to muscling in on the elite of the North? Rix pinpointed the coaching at the pre-season Umbro tournament: 'As an experiment, Ruud had us man-for-man all over the pitch against Ajax and we slaughtered them. The players started believing how good they could be. Also, for me, the signing of Zola was interesting. Coming shortly after Matthew Harding's tragic death, it sent out a statement that we mean business. We are building a team, a club, a stadium to compete with the best. That was the legacy Matthew would have wanted.'

Next for Zola was Elland Road. Few fixtures evoked memories of the seventies more than this one – those flying wingers, silly sideburns and colourful characters. The cultures of Elland Road and the King's Road were more than a World's End apart. 'They hated each other, kicked lumps out of each other, didn't they?' said Rix, a Yorkshireman, and then an Arsenal player. Little changed. 'Leeds will be steaming in, tackling for everything; the crowd will be booing Gianfranco Zola and Luca Vialli, calling us southern softies and all that,' said Rix.

He added: 'There are two kinds of courage in football. There is putting your head or foot in, and there is sticking to your principles, playing with the pressure, not getting carried away by the taunts of the public. The likes of Zola, Vialli and Frank Leboeuf have the character and belief in themselves that comes from having seen it all. They have a mental toughness that maybe this club has lacked at times.'

As the month came to a close, Kevin Keegan and Alex Ferguson believed it would be the most open title race for years. Keegan argued: 'Nobody is going to run away with it this season and I think it will go to the wire. Any one of five or six clubs could win it, and I would include Chelsea in that.' The Manchester United boss felt it would be limited to five clubs. 'As for Chelsea, they have bought big to get in touch with the big time. The way they keep buying, yes, they could be there as well. Nobody has been flying away with it and, at this moment, the League is looking really close.'

Gullit was sure his side were shaping up: 'We are doing well. With a third of the season gone, however, we can still improve a lot of aspects. But that is normal. I expected improvement by this stage, and it has come. But we are not yet where we want to be. Everybody, I am pleased to say, is aware of this, which makes it easier for the management. You can see it in people in training, not going home immediately they've finished work together, but maybe going in the gym or staying on the pitch doing exercises. They are aware of how to improve themselves. The management doesn't have to tell them anymore. In other words, their awareness of being professional is much greater now.'

The first day of December was another setback, a crushing 2–0 defeat at Leeds, as Zola continued his initiation period with his new team-mates while Gullit worked out the best strategy.

Zola was provided with an insight into the brutality of the English game, if he ever thought cynicism was restricted to *Serie A*! Mark Hughes was lucky not to have his leg broken, stretchered off after being pole-axed by a high tackle from striker Brian Deane. Six stitches in an ugly gash above his ankle left him grimacing as he hobbled away: 'He came in high and when someone does that, you know you're going to be in real trouble. I feared the worst. I'm lucky, I think I got away with it. Once a challenge comes in higher than the level of your boot, you know there's a chance of serious injury.' Leeds boss George Graham countered: 'Brian has some nasty scratchmarks down his shins. That is part and parcel of the game. You don't want to take away the sport's physical nature.' Physio Mike Banks said: 'Mark's sock over his right shin was in tatters when I got to him and the pad was broken underneath. As usual, Sparky made light of it all, but there was an extremely deep two-inch gash which was impossible to repair.' Referee Steve Dunn clocked up seven bookings but somehow managed to miss the horror tackle. Gullit was frustrated that players were confused and upset by inconsistent referees: 'A player doesn't know where he stands. He doesn't know which tackle will be punished and which one will be allowed to go. It is a big issue and we have to discuss this with the whole of the Premiership.'

Gullit's European union had come across a touch of Yorkshire grit. At a wet and windy Elland Road, from the opening minutes when Vialli fell to the ground clutching his face following the merest nudge from Lee Bowyer, it was suspected that the foreign legion didn't fancy this one. Leboeuf was once again subjected to the rough stuff. Wimbledon had given him a major battering; now Deane carried on where the Crazy Gang left off. At least Di Matteo tried to get involved in the midfield war of attrition, but he was so much out of his depth he was withdrawn at half-time with the battle already lost.

Vialli managed one shot – in the eighty-ninth minute. Zola managed a couple of tasty corner-kicks, but he was completely snuffed out by South African defender Lucas Radebe, beginning the debate about whether to man-mark the latest Italian recruit to the English game.

Chelsea hadn't lost often on their travels, but when they did it was normally pretty comprehensive. Gullit had arrived with fifth place in his sights and left fortunate to have conceded only two goals. Instead of the skills of Zola and Leboeuf, the more prosaic talents of Deane and Beesley took the eye. 'Our tactics were spot on,' Graham said. 'We knew they would want to slow the game down, and it was our duty to impose the pace of our game on them. We denied them time and space to show their ability. Zola is one of my favourite players, but we gave Radebe a job to do and he was up to the task. Their defence looked a bit suspect.'

Graham, a former Chelsea player himself, concluded: 'Chelsea have to start winning things soon. With the players they have at the club now, they have got to win trophies.'

4

Zola In – Spencer Out

As a player, Ruud Gullit transformed AC Milan from a mid-table team going nowhere to one of the world's most powerful club sides. He, van Basten and Rikjaard, the three Dutchmen, were the driving force, the intoxicating foreign influence that made for a tantalizing mix: Italian flair and efficiency and the Dutch mastery of the unexpected.

The key to the team built by Silvio Berlusconi's millions was a formidable squad system, the rotation of several international-class players. Sometimes it meant a player of even Gullit's calibre missing out, as he indeed did in a European Cup Final. He experienced first-hand the bitterness towards his coach and the humiliation that drove him to walk out on his beloved Milan for Sampdoria.

Gullit knew that the arrival of Zola at Chelsea would increase his managerial options, and that someone would be 'disenfranchised'. Sure enough, a mere five days after Zola's debut for Chelsea at Blackburn, John Spencer became the first big-name casualty of the Ruud Revolution.

In truth, Spencer's future at the club had already been the subject of prolonged speculation. He had failed to hold down a first-team place since the arrival of Vialli. Now the signing of Zola made his departure inevitable.

Gullit had a straightforward, simple philosophy. Anyone willing to stay and fight for a first-team place would be welcome to stay.

Anyone moaning about the squad system could leave if they wanted to.

The long-running Spencer saga was finally concluded with his £2.5 million move to Queens Park Rangers, as he became the Loftus Road club's record signing. He said: 'I'm just glad to get this chance with a club that has faith in me.'

Spencer had joined Chelsea in 1992 for £450,000 and become a favourite with the fans. He was the club's top scorer with thirteen Premiership goals in the last season under Hoddle, having been joint top scorer the previous campaign. But he was frozen out following the Gullit revamp up front. Under the new manager, Spencer made just three starts, all in the Coca-Cola Cup, with just four Premiership appearances from the bench. The 5ft 6in Scot made clear his displeasure at the start of the season, and while Gullit had gone on record as saying that nobody would have to leave to balance the books, the arrival of a third Italian tipped the balance.

Spencer insisted that Gullit was wrong to leave him out: 'I don't care what big names they have signed or where they have come from, I felt I was good enough to be in the side. But I wasn't going to hang around in the reserves. At twenty-six, I needed first-team football, especially as I have international ambitions. It was a difficult decision to leave. I got on well with the other players, but it was frustrating not being picked. Now I have to forget about it because Chelsea is finished for me and I have to think about QPR.' He had no regrets dropping down to the First Division. 'QPR offered me first-team football. Just speaking to Stewart Houston for ten minutes made me realise it was the right decision. He is ambitious and QPR won't be in Division One for very long. I wasn't in the first team at Chelsea and I'm not the kind of person to sit on my backside and take the money for playing in the reserves.'

Houston also snapped up Gavin Peacock on loan, pending a permanent transfer. Next out the door from the Bridge was Mark Stein, who rejoined his former club Stoke on a month's loan. QPR also went back for Craig Burley, but baulked at the same asking price as Spencer. But Burley would eventually become part of a summer clear-out.

Spencer trebled his pay-packet by quitting Gullit's Chelsea revolution, but insisted money played no part in his decision. He said: 'I could have stayed at Chelsea and picked up good money just for sitting on the bench. But no matter what fans think about the glamour at Stamford Bridge, it wasn't much fun for me being out of the team. It doesn't matter if you're Italian, Scottish, Brazilian or a Frenchman, footballers have one thing in common – we all want to play. We need to be wanted. So the moment Chelsea signed Gianfranco Zola, I knew it was time to go.

'He's the best player I've ever seen. It was actually worth training just so you could be there when he was practising his free-kicks.'

'His bad foot is better than my good one!'

But the self-deprecating humour failed to conceal the hurt Spencer felt at being edged out of Chelsea by what he considered to be the ruthless decision of Gullit: 'He didn't think I was good enough and we did have rows about it. He is one of the finest players I have played with or against. He is Glenn Hoddle with pace and power. I knew he was world-class but he thought I was second-class. That's fair enough, it's his opinion. He brought in other players and has been proved right, because Chelsea are now in their best league position for years. But Glenn Hoddle used to pick me and I know I played very well last season. In fact, Gullit didn't do any better than me on the park.

'Everything was fine between us when he was a player. But when he became manager, it became very obvious British players just weren't good enough for him. He was only interested in foreigners. And, to his credit, those he's brought into the club are world-class. But I must have been doing something right, because my value rose from £400,000 to £2.5 million during my time at Chelsea and I also became a Scottish international.

'If I do the business at QPR, I know I'll keep my place in the side. And that was never the case at Chelsea. I feel really wanted here and that is so important. Ruud Gullit was a big influence on me, but he was not happy with me. There was no point moping about it and feeling sorry for myself. I had to find another club who cared, and QPR have given me that arm round my shoulder.'

Peacock completed his permanent move to QPR before the end of the year, for an initial fee of £800,000 rising to £1 million after a certain number of appearances. He had captained Chelsea and played in the 1994 FA Cup Final, but had not featured under Gullit: 'I felt it was time to move on. I had some great times at Chelsea and I like to think I had a good relationship with the fans. But now I am 100 per cent committed to QPR and I believe we have all the ingredients we need for success.' Spencer's goals and the ammunition supplied by Peacock rocketed Rangers to the fringe of the promotion zone, but sadly they missed out on even the play-offs.

There would be other departures. Erland Johnsen opted to exercise his rights under the new Bosman ruling and long before the end of the season decided to return to Norway to join Rosenborg. Even one of the FA Cup heroes, Scott Minto, quit on a free transfer at the end of Gullit's first year in charge to sign for one of Europe's glamour clubs, Benfica. Johnsen never felt that he would win a regular first-team place, while Minto was dissatisfied with his new contract talks. Even before the Cup Final, Gullit was busy recruiting a new army of foreign stars for the new season.

Little wonder, then, that the debate rumbled on about whether overseas stars were good for the game or stifling the development of young talent at clubs such as Arsenal, and restricting the supply to Glenn Hoddle's England team.

Players' union leader Gordon Taylor was outspoken about the quantity of overseas labour, although he was not against the arrival of quality stars to enhance the English game. With Zola's impact encouraging clubs to pursue even more foreign talent, the new season was to see a near fifty per cent increase in overseas players – there are now more than 130 in the Premiership and a further 100 in the Nationwide League. Taylor said: 'If our own youngsters aren't going to get an opportunity, they will look to other sports and perhaps other professions. It has become fashionable to look abroad for the products of other country's coaching systems. Managers are looking from week to week because of their insecurity of tenure. But we have to look to the long term. Going abroad for talent is a quick fix, but sooner or later the foreign clubs will raise their prices and if there is nobody to turn to domestically, the clubs will have been hoist by their own petard.'

Zola's agent Jon Smith, who also represents Ruud Gullit, looked at the other side, the benefit to the game. He observed: 'It has sparked life into our game. For a long time we had an island mentality and our football suffered from that. We used to say we produced the greatest goalkeepers. Then we saw people like Peter Schmeichel coming into our game. What Chelsea have done has created excitement and allowed supporters here to watch players like Zola.'

There was no questioning Zola's quality. He was hailed as the icon of foreign imports by George Graham. The Leeds manager attacked the 'whingeing' mercenaries, only here for the fast buck, and picked out Zola as a shining exception to the rule: 'Obviously financial gain had a part in Zola's decision to play in the Premiership, but he came with a big reputation and has delivered the goods. If all foreigners approached the game in the same manner, it would be superb. I have seen too many come over here and start whingeing after a few months, but Zola has worked hard, his attitude has been first-class and he has been a credit to himself and his country.'

Graham's former club captain at Highbury, Tony Adams, took a similar view. The Arsenal skipper appreciated the extra dimension players like Zola and his own team-mate Dennis Bergkamp had brought to the Premiership: 'They are the sort of players who can open a door in an instant; they have that bit extra. I wish English players were producing what Bergkamp and Zola are. Better still, I wish they were Londoners. The foreign players bring something different to our league and I have no objection to them playing here, as long as it doesn't interfere with the growth of young English players. That won't happen at Arsenal, though. We have Liam Brady in charge of the youth set-up and he is doing a terrific job. But we have some of the best players in the world at English clubs now and two of them are in London. That can't be bad, can it?'

Adams added: 'They are exciting, but I see other things in a game. Naturally, I speak as a defender and I like to see how defenders cope with them. I like watching the defensive work put in to eliminate those players. I would want to pat someone on the back for putting Zola in his place. For me, defending is an art as much as attacking.'

The Bridge buzzed with anticipation and expectancy thanks to Chelsea's foreign legion. Captain Dennis Wise said: 'I keep reading stories about problems at the club, but it's all nonsense. The foreign stars are great blokes and we all get on well – although I still haven't managed to persuade Zola to start drinking.

'As for the so-called rift between Vialli and the manager, all I can say is that it isn't apparent to the rest of us and if there is a problem, it's a matter for them to solve. Because of the number of good players we now have at Chelsea, it's obvious someone has to be left out; we've all had to put up with it and I think we all accept it.'

Zola's success was a big influence on the influx of more foreign talent to the Bridge. The Nigerian left wing-back Celestine Babayaro was signed for £2.25 million as Chelsea beat off competition from Juventus, Inter Milan, Ajax, Deportivo La Coruña and Arsenal. Known as Baba, he won an Olympic Games gold medal for Nigeria in Atlanta in 1996, scoring one of their goals in the final against Brazil. Babayaro had been with Anderlecht from the age of fifteen and was being tracked by a pack of Europe's top clubs after impressive performances for the Belgian team in the Champions' League and UEFA Cup, but Gullit's worldwide reputation persuaded him to join Chelsea. 'I told Ruud I wanted to sign for Chelsea after only two conversations on the telephone,' Babayaro said. 'He told me, "Baba, you're a great player. Do you like Chelsea?" I said yes, and he says okay, he'll be glad to have me. I am very happy he wants me in his team and I am looking forward to a great season with Chelsea. I've watched all the top European matches on TV and I have been impressed with Chelsea and their players. I watched them defeat Wimbledon, for whom my Nigerian team-mate Efan Ekoku plays, in the FA Cup semi-final and I was very impressed. Ruud Gullit was always one of my heroes, long before I spoke to him. Gianfranco Zola is an inspirational player and I am very excited about playing with him. It is my dream to play in England. My assets, I think, are that I'm fast, good with my head and I can score.'

Uruguayan international Gustavo Poyet was brought in on a free transfer from Real Zaragoza. He signed a three-year deal worth over £600,000 a season. Poyet, a goalscoring midfielder, played in Zaragoza's Cup-Winners' Cup semi-final first leg win over Chelsea in 1995, although he was suspended for the Stamford Bridge return, and helped the Spanish side beat Arsenal 2–1 in the final. With another deal expertly tied up, Colin Hutchinson explained: 'Although he is Uruguayan, he has a Spanish passport and has dual nationality so doesn't need a work permit.' Poyet was named 'player of the tournament' in the 1995 Copa America, which Uruguay won, and Hutchinson said: 'Players of his calibre don't usually become available on free transfers. Both the Madrid giants, Real and Atletico, showed interest, as did some Italian clubs. But it shows the pulling power of Chelsea and the Premiership that he has chosen to come to us.'

Poyet said: 'I watch a lot of English football on television and Chelsea's style of play impresses me. I believe I am well-suited to the English game and I am looking forward to the challenge and playing with great players like Mark Hughes, Zola, Leboeuf, Wise, Di Matteo and Vialli. Chelsea are ambitious and this is a great move for me.'

Diego Maradona's advice persuaded Poyet to join Chelsea. The Uruguayan revealed: 'Diego said that Zola and Gullit were two of the best players in the world. The fact that they are both at Chelsea definitely influenced my decision.'

Roberto Di Matteo believed Italy's superstars were queuing up to come to England; he found himself being grilled on English football every time he reported back to Italy for international duty: 'There is now a huge interest in English football. All the Italian players would like to come here. They see that me and Gianfranco Zola are enjoying the life and the football here and they want to taste it for themselves. Something has changed in England this year. In Italy, we always used to look down on the standard of football in this country. But the technique has definitely improved lately. A lot of that is down to the foreign players in the Premiership. They raised the standard of play in Italy in the past and now they are doing the same over here.'

Di Matteo paid tribute to his manager for the faith shown in him. 'I feel the confidence of the gaffer . . . I mean the coach,' he laughed. 'That is very important for me because it allows me to try things I would not normally do. London was very important in my decision to come here, but Gullit played an even bigger part. I could have gone to other Italian clubs, but knowing that he wanted me made my decision very easy. Now other players in Italy want to come here because we already have Zola and Vialli, and they are important names to attract them.'

During a season interlaced with discussions about the foreigners, Gullit turned on the critics still sniping away at his foreign captures:

'This whole thing has exploded because of what has happened with Emerson at Middlesbrough. It has given attention to the foreign players, especially ours. It is not fair to say every foreign player can be compared with what is happening at Middlesbrough. I am happy with the commitment of my players. The fans are also happy. When I was at Milan, we were not given any favours because we were so good. We had to fight jealousy from so many people. Everyone wants to beat Chelsea now, that is natural. I have told my players this and advised them now to stick together and carry on working hard. I am not looking to build a side completely of foreign players, but people should ask themselves, "What do we want, what are we creating?" We have been going up this season and now we have levelled out a bit. But that is natural.

'The trouble is, some people do not like change. Some clubs look into their wallet and do not want to spend or cannot. Because of the Bosman ruling, foreign players are coming here. It seems you want to be part of Europe in this country, but not football. My team keep playing right to the end and we never give up. I can do nothing about goals that go in off one of my player's backsides. I never see these kind of things happening in our favour. One day the luck will change. I would like to see us play badly and win. We have played some very good matches; we have deserved more than draws. I'm pleased at how we have handled the games. It is disappointing that we've lost points, but everyone is convinced by the way we're playing. It's a very good sign. I am sure our results will change. I believe it is just a matter of results now. My players know they can do better and there is a lot of hard work for us to do yet. My team have adapted well and there is a very good atmosphere here. They all get on very well.'

5

Zola the Gola

The headlines roared 'Zola the Gola' after his startling exploits for both Italy and Chelsea.

It seemed every time Zola scored, it was either an exquisite exhibition of trickery and control or a goal of monumental importance.

His goal against England, his cheeky piece of impertinence against Manchester United at the Bridge, and his explosive turn and strike against Wimbledon in the FA Cup semi-final at Highbury were among his most potent goals in his short period in English football.

Honoured by the BBC's experts as his goals became candidates for Goal of the Month and Goal of the Season, Zola jeopardized England's World Cup qualification chances with his Wembley winner, worried Alex Ferguson's champions and took Chelsea on their glory ride to the FA Cup Final.

The first of his glory goals came against Everton at the Bridge on Saturday 7 December 1996. It might have been another indecisive 2–2 draw that left Chelsea short in the title stakes, but the game was illuminated by Zola getting off the mark with a wonder free-kick, and it had Gullit drooling over the virtues of Italian imports as, in addition, Luca Vialli headed his eighth goal in the league. Gullit said: 'We had the same discussion in Italy when the foreign players arrived: is it good for the national team? Now, a lot of discussion is about the Italians that have come to Chelsea pushing out the British players. But they are having a major impact on the Premiership, they are bringing something special to Premiership football; everybody is very happy to see them play. I don't really understand what the discussion is all about. These players have brought something extra to the Premier League and they are talked about all the time. But for some reason they only talk about the Italians.'

Little Zola's first goal in English football was a gem: a thirty-yarder mesmerizing Earl Barrett and Neville Southall on the line after clearing the Everton wall. Gullit said: 'I couldn't have done that, my feet are too big! I knew he could do things like that, that's why I bought him. He's small, but he is still strong.'

Zola might have scored a second from another free-kick, much closer, just outside the penalty area, after Gullit's quick turn and right-wing cross left Vialli grounded and Barrett complaining to referee Paul Durkin. Zola's free-kick clipped the top of the defensive wall and from the corner, Vialli chased, produced a delightful back-heel and from Duberry's cross, Gullit, of all people, headed just over from two yards – kicking the post in frustration.

Gullit's presence from the start certainly lifted Chelsea but another draw did not truly satisfy either manager. Joe Royle was upset Zola had been awarded the free-kick from which he scored in the twelfth minute, after the Italian dispossessed Barrett and, while taking up possession, was brushed off the ball by Joe Parkinson. Just six minutes later the ever dangerous Duncan Ferguson touched on Andy Hinchcliffe's cross, Leboeuf was beaten to the bouncing ball and young Michael Branch equalized. A magnificent pass by Ferguson over Steve Clarke into the stride of Andrei Kanchelskis culminated in a comfortable goal in the twenty-eighth minute, emphasizing Everton's growing dominance of the first half and Chelsea's frailties at the back.

It changed after the interval, with Gullit making tactical adjustments and reverting to a flat back four. In the end, Chelsea were unfortunate not to win.

Zola was the inspiration behind Chelsea's equalizer, winning the ball in his own half and exchanging passes with Gullit before his chip to the near post was finished off by Vialli in the fifty-fifth minute. When Gullit took a throw to Leboeuf, the Frenchman produced a magnificent pass to Zola, but the shot was cleared off the line by

David Unsworth and somehow he saved the rebound from Vialli. Zola also clipped the top of the bar from a corner in an outstanding all-round display. He said: 'I was happy because it was my first goal in England. But we made little mistakes and the other team scored. That is the problem. In the second half we played well, but we did not win and we have to think about that.' Zola's interview in the press room was interrupted by his son Andrea. For a while the yellow teddy with the headscarf over his eye occupied Zola junior, but soon boredom set in!

Down to seventh place, Chelsea needed a winning run to re-establish their title aspirations. Royle branded Chelsea and Everton as 'wannabes', but Gullit's instincts told him Chelsea were not that far away: 'Everybody was really amazed the ball didn't want to go in for the winning goal. Twice off the line, incredible it didn't want to go in. We have to win these games.'

At least Royle had no objections to the foreign revolution: 'The problem arises when someone arrives from Eastern Europe with four Cs and two Zs in his name but is no better than those we have here. But Zola was different class.'

It wasn't all glory for the Italian boys as Di Matteo was dropped for the first time to the subs' bench. Gullit explained: 'There's no problem. For two weeks he has been a little bit out of form. I want him in the team, but he has to work hard to get back. He understands. It's nothing bad, a lot of players have this kind of period. As a coach, you pick the ones who are fit and doing well – Craig Burley came in and did very well for the team. It shows the choices made by the staff are right. It's only a matter of time before he is back.'

Gullit named Zola among the greatest dead-ball specialists in the modern game. 'Sometimes when he is doing his exercises, it is amazing how the ball is curving. I don't know how he does it. I only know I could never do it.'

Zola was sure Gullit would find a successful team plan: 'Chelsea are working hard to play the European way under Ruud Gullit. We need to improve, and I think we will with time. But the style of play was important to me. Sunderland will be a difficult game, but we are looking forward to this match with victory in mind.'

But it was a measure of Chelsea's inconsistency at this time that they slumped to a 3–0 defeat at Roker Park, sending their title odds tumbling from 16–1 to 33–1 long shots. Five games without a win! Zola yet to finish on the winning side! Gullit was not happy: 'There were strong words afterwards. We didn't deserve anything. I know we haven't won for five games, but I'm not worried about that. We didn't play well against Leeds and Sunderland, but we certainly had the other games there in our hand.'

Sunderland defender Andy Melville reflected on two emphatic away defeats for Gullit in front of the live TV cameras and said: 'Other teams will have noted that Chelsea can be hustled out of their stride and are bound to try it themselves. There's no doubt about it – they're going to have to cope with that side of the game if they're to challenge for honours.' Leeds had shown that raw-boned aggression could triumph over finesse and Sunderland took that as their cue. Melville added: 'They've got so many players who are top quality and who can do brilliant things on the ball. Gianfranco Zola, for instance, is a class act with an exceptional first touch. But we were determined they weren't going to have the space and time to start showing everyone what they can do. Sit back and let them play, and you're in trouble. But if you get your tackles in and work hard at closing them down, it's a different matter. That was the key for Leeds, and it was the same for us. Maybe I expected a bit more from Chelsea, but, to be fair, we didn't let them play any better. They've got great individuals, but we worked so hard as a team that they had no answer to it. Other teams are going to learn from this. They're bound to. It was live on TV, and teams due to face Chelsea are sure to set their stall out to do exactly the same as we did. Chelsea like to play to a pattern, but we didn't give them a second to settle on the ball. Now the big question is whether they can cope with that sort of close attention.'

Chelsea had always been the great underachievers and Gullit knew the sniggering and the sniping was beginning to start again. The Roker fans roared: 'Can we play you every week?' Chelsea slumped to eighth in the Premiership – a dozen points behind leaders Liverpool – their lowest position since the second game of the season. Hughes declared: 'At Chelsea, we play brilliant football one day and then fail to win matches we should have done the next. I think it takes time for a side with new players to settle down. At the moment, we are not producing the goods week in, week out, which the sides who finish top do.'

Zola did not agree he was less than effective when the opposition assigned a man to mark him: 'In every game in Italy I always had a man-marker. This is normal there. But I am a striker, so it is the same always. You always have a player behind you. That is not a problem. What is different for me is when I am not in good form. Sometimes you find a good player who can limit you. When you stay on form, then I can do the job the same. I only need one or two actions in a game. If you are clever, you can wait for your action and then you can score. Man-marking can be very hard for the defender then.'

Immediately after the disappointment at Roker Park, Zola was on the goal trail with four in three games against West Ham, Aston Villa and Sheffield Wednesday in a blistering Christmas period – and the goals continued with wonderful regularity for Chelsea fans. 'Gorgon' Zola became a *grand fromage* among the foreign legion in English football with a world-class goal and dazzling display in his first win in the Premiership, on Saturday 21 December, when the Blues beat the Hammers 3–1.

Zola was as amusing off the field as he was devastating on it, giving 'Terminator' Julian Dicks the kind of runaround that nobody else would dare contemplate. Zola dribbled one way, then the other, leaving Dicks embarrassed and searching for revenge before scoring his goal, but when the Hammers hardman targeted him, Zola's tiny feet were just too quick. So was it bravery or sheer stupidity to take on the shaven-haired assassin from the East End? Had he heard about Dicks's formidable 'psycho' reputation? In his broken English, Zola joked: 'I think they could have told me about him before the game! Had they done that, I'd have played for the other side.'

Zola knew the importance of this result in the London derby: 'Yeah, if we didn't win today, maybe I would have needed a ticket to go back to Parma. . . . I am only joking.'

He added: 'It was not only my goal, it was my overall performance for the team. I could have scored more and I can do better, but the most important thing is that today we played a very good game and everybody is happy.'

Gullit had assembled the biggest number of overseas stars at any club – other than West Ham. The Hammers had the most non-British players in the Premiership, ten, reduced from eleven after the loss of Paulo Futre. Chelsea had nine, followed by Manchester United with seven, Southampton six, and Arsenal, Aston Villa, Coventry, Derby, Middlesbrough and Sheffield Wednesday with five apiece in a Premiership that shared ninety-seven foreigners among its twenty clubs. Zola was up there among the elite already. He said: 'I can be more effective for the team, that's my target. We all have to work a lot to improve, but it helps to have an intelligent person like myself!'

The Zola–Hughes partnership had come together with startling effect in the absence of Vialli. Two goals from Hughes and one from Zola was the start of a formidable pairing that would soon lead to discontent from Vialli when he felt it was time to return. At the time there was only deep satisfaction that the Chelsea attack had begun to take shape with Zola playing a key role.

When he was handed a glass of Coke, Zola asked, 'Is it wine?' The press steward duly ran off to fetch a glass of white wine to put before him. 'I was only joking,' he said.

Still finding it difficult with his pronunciation, grammar and sentences, he called his new team 'Chels' as he tried to explain their frustrating away form compared to the successes at the Bridge: 'It's not only a problem for Chels, it's a problem for other teams. At times English football is very physique [physical], aggressive, but if you are organized you can win. It is a small margin between winning or losing, and I think we can still win away.'

Zola expressed his utmost admiration for Gullit: 'He's a good coach because he knows the football, he knows how the football must be played. I don't have a problem with his ideas. I think he will give Chelsea a lot of satisfaction. Football is interesting here, but I see good things from the coach and it's very interesting.'

With a cheeky backheel, Zola had set up Mark Hughes for the opening goal after five minutes, the Premiership's fastest of the weekend. Then, Gullit started the move that ended with Zola twisting Dicks in all directions for the second, after just nine minutes.

It was a Gullit tackle that gave Hugo Porfirio the shooting chance to haul the Hammers back after eleven minutes. But from a Burley break and Petrescu cross, Hughes headed Chelsea back into a

commanding lead after thirty-five minutes. Two minutes later, from a
Gullit pass, Hughes's shot was deflected off the line by Dicks and
onto the post. Hughes might have scored more, but it was a triumph
of courage, with his ankle heavily padded, that he survived the entire
game despite taking some nasty whacks. Di Matteo struck the post
eight minutes from the end after a move involving Gullit, Zola and
Hughes, leaving West Ham boss Harry Redknapp moaning about
defensive frailties: 'I didn't try to man-mark Zola because we haven't
a marker – neither, on today's showing, have we defenders who can
pick up Mark Hughes.'

Gullit said: 'Everyone can say whatever they like. Criticism and
compliments are part of the game and you have to accept it. This was
a good, solid performance; I never had the feeling we'd throw this
game away. Zola's goal was world-class, both strikers were world-
class. I'm happy about every foreigner who has come to this club and
Zola has brought something in particular. His skills have stolen the
hearts of everyone; the crowd like him. The players we have brought
have given something extra to the Premiership and I am very happy
for Franco; this was his best performance.'

Gullit's purchasing policy was based on a simple truth, that 'good
players can adapt'. He explained: 'You must understand, the first
thing you talk to them, you say it is a different ball game. But I know
exactly what I want. I don't buy a foreign player because he is foreign
and I must go with the fashion. I buy players I need. I think, "I need
a midfielder, what skills do I want from him? Who can do that?"
Then, "Is he available?" It is incredible the phone calls I get. Really
great players are offered. I think, "That's not possible," but you have
to check everything. But it must also be someone I can use. If I
already have three strikers, why buy a fourth?'

More to the point, how would Gullit accommodate Vialli? That
became a constant question for the Chelsea manager, though at this
stage it wasn't such a contentious issue. But in any case, Gullit was
unconcerned: 'It's nice to have that problem, especially now that
Gianfranco Zola has stolen the crowd's heart.' Gullit's selections
were based on form and fitness. He didn't judge anyone on reputation, not even Vialli. He himself planned to drop out when Leboeuf's
suspension was over, and if the manager axed himself, it seemed a fair

enough policy! Gullit added: 'I am comfortable with the players I have to do a job. There is always somebody who can create in this team, there are a lot of options.'

Zola not only had to acquaint himself with the English peculiarity of playing matches during the Christmas period, he also had to join the training session on Christmas Day. It was something that Gullit disapproved of, but he was determined to keep his players at optimum fitness over this crucial period. 'Christmas is a family day,' said Gullit, 'but in England it's a bit different. I must admit I wish we were off this Christmas. It still should be a family day for everyone. Unfortunately, the rules are different in England to elsewhere. Elsewhere, we would be off. They have a break in Italy, Holland and Belgium – everywhere has a break apart from England. We have to play so many games now, it is like a mini-marathon and we will have to divide our forces to get through it. There are a lot of points to be won and lost. I've heard the FA are thinking about introducing a break, so that's okay.'

Gullit planned an overnight stay in a Midlands hotel to prepare for the Boxing Day match at Villa Park, after training at the Bridge at 6pm on the heated turf. He explained: 'I shall allow the players to stay as long as possible with their families and we shall only go away in the evening.' Ruud trusted his 'professionals' to 'take care of their bodies'. He did not expect them to 'eat or drink a lot'. Zola was aware of the concentration of fixtures, five games in fifteen days: 'We shall need a lot of . . . how you say . . . strength. We hope to give our supporters good games, so they can have a good Christmas; that will be our present. I shall spend Christmas with my family and some friends from Italy. We know we are going to play a lot of games.'

Zola preferred an attacking position as the 'second' striker but was ready to adapt, despite acquiring a reputation on leaving Parma because he did not like being played out of position. He felt, though, to get the best results in signing him would be to play him in an advanced position, rather than wide or behind the front two.

He had no problem with being asked to switch roles: 'If you buy Zola, you want Zola to play the way Zola knows. I have to play like Zola. I am not in a situation to say I want to play here or there. My coach will decide this for me. If he thinks Zola can play better forward, I'll play there. The important thing is the team. I came here to play because I want to give all my possibilities to Chelsea. I don't want to create problems.'

Vialli and Leboeuf needed more rest and training before they would be back. Gullit explained: 'We're getting there in terms of injuries and most of the players are almost fit. We're looking forward to playing Villa, having looked so sharp against West Ham. People are saying Villa are a championship side, but the same can be said of a lot of sides at this stage of the season.'

On Boxing Day, Zola added Villa to his list of victims with a devastating display of finishing, a decisive two-goal burst in the space of just four minutes as Chelsea won 2–0. It was his first Premiership double since his arrival, and enough to shatter Villa's five-match winning streak. But, for Gullit, making his fiftieth Chelsea appearance, the most pleasing aspect was the team's first clean sheet in seventeen matches. 'At last,' as he put it.

It was the perfect introduction for Zola to festive football, courtesy of Villa's appropriately generous defence. First, he was allowed to cut across from the right before delivering a low shot to beat Mark Bosnich on sixty-five minutes, with the aid of a slight deflection off Ugo Ehiogu. Four minutes later, Zola was first to react to another Bosnich blunder when the Australian keeper hesitated, then missed as he came out to collect a back-header from Fernando Nelson. Left all on his own at an acute angle, Zola didn't hesitate before squeezing his shot inside the near post for his fourth goal in seven games.

Villa manager Brian Little complained: 'Bosnich could have done better with both goals. The first was slightly deflected, but he certainly should have dealt with the second goal long before there was any danger.'

Gullit was just full of praise for Zola again: 'The rest of the team have been supplying the bullets and he's our big gun to finish them off. His first couple of weeks were always going to be difficult, but now he has moved into a house, has settled in and is beginning to feel appreciated by everyone else here. The other players like the fact that even though he is such a very good player technically, he is still prepared to work hard, run back and do his fair share of defending.'

Just as crucial was Gullit's own role in the middle of a three-man defence. Deputizing again for the suspended Leboeuf, Gullit showed the class to blunt Villa's previously rampant attack. He said: 'Our defence was very good and very disciplined. We didn't give away many chances – that was the key to us playing well. Having got that right, we could rely on the talent in our team. When we have the ball, we can do so many good things.'

Villa managed just one real effort only seconds before Zola's breakthrough, when Dwight Yorke's header was blocked by Clarke before Ian Taylor miskicked in the six-yard box. In the end, Chelsea could have won by a much greater margin, with Bosnich making amends for his blunders by defying Newton and Zola. Little refused to condemn his side, insisting it was the presence of Gullit which had made all the difference: 'Whenever he is at the back for them, he keep things very tight. He doesn't lose possession, and tactically he is so aware of everything going on around him.'

Gullit warned absent stars Vialli, Leboeuf, Wise and Minto that there would be no quick return: 'I'm glad that my players are all available again, because it gives us greater competition. It's not so good for the players themselves, but it is for me as a manager. Zola and Hughes are playing very well as a pair together up front. It's unfortunate for Luca, but he will have to start on the bench when he comes back – not because he's not a good player but he has to be aware what is happening and happy for the team to be playing so well.'

Master strategist David Pleat now wondered whether he should be the next manager to put the shackles on the free-flowing Zola. The Sheffield Wednesday boss used his skipper Peter Atherton as an occasional man-marker and contemplated a similar role on Zola in the next Christmas fixture at the Bridge. 'I hope he does,' said Gullit. 'It will mean he will have one less player playing for his side and give us more space. Franco is used to it in Italy and so was I. I loved to be man-marked, it was a compliment to me.' Atherton, normally a centre-back, had been used to stop Steve McManaman and it worked so well that Wednesday won 1–0 at Anfield.

Vialli, Leboeuf and Wise on the bench! That signalled a powerful squad, but did not help Vialli's bid to return to World Cup football with Italy. New Italian coach Cesare Maldini was at the Bridge for the

Sheffield Wednesday game to check on the four Italian players on show. Gullit insisted: 'I'm happy to have Luca back and it's good he wants to be in the team, but we'll have to see. I must do what is best for Chelsea and the players understand that. It is not personal and I would never let personal business harm what is good for the team.' So Maldini watched Zola and Di Matteo as well as Wednesday's Benito Carbone before moving on to Highbury to check on Ravanelli. Being stuck on the bench with Maldini in town did nothing for Vialli's mood.

Carbone might have considered himself a rival to Zola, but the Chelsea man was in outstanding form. Gullit said: 'It wasn't easy for Franco at the start, because he was living in a hotel rather than his own home and couldn't get his rhythm. Now he is at home, feels appreciated and the team appreciates him, and that is what he needs.' Zola's swift acclimatization to English football pleased Gullit more than anything. His goals and his skill had enraptured the fans. 'Don't worry about him playing too much,' advised Gullit, 'or that it is cold. It is cold in Italy now. It is no different for him than playing two matches a week in Italy. If you play a lot of games and maybe one of them is a not-so-good game, you have the chance to forget about it because another game comes along so quickly. But if you are winning these games, you can jump three or four places and that is good for confidence. But we must aim for consistency and not lose matches we should win.'

Gullit reckoned the foreign legion made the Premiership the envy of the world – even the Italians were jealous of the cash and glamour generated by English soccer. He was convinced Vialli, Zola, Ravanelli, Vieira and Cantona had improved the quality of our game: 'I've a feeling the Premier League is becoming better all the time and more teams than ever can now challenge for the title. It is a very open championship because there are more foreigners bringing extra quality here, while the Englishmen have gained confidence because of the performances of the national team at Euro 96. The attention the Premiership gets from abroad has boosted all the players here, and the standard is so much better. There is now a whole page every day in the Italian papers about English football. The Fiorentina president Vittorio Cecchi Gori has just been complaining about the number of Premiership games being transmitted on Italian TV.'

Zola's two-goal blast at Villa Park had made the front pages of the Italian sports papers and now his goalscoring exploits continued in yet another high-scoring Chelsea draw. Terry Phelan, in his first full game of the season, linked with Hughes, whose low cross was slid in by Zola, lurking at the far post. Then in the twenty-second minute, Gullit stepped forward to make the perfect defensive interception and Di Matteo launched a perfect pass to Zola, whose cross was headed into the corner by Hughes, marking his fiftieth league appearance. But within seconds, a routine clearance was struck from thirty yards into the top corner by Mark Pembridge for Wednesday. Pleat, in his haste to move down from the stands to the dugout, got stuck in the lift and missed it! 'I nearly fell off the roof of the stand,' he said. 'It was suicide stuff because I thought it would be nasty for us, as Chelsea were superb. It's splendid for the game, the way they played. I love their movement, it was superb. I was glad I was here today, it was a very good game. With ten minutes to go and 2–1 down, I'd have had no complaints if we'd have lost, because we were playing such a good side. I'll take the video of this one – Zola was superb.'

Pleat had the honesty to admit: 'We were two–nil down and going nowhere at quarter-past three. It was like trying to deal with an avalanche; they were coming from all directions. If you'd have had a sweep, nobody would have had 2–2.'

Atherton was praised for subduing Zola in a man-marking role, having been assigned belatedly to the task after Zola scored. Personally, I felt Zola came out on top by some distance. Pleat said: 'A journalist rang me to say that Zola ran the game against West Ham. Did I plan to man-mark him? I had another plan – it didn't work!'

Atherton certainly got tighter on Zola, but the Italian was hardly fazed by the experience. He even joked that he would have 'preferred his wife' to the close attentions of his marker. He added, significantly: 'I know that I'm preparing myself well and I'm improving, running better than before. It is not a problem to find a player marks me like that, I had it all the time in Italy. But by the second half I was getting tired, after playing in a match two days earlier. I'm not used to that. . . . Now I'm going home to bed.' However, he would be 'watching *Match of the Day* first'.

Pleat was enthusiastic about the way Zola had been marked. He said: 'Atherton was splendid. He's a rarity in our game. He can tackle and mark but doesn't do it in a dirty way. Zola was superb, but not so superb when Atherton went onto him.'

Zola was cheered every time he went to take a corner. It was the sort of adulation he had never experienced before: 'I am very, very pleased; the people are important. They are very, how do you say, keen. Very supportive.' In just a few weeks, he'd become the idol of the Bridge. Gullit said: 'The fans need someone to identify with, especially the youngsters, and he's growing with every game.'

I suggested to Gullit that at 5ft 4in Zola *needed* to grow! Gullit laughed. 'It's very good to see good footballers in general,' he said. 'People come especially to see him, and you have that with players like Shearer and McManaman. It's the same with the good foreigners who come to the Premiership. When we go to other stadiums, they want to see us.'

The Italians were shocked by the extent of the passion in the crowd. Even Vialli, overcoming his disappointment at being on the bench in the presence of the new Italian coach, had to laugh when he spotted the famous Sheffield Wednesday fan, 'Tango Man'. Wearing any number of sweat tops and sporting a woollen hat and gloves, Vialli couldn't believe the bare-chested, bald-headed fan chanting throughout the game yards behind the dug-out.

Maldini was content with Zola and Di Matteo, less so with the substituted Carbone. Gullit said: 'I've been speaking to Mr Maldini and he is very impressed about the way people here live the game in a different way. He was not basing anything on one match, he had come to see the players and to talk to them after the game; that's normal.'

Would Vialli be back? Hardly an original question, but it was certainly the big talking point for the regular large contingent of Italian journalists. Di Matteo said: 'I'd rather have him on the pitch, but that's up to the manager and I have to accept it.' Zola also felt for his fellow countryman: 'It's very hard for him sitting on the bench, and he has to be a very strong man. But he's overcome more difficult circumstances and will do so again.' Gullit defended his decision: 'Vialli has been injured and he has to work hard to get back in the team. I asked him if he was ready to sit on the bench and he said yes. Everybody has to work hard to get in the team. Somebody plays good, he will stay there. It's not my concern what the national coach of Italy thinks.' Maldini, who had arranged a friendly with Northern Ireland, said that he knew Gianluca well, 'so I didn't have to see him today, but I will be back to take another look'. He added: 'When I see him, I will embrace him.' But there were no clues as to Maldini's selection for the clash with England. 'All roads are open,' he said. 'I didn't come to find anything new, just to see what form they were in.' But he was impressed with Zola: 'I know him very well. I thought he was in very good form. I was pleased with the reaction of the public towards him whenever he touched the ball.' Maldini was also pleased with Di Matteo: 'He was good in the second part of the game.'

While the Vialli question persisted, there was no debate about Zola's importance to the team. He superseded Vialli in the popularity stakes, and even overtook Leboeuf.

Zola's progress was so rapid that in February, his wonder goal against champions Manchester United at the Bridge in a 1–1 draw opened up a new debate – might he even become Footballer of the Year? The goal was so stunning, it was destined to become Goal of the Month. More significant was the concern about fatigue levels. Gullit's nostalgic excursion with Chelsea to his 'home' club Milan took its toll, a second-half collapse against United overshadowing some dynamic football, of the kind that had destroyed Liverpool in the FA Cup. Zola said: 'I knew in the second half we would suffer, because we were very, very tired. During the week we couldn't train a lot, because of the friendly game in Milan. We were very, very tired in the second half. We had to score again in the first half, that was the only way to win.' So was it a mistake going to Milan? 'I don't know, it is not my job,' said Zola. 'We had to play in Milan, because the game was already "organized".'

'Organized' was a word supplied by the ever attentive Gary Stalker. Zola nominated Gary as his 'unsung hero at Chelsea' in the matchday programme: 'He is a good person. Poor Gary will have a fit, he helps me a lot. And Dennis helps me out a lot, too. It's important to have people like that when you are new in a country.'

Zola and Di Matteo were playing their fourth game in eleven days and it showed. The pair ran the first half but, as at Leicester the week before, tired in the second. The first of those games had seen Zola and David Beckham, who scored United's goal, in opposition at Wembley, when Zola's opening strike proved to be decisive. Shame, that Beckham hadn't been able to equalize against Italy as well! When that was put to Zola, he smiled: 'Why? It's okay.' Significantly, he added: 'Today he played very well, but not at Wembley, because we marked and didn't give him a lot of opportunities, that's the key. I knew he could be a big problem for us and he did give us a lot of problems today, he played a very big game, a great game. And he scored a beautiful goal, a fantastic goal.'

So, too, did Zola. After two minutes, he outfoxed Denis Irwin as the full-back slid along the ground, expecting the cross. Zola kept possession, took him out and then weaved past Gary Pallister before shooting inside the near post, leaving Schmeichel standing.

Then, when Zola broke, leaving United stretched two against two, the Italian dazzled their defence and Hughes was left unmarked, but his sidefoot attempt was saved. 'I'm glad he tries to place it. It could have been different if he had blasted it,' said Alex Ferguson of his former striker. A second goal would have given Chelsea a cushion for the second-half onslaught by United once Beckham's volley put them level on sixty-eight minutes. As Ferguson put it: 'The chances we had . . . yet we scored from the most unlikely opportunity. It was a fantastic hit.'

He added: 'Of all the teams we have played this season, Chelsea had the best imagination in the last third of the field and we had to cope with that. I am glad they didn't win this match, because they could go very close. Ruud Gullit tried to change it, Di Matteo was pushed further forward, but the momentum was with us and it was difficult for Chelsea to do anything about it.' As for Zola, Ferguson said: 'We watched him in the last three games and saw him against England. We pushed Roy Keane into his space, but he was clever enough to go wide and still cause us problems. He's a clever little bugger. Zola has got a very good head on him. He sorted out how we were playing very early and was clever enough to hurt us. He is a better player than I thought.'

Zola explained: 'You can find space when you play in the right position and make the right movement; you can find space in every game. There's not a game where it's impossible to find space. I do my job when I try and find space.'

Chelsea might have had two games in hand, but, twelve points off the lead, they had a colossal gap to bridge. Zola felt that Liverpool were most likely still to challenge United for the title, or, as he put it, 'the season'. He said: 'Both teams can win this season, I can't judge which one. It was not easy for us to upset Manchester United. A win would have made me more happy, but I have to think we played against the Manchester United who will be first in the season. So I have to be happy with that.'

Analyzing Zola's contribution to that game highlighted how his influence on the team effort amounted to more than just scoring from free-kicks or notching spectacular goals. These were his match statistics:

First half

Passes completed: 15
Passes incomplete: 2
Shots on target: 1
Dispossessed: 3
Offside: 1
Free-kicks: 1
Corners: 4
Dangerous crosses: 1

Second half

Passes completed: 8
Passes incomplete: 3
Shots off target: 1
Dispossessed: 2
Corners: 1
Dangerous crosses: 1

6

Zola Takes Over From Vialli

Zola once said in Italy that if he had to name the one player he was envious of in his career, it would be Gianluca Vialli. So when he was keeping Vialli out of the Chelsea side soon after his arrival from Parma, Zola observed: 'I am embarrassed about it, and I feel so sorry for Luca. They signed me to play behind Vialli and Mark Hughes, but when there was a lack of balance, they moved me forward.'

The Italian media were obsessed by the Vialli question. How could Gullit accommodate all three attacking players, Zola, Hughes and Vialli? Gullit played all three in Zola's opening three games, resulting in two draws against Blackburn and Newcastle and a defeat at Leeds. The three strikers would only play together once more that season, and that was in the second half of the FA Cup thriller against Liverpool at the Bridge.

Gullit had originally intended to utilize all three, with Zola either wide on the flank or behind the front two. But the new manager discovered, through Vialli's injury and illness, that the most potent combination up front was Zola and Hughes.

That was confirmed as Zola continued to rattle in the goals. By the time Chelsea faced title contenders Liverpool on New Year's Day, he had collected four goals in the previous three games, taking his run to five goals in five games. Zola's performances underlined to Gullit that Vialli could no longer be regarded as first choice.

In the build-up to the Liverpool game, David Pleat, whose

Sheffield Wednesday side had been the latest to fall victim to the Zola magic, said: 'I enjoy Liverpool because the way they play is patient – passing, working, chess-like; not too direct. Chelsea are becoming like them, a very good team, too. People automatically think that because it's close at the top, the quality isn't so good. They think it would be better if one team was streaking away. I don't follow that argument at all.'

Zola, looking forward to the Liverpool game said: 'I saw Liverpool a little in action, but I will see them on TV. We have possibility to do it; I don't think it will be easy, but we will try.'

The title? 'I don't know. We are a team improving; we're getting better. But we have to work more, it is not easy to win the title. Chelsea are a very, very good team.' English improving – he'd got his tongue around 'Chelsea' and was relying a little less on Gary Staker who had now taken on the role of steward/official interpreter. 'We can win the Premier League, but we have to work hard getting results. There are a lot of teams like Chelsea [in the same position], about four who can win the Premier League the same. The difference will be the work done in training; that is the key issue.'

Could he keep on scoring? 'I'll try to score in every game, but it is impossible to say whether I will. I'll try to score ten, twenty, thirty. I'd like to score thirty, but it is not likely. The best I have managed in one season, excluding the national side, has been nineteen with Parma.'

Vialli went down with the flu and was sent home from training, missing the Premiership return with Liverpool. In September, Chelsea's unbeaten record had been smashed to smithereens at Anfield, where Vialli stormed off the pitch in disgust with the barracking he took from the Anfield coaching staff. But Gullit insisted: 'If you ask anybody, that wasn't a 5–1 game.' However, it illustrated where they had to improve.

Zola was one such major improvement. Now he expected close attention: 'Football is a game for men and it is not a problem when teams try to stop me. In Italy, I was closely marked all the time, sometimes too closely. I have played against Gentile, Costacurta, Vierchowod and Ferrara, so there is nothing defenders can do to me here that is any worse than I've already had. The biggest difference is that in Italy, the referees whistle more for fouls. That makes it difficult for me here, but I prefer it that way. I am not a child. I am thirty. I know how to cope with this sort of thing. Defenders in England don't give me any presents and sometimes they say things to me and try to be rude. I don't know if they're being rude to me over here, because I can't always understand them as I don't speak very good English, so it doesn't worry me. And when I have a problem, I just call "Marco" and Mark Hughes comes over and sorts everything out, then it's no problem!' Zola anticipated his toughest assignment yet: 'Life will get harder for me because teams are more aware of me now. Liverpool are maybe the best team in the country this year and Di Matteo has told me they are very organized. So it is going to be difficult for us.'

John Barnes, returning for Liverpool after recovering from a hamstring injury, had no doubts about the dangerman: 'Zola is an exceptional talent and I really don't think we've ever seen anyone like him in England before. He has given Chelsea a new dimension and made them a real threat. He is his country's best talent.'

Liverpool's fluid play had been stifled by the likes of Sheffield Wednesday's Atherton and Southampton's Ulrich Van Gobbel keeping the tightest of reins on Steve McManaman. Their manager Roy Evans conceded that his side had been restricted by the tactic. But Gullit would not follow that example: 'I want to use all eleven of my players. If one of mine is just offered to stay with one of theirs, he's not playing and I'm down to ten.'

Trevor Brooking provided his Chelsea end-of-year assessment in his London *Evening Standard* column: 'Gullit will be able to gauge the progress of his emerging team when Premiership leaders Liverpool visit Stamford Bridge for the opening fixture of 1997. The West London club are ten points behind the men from Anfield and, even with a game in hand, must collect maximum points if they are to sustain their championship hopes. But maximum points have not been easy to obtain at home, with only four victories coming from ten matches at the Bridge. Of the remaining six games they have drawn five, conceding thirteen goals in the process, and that is the main reason why they are not higher up the table alongside Arsenal and Wimbledon. Chelsea have developed an international flavour this season with the arrival of Frank Leboeuf, Roberto Di Matteo,

Gianluca Vialli, Gianfranco Zola and Frode Grodas. They have given
Chelsea greater strength in depth and, with the recent arrival of Zola,
more goalscoring potential in attack. This little man will prove a giant
of an acquisition and go on to become one of the most successful
foreign imports anywhere. He possesses a refreshing willingness to
run at defenders and his superb balance and vision enable him to
hurt the opposition by selecting the most perceptive passing option
available. . . . They have enough talent to beat Liverpool but, even if
they do, I can still see them slipping up in the sort of fixtures where
they should be taking three points. Therefore, the start of this
season's FA Cup campaign on Saturday offers a more realistic chance
of success . . .' Trevor should really take up fortune telling!

The game was billed as the potential champions against the championship pretenders; it turned into sweet revenge for Chelsea.

Liverpool began with the airs and graces of champions elect.
Sophisticated stuff, retaining possession with McManaman a central
figure but often deep. Fluent passing movements, but strangely no
cutting edge. Robbie Fowler, who had raced to a century of Liverpool
goals faster than Ian Rush, was twice foiled by Grodas when he
should have been sharper. He might have finished off Chelsea, but
from a corner, Grodas pushed the ball away to Minto, sprinting down
the flank, and Di Matteo sent Zola clear. He weaved inside before
bringing David James to his first important save. When Hughes put
Di Matteo under pressure, the defender managed a pass to Mickey
Thomas, who didn't have time to look up and Roberto Di Matteo
intercepted his pass intended for Wright, who moved on to wrong-
foot James with a shot into the corner. In the second half, collecting a
pass from Zola, Wise sent Hughes into a shooting position, the
Welshman cracking his shot against the bar with James beaten.

Chelsea celebrated a significant win and Zola sensed their title
aspirations had become a reality: 'On the pitch today were two teams
who could win it. The championship is very unpredictable and I still
think that Liverpool are the best team. I haven't changed my mind
about that, but we have some chance, too. Arsenal and Manchester
United are also the best teams and I don't know if we can win it, it
will be very hard. Liverpool play very good football and today they
gave us problems, but we played with intelligence, we didn't give no

chances. This game was very important for a lot of reasons. We merited the win, we played better than them.'

The outstanding Hughes revelled in his blossoming strike partnership with Zola. He assessed the most open championship for many years with the experience of a title with Manchester United: 'It will be very open and it's going to be exciting, with teams at the top taking points off each other.' Did Chelsea have a shot at the title? Hughes said: 'That's a difficult one, but if we keep surprising ourselves and perform the way we did today, then we must have a chance. I know it's boring but it's too early to say who will win the championship. We're just pleased we've had a great Christmas.'

'Sparky' thought he would be ousted by the arrival of Vialli and Zola. Instead, there was no guarantee now that Vialli would win back his place, even though he was the most respected and revered of all the Italians to depart *Serie A*. Gullit said of Hughes: 'You can see it on his face, he is happy here; he is fit and is helping the team as one of the leaders of the team. The crowd are cheering him. He is having one of his best seasons ever and I have asked people who have followed his career, and that's their view.'

It had been assumed that Zola would be better served by the subtle skills of Vialli alongside him rather than the sledgehammer method of Hughes. But Zola was won over by the player he called 'Hughses'! 'I play very well with Hughses; a player who allows a player like me to do well. My best position is not the first striker, but the second.'

Hughes was enjoying a renaissance under Gullit, proving that the British-based players could still excel. Hughes in turn praised Zola: 'We all enjoy the way he's played; great skill, great awareness. He makes it easy for everybody in the team. There would be something missing if you couldn't gel with Zola; it would be a bad reflection on yourself.'

This win was one of Gullit's most notable successes in English football, but his admiration for Liverpool was undiminished: 'Liverpool are a quality team, but Chelsea were very well organized also. Over the whole Premiership, the whole year, they will do well. But we were well prepared, we knew exactly where their weaknesses were. It's been a long time since we kept a clean sheet at home, but I liked the way the team responded to the tactics. I knew the game depended on small details, small mistakes. It was down to who would make less mistakes. The team did exactly what I asked them to do, especially in midfield.' When Patrik Berger came on, Gullit brought on Dennis Wise to counterbalance the midfield: 'That gave them one more man in midfield. When we changed it, we were in control again.'

By the middle of January, the frustration boiling up in Vialli began to spill over into public outbursts.

He was recalled for the FA Cup fourth round tie with Liverpool as Hughes dropped down to the bench. But although Vialli scored two goals in the epic victory, it wasn't until Hughes started the second half that the unlikely comeback from two goals down began.

Vialli was ecstatic, yet still there was bitter disappointment for him in the next game against Spurs. Dropped despite his brilliant display against Liverpool, he never kicked the ball in the 2–1 win at White Hart Lane that lifted Chelsea into fifth place in the Premiership.

Vialli packed his golf clubs, not his bags, that evening, for the team's Cyprus sunshine break – not, as he had hoped, for a return to Italy on international duty. He was spotted puffing away on a cigarette after sitting apart from Gullit and the rest of the substitutes.

Inside the Bridge, they played down Vialli's predicament. Gwyn Williams said: 'Yes, Luca had a fag, but it was after the game while he was waiting for Zola, who caught his taxi at 5.30 from the ground to catch the 8pm flight back to Italy. Roberto caught the 8am flight as the two Italians went back to prepare for the England match, and Luca was coming with us to Cyprus. In fact, the only reason I've got my mobile phone still switched on is I'm expecting a call from Luca – he wants to borrow my golf bag to put his clubs in, and I'll be playing golf with him as soon as we get to Cyprus. Luca likes a fag and he's entitled to have one if he wants it. It's nonsense that he stormed out of our dressing-room before the kick-off once he heard the team. The team was announced at our hotel during a team meeting before we even got to the ground!'

While Zola was again the focal point of attention against Spurs, Di Matteo produced the scintillating finish with a blockbuster thirty-yard shot into the top corner seven minutes after the break. It capped a brilliant performance, a wonder strike with his supposedly weaker left foot. Chelsea took the lead after just fifty seconds when Stuart Nethercott fouled Hughes and Zola lined up for what the Spurs defence expected to be one of his specialist free-kicks. Instead, he floated the ball across to the far post where Newton headed down, Hughes's shot was saved by Walker's feet and it bounced in off Campbell. Gullit took off Zola two minutes from the end to send on an extra central defender, Johnsen. Three minutes over time, Minto hooked off the line as Gerry Francis said: 'All our plans went out of the window and it was a big disappointment to concede a goal after fifty seconds. Zola has had quite a lot of success with those free-kicks, so Stuart was caught when he disguised it well with his ball to the back post.' Francis stressed that half his team were missing: 'You need a strong squad and Ruud has that. We've got a strong squad, but eighty per cent of it wasn't out there and we needed them to match the likes of Chelsea.'

Vialli could take it no more. He joined Fabrizio Ravanelli in expressing his frustration at life in the Premiership, stating his case in no uncertain fashion during an Italian TV sports programme: 'It is not a particularly happy period for me. Ruud Gullit has used me very little and I am not satisfied about this. I think if the manager keeps the captain of the side that won the European Cup six months ago on the bench, it would mean his team are top of the league. But this is not the case at Chelsea. So it must mean either the manager is not doing an exceptional job or there is something wrong. I feel there is something wrong. I wait with patience, I continue to train and I just grit my teeth. I did not come here on holiday or to enjoy myself. I came here to play and become a legend in London with Chelsea. Staying on the bench is frustrating for me and I hope things change in the future. Certainly I am not happy and not prepared to bear this situation for much longer.'

Sidelined with a hamstring, then flu, Vialli had watched the partnership of Hughes and Zola flourish in his absence. Gwyn Williams said: 'When Gianluca is on form, he will return to the side. I have spoken to him and was happy.'

Vialli could expect no special treatment from Gullit. He was told to fight to get his place back and to keep it. If he deserved to play, he would be picked. Otherwise he stayed on the bench. Gullit operated a 'no favouritism' regime. Williams added: 'Luca has spoken to Ruud about this. We understand his frustrations. The team will be picked at 1.20 on Saturday afternoon. Then we shall all know who plays.' Williams insisted Vialli's future was not in doubt. 'We understand how he feels, but he appreciates the situation. He accepts it. We didn't want him injured, he was outstanding against Everton, scoring a great goal. Then he damaged his hamstring. A team needs a large squad, to cope with injuries and suspensions.'

Ravanelli, for his part, still couldn't understand why Juventus had sold him to Middlesbrough after winning the European Cup; he dreamed of returning to *Serie A*. In an interview with the Rome daily newspaper *La Repubblica*, he sympathized with Vialli. The two of them had spoken to each other and could hardly believe what had happened to them. Boro were bottom of the table but Ravanelli said of Vialli: 'He is worse off than me. He told me about his knee, about Gullit who never plays him. Incredible. If I close my eyes, I see myself with Luca at the Olympic Stadium while we are kissing the European Cup. And now we are here. The England that I was expecting was not a last place. Even a child could understand that.' Middlesbrough had also been docked three points for failing to play a match against Blackburn on 21 December after Bryan Robson reported that twenty-three of his players were either ill with influenza or injured.

Di Matteo had a philosophical approach to developments under Gullit, having been dropped himself: 'Every player who sits on the bench is unhappy because naturally everybody wants to play. But you have to wait your time, work hard and then you get back into the team.' Graham Rix said of Vialli: 'He just has to bide his time. He has to keep himself fit so that he's ready to come back in, as he surely will.'

But Vialli remained Gullit's major problem. 'I would hope anybody would be unhappy when they're not playing,' the manager said. 'It means they are prepared to do the business when they come in. But I don't speak about things in the paper with players – if they have something they want to say to me, they should come and see me.' Gullit reiterated that he didn't want his players publicly moaning, and he warned: 'Supporters do not want players who moan, they will not tolerate it. They want them 100 per cent ready to do the business for the team. They will listen to it for so long. If it carries on, there is a danger the crowd could turn against those who only think of themselves. Supporters like what they see here. But, despite that, every month there is a player unhappy. I've had it from John Spencer, Gavin Peacock, Terry Phelan and Dennis Wise. They did not want to be part of it and if someone can't cope with the new situation, there's only one solution. If you can't stand the heat, get out of the kitchen. It's not my solution – they reach that conclusion themselves.

'I could see this situation arising with Vialli, as no-one likes being left out. If he was happy being out, I wouldn't be happy with him. There is no star status here. Vialli is a friend, but I can't let that interfere with running the team. I have to be honest in these situations. If you make concessions, give one player the benefit, then others will moan. I have a responsibility as head coach to pick the best team. I am not doing my job properly if I am affected by my personal relationship with some of the players. I have to separate my feelings from the players in the team because of my job. I have to stand on the outside.'

Gullit indulged in a couple of gentle digs. In Italy the previous season, Vialli had refused to talk to the press. Yet now he went on Italian TV to air his grievances. So Gullit said: 'I remember when Vialli didn't say anything to anyone, but it is convenient for him to come out and say things now. I am comfortable with the way I run things at Stamford Bridge.'

Had they discussed Vialli's TV comments? 'He has said nothing to me. I said to him: how was your trip? How was the weather? Your car? He says nothing. That is up to him.'

Ruud really wasn't that perturbed. He had bought Zola to play behind Vialli and Hughes, but the Zola-Hughes pairing, thrown together when Vialli was injured, had undeniably worked. Gullit said: 'I can sleep easy at night. My conscience is clear, because I am doing what I believe is best for Chelsea. Zola and Hughes are doing well. I admit I did not believe they would, but they are. It is as simple as that. If anyone wants to replace them, then it is down to them. Work harder, I say.'

Gullit had no plans to sell Vialli. In fact, Gullit said: 'Vialli can still

Zola, playing for Napoli, slips past AC Milan's Nava. (*Action-Plus*)

Taking on the mighty AC Milan defence again, this time for Parma. (*Allsport*)

Zola mid-kick, Parma vs. Piacenza in 1995. (*Allsport*)

Gianfranco and Gianfranca at home in Parma.

Zola with his two children.

Draped in his national flag, Zola contemplates a kick-about.

Zola arrives in London in 1996 and soon sized up by Ruud Gullit for new Chelsea shirt.

Zola in his home début against Newcastle in 1996. (*Allsport*)

Zola-Power grips London and Tesco's name a pizza in Gianfranco's honour.

During the game against Leeds in 1996 (*Allsport*), and below right, Zola and Dennis Wise brace themselves for a free kick.

ola holds off David Beckham.

The Italian Job – Sol Campbell cannot get to Zola as he scores against England in the World Cup Qualifier at Wembley, and below, Roberto Di Matteo joins in the celebrations that followed.

be the shining star here, I don't want him to go.'

Zola joked: 'I'm surprised Vialli is not playing . . . If it was me, I'd murder someone to get back in the side.'

But Vialli was clearly unhappy stuck on the bench: 'I am not one of those players who don't care sitting on the bench so long as they get their money. I want to play – for me, for the fans, for everyone.' With his English improving to give him a greater ability to express himself, he added: 'Believe me, I love Chelsea. Perhaps it is something to do with the fact they have struggled to live up to their big past; the fact that it has been up and down for so many years. I know that Zola, Di Matteo, Leboeuf and myself can bring back the good times. If I leave before Chelsea have won something, it will be the biggest regret of my career. I am still very happy at Chelsea. But it is the first time in my career I am not playing when I am fit. It is a new experience that I am trying to come to terms with.'

7

The FA Cup Adventure

Glenn Hoddle, of all people, started his old club's FA Cup adventure. The England coach pulled out the ball with Chelsea's number to start the Blues' FA Cup campaign with a third round home tie against West Brom.

The draw was live on television on Monday 9 December, with Hoddle responsible for drawing out the home sides and former England boss Bobby Robson the away teams. Hoddle reminded viewers that Chelsea's biggest scare en route to the 1994 Final, when he was in charge, was in the third round against Barnet, when the Third Division side came close to snatching victory with a late chance.

But Gullit knew West Brom could not be underestimated. So, too, did his players. Zola smiled politely but had clearly never heard of West Bromwich Albion: 'No, I don't know them very well, but Leboeuf said the games in the Cup are very difficult.' The Frenchman himself said: 'Everyone in the country is very interested in the Cup. It is going to be hard, but this is the target, so it is very important. We shall try to get it; the supporters want success.'

Leboeuf, being interviewed in his native tongue by a reporter from *L'Equipe*, virtually drowned out the quietly spoken Zola, struggling to concentrate on his English with less and less prompting from bilingual journalists and Gary, his interpreter. 'I don't suppose you spoke in English, did you?' smiled Leboeuf as Zola moved towards the exit of the press room. 'Yes, I did,' responded the Italian. 'I don't think so,' said Leboeuf.

'Well, I am learning English,' said Zola and provided the Frenchman with an example: 'F*** off.'

Zola was 40–1 along with Les Ferdinand, Eric Cantona and Ole Gunnar Solskjaer to score in every round including the Final, while Alan Shearer, inevitably, was favourite at 20–1. Realistically, although Chelsea maintained a challenge for the title, they were struggling even to qualify for a UEFA Cup place, so their best chance of glory was the FA Cup. They were initially installed as fifth favourites at 8–1, behind Liverpool, Arsenal, Newcastle and Manchester United.

Alex Ferguson, though, placed Chelsea among his personal favourites: 'If it's not going to be ourselves this season, then I have a fancy for Aston Villa or Chelsea.'

So it was Chelsea against West Brom – David Baddiel against Frank Skinner! And it was Chelsea fan Baddiel who could begin to fantasize about a Wembley triumph after a proficient rather than spectacular 3–0 win on Saturday 4 January. It came as something of an anti-climax after all the hullabaloo of beating the highly fancied Liverpool at the Bridge in the Premiership, but as Gullit pointed out: 'Everybody thought it would be typical Chelsea to beat Liverpool then lose to a team from a lower division.'

The Italians made their FA Cup debuts fully conversant with the reputation of the world's premier knockout tournament. No-one told them, though, that the Cup can be played in Arctic conditions. Vialli, who sat on the bench until ten minutes from time, peeled off layer after layer that protected him from the winter's chill: a coat, a warm suit, a sweat shirt and, finally, off came a white T-shirt over his blue Chelsea kit – no doubt there were a few layers of T-shirts underneath. He decorated a match already won, with a deflected shot that struck the post to provide Zola with his sixth goal in seven games.

Gullit shrugged and smiled when the Vialli 'sub' debate opened up again. He insisted it was a coach's dream to choose from Zola, Hughes and Vialli: 'It's a luxury and we shall have to see if they can all play together. All I do is pick the best team on the day. Everything is OK. Everybody knows the situation. There is an attitude among the players and it's team spirit.'

While Albion gambled without a substitute keeper, Gullit had
Hitchcock on the bench with Burley and Vialli. He explained: 'You
need players for different places on the pitch, you can't always take a
risk with only two. I thought I took the right one – one came on and
did the job.' Namely Burley, who scored the decisive second. Can't
argue with that!

How much longer would Vialli be content to sit on the bench?
Gullit said: 'I was happy the way he came in, it was a good moment
for him. It gave the team an extra boost at that moment. Hughes
deserved to come off to applause, but if we'd have been one-up, no
coach in the world can make any moves. You must be sure of the
result.'

Huge intakes of air greeted the draw for the fourth round:
'Chelsea . . . will play Liverpool.' Well, at least it was at the Bridge –
and Chelsea had already beaten them there in the league. Could
lightning strike twice in the same place?

First there were a couple of league games, at Nottingham Forest
and at home to Derby.

Chelsea lost 2–0 at Forest. 'I ordered my players to go up one gear.
I should have said *two* gears,' said Gullit. Much was made of the way
Zola was man-marked out of the game. Gullit said: 'With more top
players coming over, the Premier League could get like *Serie A* for
man-marking. In Italy I was marked all the time. I would go to the loo
and they would be waiting for me. I would say, "While you're there,
hold this, would you?" ' Gullit treated such tactics with disdain and
wanted Zola to do the same. After a chat with his former Forest pal
Des Walker following Sheffield Wednesday's draw at Stamford
Bridge, Stuart Pearce told full-back Des Lyttle to man-mark Zola.
Zola hardly got a kick, and probably wouldn't have been surprised if
Lyttle had followed him into the Chelsea dressing-room at half-time!
'I was aware that Zola could have ripped us apart. Des was magnifi-
cent,' enthused player-manager Pearce.

In the end, Zola's temper snapped. He petulantly pushed Lyttle's
chest, a gesture which summed up all the frustration felt by Chelsea.
Gullit claimed: 'I don't quite understand how we lost. We had lots of
possession and opportunities, but didn't produce. We never enjoy the
luck which is so important in football. What I would give for one

fixture full of bad football when we actually emerge as the winners.'
As for the attention Zola was attracting from opponents, Gullit said:
'It does not worry me if teams decide to man-mark Zola; it will mean
there will be more space and opportunities for other players.' But
there were worrying signs that with Zola contained, the team had less
of an effective cutting edge. As Gullit said, 'nothing happened' for
long spells. With Zola ineffectual, Chelsea were a shadow of the side
which beat Liverpool. Gullit despaired of the banality of their final
ball, often lofted towards the diminutive Zola as if he were Duncan
Ferguson. They ended in disarray, with Sinclair up front and Vialli in
midfield.

Zola still felt there was a chance of the title, with none of the sides
above them winning either. 'We are still in the race,' he said.
'Obviously this defeat is a setback, but we have shown we have the
consistency to make a challenge. We have to learn from our mistakes
and we are doing that. As a team we are improving all the time. At
this stage, the title is not beyond us.'

When Michael Duberry was ruled out for the rest of the season
after undergoing an operation on a snapped Achilles tendon, losing
the England Under-21 captain did as much as anything to lessen the
team's chances of sustaining a title challenge. The bad news came the
day before the Derby match.

Their manager Jim Smith decided not to put a minder on Zola.
Smith said: 'I've never been a fan of man-to-man marking. You might
stop their guy playing, but you lose a player yourself. It's everybody's
job.' Derby had not won since late November, and Dan Petrescu
wanted to know why did Chelsea beat good teams and lose to less
strong ones? The question was partially answered with an emphatic
3–1 win over Derby at the Bridge, Zola for once not getting among
the goals.

Next it was back to Cup business and Zola talked about his love
affair with the supporters: 'My relationship with the fans is one of the
most pleasing things in my English experience.' Zola was described as
a 'box of tricks' in Italy after his goalscoring performance against
Northern Ireland, watched by Hoddle and his assistant John Gorman.
Zola knew the English fans would not be cheering him at Wembley!
'It is not a good thing for us to play England, because they are very

good. I think English football is going to get better and better.'

Liverpool's Dominic Matteo had a special reason to look forward to facing Zola – Zola was his dad's favourite player! Matteo knew stopping Zola would considerably boost Liverpool's hopes of keeping alive a League and Cup double. It might also help his own chances of earning a place in Hoddle's England squad. 'My dad Alberto watches Italian football and he really admires Zola,' Matteo explained. 'He was always talking about him when he was at Parma, scoring free-kicks and other wonder goals. You can't help but rate him, because he is a great player. I've worked in training this week on how Zola might play, but it is on the day that counts. I'd be lying if I said I didn't relish this sort of challenge.'

Liverpool aimed to avenge the 1–0 league defeat, but they were unlikely to repeat the scoreline from their meeting at Anfield. Matteo said: 'That was one of our best performances of the season in beating them 5–1, but they did a professional job on us at Stamford Bridge. Everyone admires Ruud Gullit as a footballer and he has taken that ability into management. He knows what he wants and he seems to be getting it from his players.'

Vialli was still sweating on a recall, but Zola was guaranteed centre stage. Zola was asked whether this side had a chance of ending twenty-six years without a major trophy: 'I don't know what the sides were like before me, so I cannot talk of them. But this is a good team. I definitely think we can win the Cup this year. It's so important to everybody at the club that we win a trophy, but we will have to be very careful about the way we approach the Liverpool game.' Zola sympathized again with Vialli's plight: 'There is not a stormy relationship between Luca and Ruud Gullit. I have never seen them argue. Certainly Luca is not happy on the bench, but no player in his position would be.'

Vialli would surely stay on the bench. Or did Gullit plan a major surprise? Gullit said: 'Luca has trained hard and if his attitude is good in these situations, he is still setting a good example to the younger players.' Paramount for Gullit was to select the team that he believed would win – irrespective of reputations: 'Everyone had their opinion of how I would do and where I might go, but the job is here and is one I feel I can complete successfully. For now, it is time still to be patient

– slowly, slowly. Chelsea is not where I want it to be yet, but that takes time. The fans have less patience than I have, because the coach needs patience.'

Gullit and Vialli are friends; friendship was set aside. Just as it had been when he dropped Dennis Wise. 'That has been the most difficult part of management for me,' Gullit admitted. 'My decisions are done for the benefit of Chelsea, not for me. I knew there would be conflict. I don't hurt players on purpose. What would be the point of that? My solution has to be what I believe suits the players, so they can play at their best. That is the point.

'The hardest decision this season was to leave out Dennis Wise. It was the first one, the big one for me and for Dennis. I know him well, I have gone out with him, we've played golf together. That made it difficult, but he wasn't playing well. I needed some power in the middle.'

Sunday 26 January 1997 will go down in Chelsea folklore. It was the day of the Great Comeback. Vialli unleashed all his pent-up frustrations to lead Chelsea to one of their greatest FA Cup triumphs ever, as Gullit ended his exile on the bench and Liverpool suffered one of the greatest Cup shocks of their existence.

Stamford Bridge had seen nothing like it since Liverpool, as European champions in 1978, were stunned by a Clive Walker double that produced a 4–2 scoreline. But, nineteen years on, no-one would have put a penny on Chelsea's chances when they trailed hopelessly 2–0 at half-time and might have gone into the dressing-room three or four goals behind.

Gullit was relentlessly taunted – 'What's the score?' – after his side went two-down just twenty-two minutes into the game. Finally, he turned round and gave the Liverpool fans the answer: 0–2. He brought fits of laugher during his after-match press conference when he explained: 'They asked me what the score was and I told them; it was 2–0.' There can't be another manager in the game who would have responded to the jibes of the opposition fans in that way.

Gullit gambled at half-time by sending on Hughes in an all-out attacking formation – Vialli, Hughes and Zola all operating in a single forward-line. It produced a scintillating four-goal burst. Every one of the 27,950 crowd was on the edge of their seat and the millions watching on television witnessed an epic tie. In front of England boss Hoddle, Chelsea's Italian contingent mastered the Premiership leaders, with Zola issuing another grim warning before the England–Italy clash.

It was the most unlikely outcome as Liverpool, on cruise control, were in total command after Fowler's tenth-minute opener. The Chelsea defence was a shambles as Liverpool engineered a prolonged movement from one flank to the other. McManaman's cross caused panic as it flashed past everyone to be rescued by McAteer, whose cross was completely missed by Frank Sinclair. It finally fell to Bjornebye, whose low cross was turned in, inevitably, by Fowler. When Zola was hassled in possession by Mark Wright, his hurried pass was miscontrolled by Eddie Newton. Collymore romped forward gleefully, sliding his shot under the body of Hitchcock.

Vialli squandered his first chance in the thirty-first minute, latching onto Zola's attempt to control a long ball, body swerving to give himself space, but lifting his shot over the bar. . . . stomping on a *Mirror* sausage – the latest inflatable craze – in disgust with himself! A minute later McManaman weaved some more magic, Bjornebye crossed but Fowler headed over. Then McManaman eluded Leboeuf to break clear, but his weak shot was straight at Hitchcock. In truth, that should have finished off Chelsea.

Gullit sent on Hughes for Scott Minto at the start of the second half. After just six minutes, Clarke's pass to Hughes produced a sharp turn and shot into the corner. Chelsea were back in it and everyone wondered why Hughes hadn't been on from the start.

Hughes changed the course of events. Gullit admitted: 'When we got that goal, Liverpool were afraid. I could hear them talking about it from where I sat on my bench. When a team feels like that, you just have to take advantage of it.'

As crucial as the Hughes substitution was Gullit's other tactical switch. John Barnes was the focal point of Liverpool's domination of the first half, always available for the ball, playing it simply but effectively. After the interval, Gullit delegated Di Matteo to force Barnes to operate deeper. Gullit said: 'The first-half goals were a present, we gave them away. We had no concentration and they played it simple. But in the second half, we adapted our tactics and the players did exactly what I asked them to do. They were great. I was surprised also, but they really did the business. We put Di Matteo on Barnes and that was the most significant thing. But this was an easy game, in a way, because you are motivated, it's a great club and you have the crowd behind you.' Newton gave a second-half dressing-room insight into the game plan: 'Ruud said to give it all we had in the first fifteen minutes of the second half to try to get a goal as soon as possible. Fortunately, we did.'

Gullit had felt real anger for the first time: 'I was angry at half-time because we had given away two goals that made it easy for Liverpool, and in the second half I knew we had to do something drastic. All the time this team are doing things that show me they are improving. Each week they please me even more. But we can't keep making the mistakes that in big matches can be so vital.'

Of his decision to leave out Hughes, Gullit said: 'It came out right. It was difficult not to have Vialli playing and I don't think the decision affected us in the first half, because we gave away two sloppy goals. Mark made an important contribution because when he scored, I could sense that there was fear in the Liverpool side and we responded to that.'

Another turning point was a decision by the referee to award Chelsea a throw in the fifty-eighth minute when it was a Liverpool ball. Zola gained possession after a Hughes challenge and whipped a shot into the top corner. Breathtaking! Zola's seventh goal was his most valuable, as the equalizer left Liverpool vulnerable. And so it proved when within six minutes, Vialli latched onto a Petrescu pass and coolly beat David James to put Chelsea ahead for the first time.

Finally, Evans threw on Berger for Bjornebye but it made little difference. Vialli held back in the seventy-fifth minute, Zola zipped in one of his specialist free-kicks and Vialli read his compatriot's pass, meeting it at the near post with a fierce header. 'Vialli did touch this one?' – an Italian journalist recalled how Vialli had claimed Zola's free-kick against Everton. 'Yes, I think so,' said Zola with a huge grin.

No-one could recall the last time Liverpool had conceded four, particularly all in the second half. The stats experts put it at thirty-three years. A few Chelsea fans stripped off their shirts and, bare-chested, celebrated in the new Matthew Harding Stand.

Hughes and Zola strolled into the press room, spotting just one chair. I suggested that Zola should sit on Hughes's lap. Hughes smiled and Zola fetched a second chair. Hughes made no secret of his shock at being left out at the start, but illustrated the new bonding of the team by accepting Gullit's decision without question. With typical Hughes understatement, he said: 'Yes, I was a little disappointed to be left out, and also a bit surprised. I wasn't expecting it. But I'm not making anything about it as Ruud explained it and I accepted it. Rudi felt we could cause them a different problem and I am not making any bones about it, he just wanted to try something else.'

Hughes made his point on the pitch, and revealed the dressing-room switch at half-time: 'He changed the way we lined up, pushing three up, and it took them a while to sort out our new formation. By then, it was too late. It was a great performance in the second half. But I wouldn't want to be two-down every week.' Hughes joked: 'When we get two halves the same, we'll be really dangerous.'

Not surprisingly, the 'Name on the Cup' talk now started. Hughes was having none of it. Looking at the massed ranks of the media, he smiled: 'We shall have to be careful what we say about things, or you lot will install us as favourites. That will be the kiss of death.'

Zola's English tuition had been so successful, he was now confident enough to be interviewed without his interpreter: 'In the first half, the way Luca and I played was a bit limited, a bit stagnant, but when Mark came on, the three of us played with intelligence and gave Liverpool some surprises they couldn't deal with.'

Asked about the next league match with Spurs, Zola said: 'It's another kind of game; we will need more organization, more application, more concentration.' (He meant more of the same, rather than an extra amount.) Hughes admired his command of the language. 'Very impressive,' he said to Zola. 'I have to change my cassette!' joked the little guy. The humour level in the dressing-room was clearly upwardly mobile.

Zola, though, was still struggling with the colloquialisms: 'We must stay with our feet on the floor, that is very important. This has been a great performance.' He praised Luca: 'Today the game was not easy for him because he had a lot of pressure on him, so it is always difficult to play well. He had a lot of reasons to play well. When a player like him, big personality, can do bit things like today.'

'What, rise to the occasion,' said the reporter from the *Express*, cigarette dangling limp on his ageing lips. 'What does that mean?' said Zola. Hughes promised to translate later. To emphasize the team spirit, Zola added: 'Today Vialli scored two goals because the team helped him.'

The players sat in the dressing-room watching TV replays of the goals. When Zola's appeared, he leapt onto the bench and took a small bow. Spontaneous applause. The players had taken Zola to their hearts as well as the supporters.

The draw for the fifth round sent Chelsea to Leicester and made them the new 4–1 favourites for the Cup, ahead of Arsenal and Manchester United who had not yet come through their fourth round ties.

Zola made a valid point: 'We're a strange team. We can make some banal mistakes, and both the goals on Sunday were due to those sort of errors. In the second half, the whole team played very well and everybody playing like that made it possible for us to come back. But it would be hard to have to repeat that every match. We have to play more like this, with intelligence. Otherwise we can win against Liverpool and lose against Nottingham Forest; we can surprise!'

Wise stood in the corridor adjacent to the players' room wearing a smart suit and broad grin, discussing the virtues of Zola. On the question of England's impending clash with Italy, he said: 'I expect Glenn will consider man-marking him because Zola is the sort of player you can't afford to give any space. Even then, he has the ability to hurt the opposition. Perhaps man-marking could help. Nottingham Forest put Des Lyttle on him and he did okay, but I'd still blame the team not playing well for us getting beat that day. It wasn't down to Franco.

'There's only one word to describe him: class. Frightening, sometimes. I saw his goal against Northern Ireland last week and when he scores like that, it scares you. When he's left in a one-on-one situation, he's deadly. He just says: "See you later." As he showed against Liverpool, he is as lethal with his left foot as with his right. He's a natural. He scored against Liverpool with his left, when I think he's right-footed. Actually, I don't know what foot he is, because he hits the ball so well with both.' Wise added: 'I can say with confidence he's the best player I've worked with, and when you consider the only player who's kept him out of a team was Maradona, it says a lot. I can't think of another foreign player who has made such an impact on our game.'

Vialli declared a complete truce with Gullit: 'I'm so euphoric that it will be okay if he leaves me on the bench for the rest of my days. Two goals against Liverpool have wiped out any ill feelings and I've found total happiness.' The euphoria had gone to his bald head! He gleefully relived the high drama that had changed his fortunes in English football: 'In sixteen years of my football career, I've never experienced such an overwhelming adventure like the win over Liverpool. Just imagine, I arrive at the ground thinking I would have to sit on the bench, as it has happened for so many games before. Then, just one hour before the kick-off, Gullit told me I would start in place of Hughes. But it didn't go well, Liverpool were in full control. We are not able to settle and concede two silly goals, but in the second half Hughes come into the attack and Ruud asks Di Matteo to control Barnes – and it works. After Hughes's goal we realize that Liverpool have shaky knees. Zola equalized with a masterpiece of his own, then Petrescu puts the ball onto my right foot for me to make the score 3–2. Then Zola services onto my forehead his free-kick and it's 4–2. We were already with one foot in the grave but it turns out to be a triumph. We've taken a lap of honour at the end and I could have stayed on for ever. I'll remember this match for a long, long time.'

Gullit put Cup aspirations and the win over Liverpool into perspective as he concentrated on the next round at Leicester: 'I went back to work with the players straight after that match, and I wanted them to forget the Liverpool game. I had to bring them back down to earth. The Liverpool game was a good battle, but we still haven't won the war. Becoming the first team to overturn a 2–0 deficit against Liverpool for thirty-odd years is nice for the record books, but it won't mean a thing if we get knocked out at Leicester in the next round. That's why nobody has yet mentioned winning anything to me.'

Hughes likened Zola in influence to his ex-Old Trafford team-mate Eric Cantona: 'They have the same influence on games because of their sheer quality. To have achieved what Zola has done in such a short space of time is all credit to him. Zola can influence a game just like Cantona; he's a tremendous player with real quality. We thought he might need some time to settle in, but after the first training session, we knew it was no problem. Chelsea can achieve anything. We just need one trophy to get going. It's the place to be and we're all very excited by what's happening. As soon as United won the championship, everyone at the club really believed in themselves.' Gullit agreed: 'When I signed Zola, I knew I was buying class. Like Cantona, he can change things round in a second. World-class players need only a few moments to make a difference. When the chance comes to kill the game, Zola is at his best.'

Leicester's Steve Walsh relished the job of shackling Zola: 'Naturally, he is a world-class footballer and it is up to us to try to cut off his supply. If we can do that, then hopefully he will become less effective.' Their manager Martin O'Neill added, after Zola had marked his card with the winner against England: 'We know that Zola is one of the top players in Europe at the moment and obviously he is going to be a real handful. But I am not considering a man-marking job on him because we have no-one available to do it. He scored a brilliant goal at Wembley. When he came off near the end, I was hoping that he would be hobbling, but unfortunately that was not the case; but we do respect him. If we can stifle his talent, then we must have a good chance of going through.'

Filbert Street proved a far more intimidating venue than Wembley for Zola. He suffered shock insults when he stepped off the team coach and was shaken by a group of aggressive fans screaming '*stronzo*'. There can be few more offensive Italian words – literally translated '*stronzo*' means 'turd'. He was targeted because of his match-winning World Cup goal, booed by Leicester fans from the moment he touched the ball until he was substituted in the sixty-seventh minute to taunts of 'England, England' after one of his least effective matches in English football. Zola said: 'I heard the boos and jeers. I was not bothered. It was Italy who won at Wembley.' At least the Chelsea fans gave English football's latest public enemy No. 1 their moral support. A banner fluttered in the wind: 'We still love you, Zola.' Zola had struck a blow against English football in the World

Cup, but he found English hearts belonging to Chelsea fans of sterner stuff in the FA Cup.

It had seemed to be a stroll at the start for the Italians again as Chelsea raced into a two-goal lead, the first an exquisite strike from Di Matteo. When Hughes added the second, Chelsea's passage to the quarter-finals looked a formality.

During half-time, Alan Birchenall suggested Leicester could emulate Chelsea's performance against Liverpool in the previous round and recover their two-goal deficit. It was not only the Chelsea supporters who tittered. The home fans reacted similarly. Even Birchenall, the former Leicester and Chelsea midfielder, now City's half-time MC, did not sound as if he believed himself, so completely had Chelsea dominated the first period.

But Leicester did, indeed, stage a magnificent comeback, their cause ignited by Walsh with a thunderous header just seven minutes after the break. Defending is hardly Chelsea's strong suit and they suffered a shaky second-half experience. Hitchcock had already come off his line to be beaten by Walsh's header, and the equalizer just three minutes from time was a typically calamitous Chelsea mix-up. A Garry Parker curling free-kick tempted Newton and Hitchcock to go for the same near-post ball without a Leicester striker in sight. Newton deflected it into his own goal.

Gullit had sent Vialli on to replace Zola, and the player-manager himself came on for the last four minutes in place of a tiring Di Matteo. The efforts of guiding Italy to victory had obviously taken their toll on both Zola and Di Matteo, though there was no denying the sheer class of Di Matteo's opening goal after fifteen minutes. He cut inside to crack an angled drive that curled in the air into the corner for his sixth goal of the season.

But if Chelsea thought it would be an easy passage to the FA Cup Final on the back of their magnificent win over Liverpool and all the other big names falling in the early rounds, then they hadn't counted on the spirit of a Leicester team with only an American goalkeeper for a foreign star. And Zola's exhausting schedule had caught up with him: 'I was very, very tired. I just could not play at my best.' Chelsea wilted, but not to the degree of falling apart completely. Hughes said: 'Possibly in the past we might have folded under the kind of pressure that Leicester exerted in the second half. But we are made of better stuff now and we have the home game to come. We are still very much in the FA Cup and that's the important thing. We are naturally disappointed that they got back into the game with two free-kicks, and we weren't happy about the second one. I didn't see anything wrong with the tackle Steve Clarke made which gave away the free-kick. I thought he won the ball cleanly and there was no offence in the first place. But give Leicester credit; they never gave up and threw everything at us.'

Even with the replay still to come, Chelsea were made 2–1 favourites for the Cup by William Hill after the quarter-final draw gave them another away tie against First Division Portsmouth. First, though, they had to get past Leicester.

From the start of the midweek fifth round replay, Zola was in majestic form, so tricky he could have wriggled through the legs of giant centre-back Matthew Elliott. Zola set up numerous chances. Leboeuf headed off the line from an Elliott header one minute from the end of normal time, but in extra-time it seemed to be Zola v Keller. Twice the American keeper saved mesmeric free-kicks.

Finally, the outcome hinged on a dubious penalty decision that left Leicester and their manager Martin O'Neill bitter: 'I would rather that Zola or Vialli had whacked one in from thirty-five yards or even the keeper had let it through his fingers,' O'Neill said. 'I don't want to take it away from Chelsea, because they are a talented side who could well go all the way to win, and it isn't sour grapes. My players are absolutely down and I won't even try and lift them tonight.' Leboeuf converted the penalty after Erland Johnsen's controversial tumble in the area. The amiable Frenchman was already so popular he was favourite to pip Zola as the Chelsea fans' player of the year. Now his nerveless spot-kick conversion endeared him to them even more. Leboeuf's dream was to emulate Cantona and become the second Frenchman to triumph in the FA Cup: 'I saw Eric Cantona lift the Cup three years ago – I cannot remember who the team was. But it caught my imagination. I wanted to win the Cup like him, and I *will* win the Cup.'

Reaching the quarter-finals had taken its toll; after the extra-time against stubborn Leicester, Zola was rested for the league game at Derby and Chelsea fell to a 3–2 defeat. Gwyn Williams explained: 'It has been a long time without a break for Franco, and people also have to remember he has been travelling with the Italian squad as well as coming to terms with a big move to England.' Zola was carrying a pelvic strain and Gullit was urgently seeking replacements for a depleted squad. He said: 'It is difficult getting the type of players we want at this stage. We will see what happens in the next few days. There may be some news. We have some injuries now and would maybe like to bring somebody in.'

Zola was recalled for the 1–1 draw with Blackburn at the Bridge when he missed two presentable chances in a dismal first half. Scott Minto's sixty-third minute left-foot thunderbolt zoomed into the top corner after some neat play from Zola. Gullit threw on crowd favourite Vialli for the last twenty minutes in the hope of pulling off a win, but he couldn't find a way through.

The quarter-final at Portsmouth was billed as a potential Cup upset for Chelsea. Zola said: 'I'd like to win the game and the Cup for everybody. For Ruud, because he is our coach; for our supporters; for the other players. When you win a Cup, I think everybody must benefit, that's what you're all playing for. But it'd be great for Ruud because he's injured now and can't play. And I think he'll be very proud of us if we can do it. He brought me here and I'm grateful to him for that, because things have gone so well.'

Zola was confident he'd be fine for the Pompey game despite his pelvic strain: 'It's such an important game for us because we need to go on in the Cup, and of course we'll be giving our best to do that. I have a little problem but I hope to have recovered by the rest of the week.'

Gullit clarified Zola's position after rumours that he was mentally and physically drained after sixteen weeks in English football and had had to recover at a health farm. But Gullit said: 'He has been given treatment and massage like several players who are feeling tired. He's played a lot of games and has spent time away with Italy, but he's 100 per cent.

'Zola and Di Matteo have played a lot of games because they were involved in Euro 96, so naturally they have been a bit tired at times. No-one is a robot and no-one can play on top form all the time. We have to use him carefully and save his energy. We did the same with Roberto Di Matteo and he is playing well again after a rest. Franco has had a couple of slight injuries, but it is not a worry. I certainly believe in Franco, just as I did in Roberto earlier this season when we put him aside for a few matches.' Zola played down the injury. 'I've had a problem with my foot, but it is something I am used to and it is not a worry.' Di Matteo added: 'We all feel a little tired, but we will be ready for this match because it means so much. We want to win the Cup to qualify for Europe and maybe win another trophy.'

Gullit, sidelined with a broken ankle picked up at the Baseball Ground, would be happy if his team pushed him into retirement as a player: 'I want to get to a position where the team are strong enough not to need me playing. I am not aiming to play again this season, although, physically, it could be possible.'

All the fears about an upset were allayed with a 4–1 win at Fratton Park on Sunday 9 March.

Mark Hughes had his shirt pulled once too often and Pompey paid the price with an intelligent Zola free-kick in the forty-fourth minute. Their defence was caught flat-footed as Zola lined up for one of his specialist efforts five yards outside the box. Instead of a vicious curling shot, the impish Zola chipped the ball to the far post where Clarke stole in unmarked; his header was saved but Wise finished off on the line. Poor old Steve Clarke had not scored for five years and he won't come closer than that.

Hughes was chopped down again a few minutes into the second half and young Paul Hughes supplied Roberto Di Matteo, who burst into the box, changed direction and curled his shot inside the post. Pompey were really finished off by the third in the fifty-fifth minute. Awford miscontrolled and then slipped, allowing Mark Hughes freedom to attack. He linked with Di Matteo and the final pass was perfect for Zola to slide past the keeper.

Pompey boss Terry Fenwick said: 'We've obviously been beaten by a much better side. The younger elements in our ranks choked up a bit; the occasion was perhaps too big for them. Two or three of our players eighteen months ago were playing non-league football and we were up against not just international but world-class players. The movement of Zola, Hughes and Di Matteo was terrific. And a massive learning curve for my players.'

Another setback in the league straight after a Cup success came with a 3–2 midweek defeat at West Ham. The decision to rest key players Hughes and Di Matteo meant a rare start for Vialli and a return to the team for Craig Burley, but perhaps the player missed the most was the influential sweeper Leboeuf, out with a calf tear. There were four changes from Portsmouth, with Vialli making only his third start in seventeen games. Slick in their passing and cutting the Hammers' defence wide open, it was no surprise when Chelsea scored, albeit from a horrendous error from Ian Bishop in the twenty-fifth minute. A poor pass intended for Tim Breaker was easily cut out by Zola and once he attacked down the flank, it was ominous for the Hammers' defence. Zola's square pass was perfection and Vialli was able to pick his spot for his eleventh goal of the season.

The Hammers staged a rousing comeback to lead 2–1 but five minutes from the end, following a Zola backheel, Minto showed superb control and accuracy with a deep cross to the far post, where a towering header from Hughes conjured the equalizer. The odds favoured a Chelsea win even with just the last few minutes remaining, but from a Michael Hughes corner, Ian Dowie won the ball in the air and Paul Kitson headed into the corner to win it for the Hammers.

Chelsea responded with a 6–2 win over Sunderland. On a balmy Sunday afternoon in west London, the three Italians must have felt they were back in Italy – except, that is, for the kind of football rarely seen in *Serie A*, as the goals flowed. Zola was the central contributor. His opening strike in the thirty-ninth minute was magical in its execution. Wise and Hughes combined as Petrescu's cross was met perfectly on the volley by Zola. Four minutes later, with so many options open to him, he bamboozled the defence before directing a precise far-post cross, picking out both Myers and Sinclair unmarked. Marginally onside, Sinclair's header bounced tantalizingly in just under the bar. Chelsea were soon three goals up when an astute Di Matteo pass, first-time on the volley, found Zola running into space. His shot was brilliantly saved by French keeper Lionel Perez only for Petrescu to follow up and whip a first-time shot past the keeper. With just five minutes left, Vialli came on in place of Zola. Sunderland manager Peter Reid said: 'Zola is a terrific player. Do you take a gamble and man-mark him? I didn't. I could have been wrong, but before they scored we had the better chances.'

Zola strolled into the press room. First, an interview with the Italian journalists; then, again without the safety net of the interpreter, a full English conference – though Gary Staker wasn't far away with a helpful word or two. Recalling how mischievous Dennis Wise had lifted his Chelsea shirt to show Vialli the message on his T-shirt, 'Cheer up, Luca, we love you' when scoring against Derby on 18 January, Zola delivered an 'I love you, too' message to Vialli, still almost embarrassed to be keeping his friend out of the team – Zola's partnership with Hughes was the reason Vialli had now started just three of the last eighteen games. Despite his goal at West Ham, Vialli was again relegated to a late walk-on role. Zola said: 'I feel very sorry for Luca because he is a good player and a good man. But I imagine it isn't easy for Ruud to leave him on the bench so much, either. Luca is a great player and when he has had the chance to play, he has always done well, like he did at West Ham when he gave a great performance and scored. I also know that it hasn't been easy for Luca to accept that he's had to be a substitute, but he respects the decision, and only a big person can do that. I respect Luca, I have to respect Mark and I have to respect the coach. The only way I know to do that is to keep playing so good.'

Since his Italian TV interview criticizing Gullit, Vialli had kept his counsel and Zola added that there could be no questioning of Vialli's commitment to Chelsea, despite his disappointments. Had he sulked? 'No, he has got on with doing his best, even though it's very, very difficult. Luca is such a big player, has won so many things with Juventus including the Scudetto . . .' Zola corrected himself: '. . . the Italian championship and the European Cup. But even so, he gets on and does his job in training without protesting. He respects the decision of the coach, and makes his job without protest. That shows how big a man he is.'

Zola agreed that he was one of the main reasons for Vialli's bit-part appearances – 'The only thing Mark and I can do is keep on playing well' – but suggested their mixed fortunes had brought them even closer together. 'I speak with him at times and I think we're friends,' said Zola, with a smile. 'We talk together about many things. It isn't just about sport, because we have adult conversations as well.'

Vialli was guaranteed a game when Hughes was suspended against Arsenal. But Zola didn't feel he needed to rest, despite an accumulation of a variety of niggling injuries. 'If I'm playing well, I want to play in every game. If the coach wants to give me a rest, that's his decision, but I want to play all the time. I'm not having a problem with my back anymore, and if there isn't a problem I will play. That's how I feel. I am getting better; during the week I can now train myself. I am leaving my problem behind me. This is a very important moment for me, for Chelsea, all the players must be in good form. If you can't train, you can't always play.

'There was a moment we were in difficulties and Sunderland could draw the game. It was imperative we win. In the last four games in the Premier League, we did not play a good football. Now we have to win; we can get a good place.' Just for once struggling with his English: 'Is it necessary . . . it is necessary.'

As fate would have it, Chelsea were to face Middlesbrough, their potential Cup Final opponents, in the league at the Riverside on mid-March. Juninho scored the winner and Gullit accused his players of lacking commitment and spirit. Having rested Hughes from the starting line-up because of a slight groin strain, Gullit gave Vialli an opportunity to impress. Gullit made the point that this was 'Gianluca's chance to show everyone what he's capable of'. Vialli's ineffective performance merely underlined that Gullit's judgment had been astute. But Vialli was not alone in failing to make much of a contribution. Zola was little better, and only when Hughes was introduced in the second half did Chelsea begin to make an impact as an attacking force. Gullit said: 'I told them at half-time they should be grateful not to be two down, and at least we were a little bit better and got nearer to their goal in the second.'

It got worse in the next match with a 3–0 defeat at home to Arsenal. Ruud felt badly let down by the worst performance of the season at the Bridge. Zola looked drained after two World Cup ties in four days and Vialli did little to prove Gullit wrong. Did Zola need a rest after all? 'You'd have to ask him that,' said Gullit.

With such erratic form in the league and a UEFA Cup place slipping away, it was all or nothing for Chelsea in the Cup. For Chelsea, the barrier to the Wembley Final was one of their toughest adversaries – Wimbledon, enjoying one of their most successful seasons. Trevor Brooking wrote in the *Evening Standard*: 'Defeat in Sunday's

FA Cup semi-final at Highbury could close the door to Europe on either Chelsea or Wimbledon. The nightmare prospect for the London rivals is several months of hard work going to waste with the closing weeks of the season falling completely flat. . . . The fact that there is so much at stake only adds to the uncertainty of the outcome. But if you compare the two sides on paper, Chelsea have to get the vote. Mark Hughes, Gianfranco Zola and Frank Leboeuf have been outstanding in the Premiership this season and if player-manager Ruud Gullit is to lead his team out at Wembley, then this trio will feature prominently. . . . The exceptional balance and close control of Zola are a delight to behold and it is his intelligent running which could unlock Wimbledon's offside ploy.'

Wimbledon had roughed up Leboeuf and the Chelsea defence in the league earlier in the season, but now the Dons had to contend with Zola. Their coach Terry Burton was asked which of the opposition players would he most like to pick up an injury, just enough to prevent them playing? 'I would have to say Mark Hughes. If you could give me the double with Zola, I would be in heaven. Hughes is invaluable to Chelsea. I know Zola can put the ball into the back of the net from twenty-five yards, but Hughes is the man for me.' Chelsea coach Graham Rix knew that Joe Kinnear's players were concerned about the magic of Zola and the power of Hughes. He said: 'Mark has been spot-on this season. He's enthusiastic out on the training pitch and his disciplinary record is vastly improved. Do you know he went thirteen games without a booking this season? Mind you, the little man Zola is different class. I remember the first day in training. I didn't know how the other lads would react to him, whether they'd try to kick him or whatever. They didn't. They responded to him, to his talent, to his smile and attitude. How do you coach a player like Zola? You don't. You just tell the others to give him the ball.'

Kinnear acknowledged that the arrival of Zola had made a huge difference to Gullit's side: 'Zola is a very good player, although I still reckon that Eric Cantona is the best foreign player in our league. Zola has not been here that long and we will have to wait and see if he can consistently produce the kind of form we have seen from him so far. I have a difficult choice to make now – whether or not to man-mark him. That said, when we travelled to Manchester United in this competition earlier this year, people were asking the same question about Cantona. Thankfully, we got a draw through Robbie Earle's late goal and won the replay. Now we will be taking Chelsea on at their own game. The thing about Zola is that he won't be used to a game like this. I know he has played in the World Cup and the big European games, but I doubt he will have seen such intensity on a pitch this tight. We won't have a problem with motivation for this game – this match is there to be won for us, if we want it. When we look back to the 1988 FA Cup-winning side, it really was a magnificent result to beat Liverpool like that. To get to Wembley and win again would be a dream come true for me.' There were no self-doubts among their players. Marcus Gayle admitted: 'I scored against Chelsea when we beat them 4–2 at Stamford Bridge. We caught them off-guard that day and they'll be better prepared this time round. They didn't have Zola then and he's the guy who really makes things click for them. We intimidated their defence. We do try to do that to teams before they do it to us.'

Zola power would be the key. He was thirsting for glory in English football: 'I have also never worried about the size of the match. This semi-final is big, but the Final is bigger. It is no good reaching the semi if you do not go all the way to Wembley. There is no such thing as tiredness when you are winning. In a short space of time, I have already been caught up in the Chelsea dream. I know how much winning the FA Cup would mean to them.

'I'd far rather score for Chelsea at Wembley than be responsible for ending England's chances in the World Cup. I get some terrible stick from fans for that goal. But you have to expect it. My teammates have had a few laughs at my expense, but the Chelsea fans have been brilliant, even though I suspect deep down they are not entirely happy that I scored against England. But I'm sure both teams will qualify for the World Cup in France, regardless of the result. It is difficult, of course it is. I regard this country as my second home and I would rather England weren't in our qualifying group for the World Cup. But, as much as I love England, I'm Italian and very proud when I play for my country.

'I adore Wembley, and it would be nice to go back and score a vital goal for Chelsea in the Cup. We have had a mixed season in the league. We are learning all the time, but you cannot expect to compete with teams like Manchester United and Liverpool overnight, because they have played together for a while. But now we have a good chance of winning something and qualifying for a place in Europe.

'It will be hard against Wimbledon. They are a good side and difficult to beat. But if we can play as well as we have done in the competition, we have a good chance to make the Final.'

Zola was surprised by the passion of the FA Cup: 'In Italy the Cup is not so big. Here it has a greater importance. When you are not involved it's hard to understand, but I appreciate it more now I'm here. I like the way the club play football, it's more European. The way Ruud wanted the team to perform was something I considered before I signed. I haven't had any problems since I came to Chelsea. My life is football. The weather and the language may be different, but you can still eat the same food, drink the same drinks and enjoy the new adventure.

'What has happened to me in England has been one of the most extraordinary moments of my life. I cannot really find the words to express how I feel. Last summer I left your country disappointed. Italy had been knocked out of the European Championships and I had missed a vital penalty against Germany. But you have repaid me with this transfer to London. I now have only happiness and pleasure. That feeling has allowed me to play without inhibition. I have the confidence like never before. I live in a beautiful city and my family have settled in well, so why should there be any problems? I only want to be happy and make others around me happy. I am not a clown, but I like to have a laugh with everybody.

'It has hurt me when people have said the Italians and other foreign players have come here only to rest, make money and to finish our careers. I have come here to achieve. I won one championship in Italy with Napoli and would like another. You must never say, "I do not want to do that." I have come to London to enjoy England and to play to the best of my ability. London is a fantastic city, it offers anyone everything he wishes. There is always something to discover. About life, about yourself. The same applies to football.'

Wimbledon was Chelsea's moment of truth. . . .

8

Accolades and Awards

Zola was a magnet for awards. His exhilarating talents, wonderful goals and inspirational approach to play made such a vast difference to Chelsea's potency. Above all, it was back to Pele's perception of 'the beautiful game', flowing, fast, accurate, and also effective.

How ironic that the England coach should be on the eminent panel of judges that nominated Zola for his first major award in English football. Zola was named Carling Player of the Month for December 1996 after just six weeks and six goals in ten games in English soccer. Phew, what a start.

Zola could hardly believe how quickly he had settled down to his new environment, and began to join in the dressing-room banter by picking up the language. He surprised himself as he began to enjoy the best form of his career.

Once the Carling award was announced, Zola was naturally a popular choice to be interviewed at the training ground. He was forthcoming about his impressive start, and his willingness to discuss every issue with the media, with his improving vocabulary, immediately endeared him to the English journalists.

He said: 'I'm surprised I've done so well. I have to say thank you to my friends and everyone at Chelsea – they give me all the things I need. I've started like this and I want to continue this way – it's not easy, but I'll try to do it. There is more to come. People have not seen the best of me yet. I don't know how much better I can get, but there is room. My confidence is growing and that will give me more chances. I love it in London. I feel at home and relaxed at Chelsea and that makes me confident on the pitch. I could never imagine it would have gone this well so soon. I always believed in my ability, but I didn't think I would settle so quickly. I now feel I am in my most relaxed state of mind ever. I am producing my instinctive football because I am at peace in England. When I first came here, I had a problem with the language and I didn't really know anything about the whole situation. But, step by step, my confidence has improved and that's helped both me and the team. I'm a different person now I'm here in England, I feel very relaxed. It's probably the most relaxed I've been in my career.'

Zola was pleased to have escaped the goldfish-bowl mentality of life in *Serie A*. He explained: 'Football is a sport and that's what I believe in – and I think that's the best way to give of your best. In Italy football is everything, a religion, and people talk about it and think about it every day. There's no time to rest. But here I can get away from it, spend time with my family. I like Italian football, but in Italy football is not relaxing. In the last few years, everything about the game has become so big, and people involved don't stay relaxed when they see a game. The first thing is they want to win, but that's not possible all the time – and sometimes you lose. In Italy, if the team does not win, "all the players are no good", they are criticized; it's not sport. It's not the right way to play, not the right way to give of your best. The fans here know that you can't win every match, know that it's still just a game. People in England understand that side of it; losing is not nice but it is accepted. They don't forget sport is just a sport, but in Italy they concentrate on football every day. I don't want to say Italian football is no good, because that's not true, but it's one of the problems in Italy. I have told Roberto Di Matteo and my other team-mates that I am like another person in England. I am so relaxed I feel I can do whatever I want on the pitch, because my football is instinctive.

'Another big different I've found here in England is that the teams think to attack first; in Italy they want to defend first. A lot of games in Italy finish in goalless draws, but I think that'll change in the future because the supporters want to see more action, more goals. I believe the game must be like a party, a festival, right? I love the ambience and the lifestyle in England – and I love playing here. It's not the same back home. Over here, when I see people in the street they say "Hello" and "Congratulations" and "Come back to Italy" [laughing]. But no-one bothers me or disturbs me. I love it here. I have a contract for three more years here and I aim to respect that.

'Ruud played in Italy, he knows what it's like over there. All he wants is to play football, and I think like that also. Ruud Gullit told me just to play and enjoy myself and not to worry about anything else. Everything has been going well off the field as well. I have a house and I have settled in with my family.'

Zola received his award on the pitch before the Premiership match with Derby on 18 January, and it was another virtuoso display from the Italian in a 3–1 win.

It was following his cross in the forty-third minute that referee Graham Poll adjudged that Mark Hughes had been pushed in the back by Matt Carbon. Frank Leboeuf converted his fourth penalty, sending Russell Hoult the wrong way for his sixth goal of the season.

An incredible forty-yard free-kick from Aljosa Asanovic after twenty-five minutes had embarrassed Kevin Hitchcock, back after a run of eleven games, but Chelsea recovered from that to equalize in the thirty-seventh minute when young Paul Hughes, yet another emerging talent, made an important contribution with a pass to Zola, whose shot struck a post and Dennis Wise gleefully followed up. Wise rushed over to the bench to raise his shirt to reveal the message on his T-shirt, 'Cheer up Luca, we love you x x'.

Steve Clarke was enjoying one of his best seasons. His vital contribution to the team effort was indicative of how some of the British players were benefiting from the influence of the world-class stars performing at the Bridge. But no-one could deny the foreigners had captured the imagination of a new generation of fans. Just ask Steve's children who are their favourite players.

'Vialli,' said five-year-old Joe.

'Zola,' said eight-year-old John.

Zola's impact earned him universal praise from inside the Bridge. Leboeuf observed: 'My confidence was high from the start at Chelsea because when I signed, I knew they were a good team to play for and we could do something. Now we are going well and I'm sure we will continue like this. Zola is a very good footballer. We can give him the ball over and over again and let him do things with it. The same goes for Mark Hughes.'

Zola wasn't the only Italian picking up awards. Roberto Di Matteo received the *Evening Standard* Footballer of the Month award for February, presented to him by Zola at the training ground; a handsome cast-bronze limited edition statuette and a magnum of champagne.

Zola's ability to transform the Chelsea team into a much more potent attacking force had made him a candidate, albeit an outside one, for the Players' Player of the Year award. But he had simply not been in the country long enough to have a realistic chance. The players start to deliberate around the end of the year and cast their votes early in the New Year. It is more of a year-on-year award, with performances in Euro 96 having a major influence on this occasion.

The Professional Footballers' Association awards are announced in March; Zola was short-listed along with Ian Wright, Alan Shearer, David Beckham, Roy Keane and Steve McManaman. Those nominated for the Young Player of the Year were Beckham, Fowler, Heskey, Vieira, Perry, Solskjaer.

Interestingly, the contenders for the main award, voted for by their own fellow players, were all British, plus the Premiership's number one Irish ace Roy Keane . . . apart from Zola. No Eric Cantona, Dennis Bergkamp, David Ginola, Tino Asprilla or Fabrizio Ravanelli.

Zola was given the ultimate endorsement by the England captain Alan Shearer, who said: 'Even though he hurt us at Wembley, he's got my vote because he's come to a foreign country, which, I imagine, is not easy, and taken everything in his stride. He's a tremendous player; he's only small but he is very strong on the ball, great with both feet and it helps not playing in a bad side, either.

'There are a lot of players who have had a good season but I've opted for Zola, with David Beckham as my choice for Young Player of the Year.'

Typically, Zola said: 'I am honoured at even being considered.'

Shearer won the Players' Player award, presented to him by Alex Ferguson at the Grosvenor House Hotel hours after Chelsea confirmed their place in the Cup Final. Shearer had voted for Zola;

now it was Zola's turn to praise the England striker. He said: 'Alan deserved to win the Player of the Year award. But if I was to judge his genius on a scale of one to ten, I would give him a nine. He played well against us and is a good striker. I would say, though, that Tino Asprilla created a lot more tension and problems for us. But I do like Shearer. He always seems capable of scoring, whether he is using his feet or his head. I know him very well and his two goals against us were not a surprise for me. He is a very important player for Newcastle and England.'

Shearer had already forecast Chelsea to win the FA Cup . . . because of the presence and influence of Franco Zola. He argued: 'Wimbledon have surprised a few people this season; Middlesbrough have got some class players like Juninho, the skill of the man is unbelievable. But for me, Chelsea are the favourites and Zola is the difference.'

Zola was asked which English players he would recommend Italian clubs to sign: 'There wouldn't be many – I'd restrict it to just three. I like Alan Shearer. Then there is David Beckham, who for me is the complete midfielder, and Blackburn left-back Graeme Le Saux is another great player.'

But he stressed that there were still vast differences in Italy: 'The English like a different type of game to our own. It is tough but fair. Very aggressive but not contaminated by malice and play-acting. That is something which is regarded as a crime. If a player goes down here without being touched, he is given hell. Not just from the crowd and his opponents but his team-mates, too. There is no room for cheats in English football and I must say I am happy. I love London and am not at all homesick. I am enjoying life more than when I was in Italy. Football is still growing here and it can get even better.'

Asprilla was a good pal from their days at Parma and Zola applauded the Colombian for fighting his way back from adversity: 'I talk a lot to Tino on the phone. He's happy here in England. He was certainly very happy against us. Tino was suffering in the game here because he wasn't playing. He needs to be, like all great footballers. That's normal for people like him and me. Now he's back in the side, he's enjoying himself.'

Of life under Gullit, Zola said: 'Ruud doesn't put pressure on his players. He gives us responsibility and allows us freedom – he has faith in us. He treats us like professionals who have their heads screwed on.'

The rules of the PFA award do not allow players to vote for their own team-mates, so the voting in the Stamford Bridge dressing-room favoured McManaman, Beckham and Shearer. Here's how some of them voted (did Di Matteo vote for Dominic Matteo because he thought he was voting for himself?):

DI MATTEO: Team: James; G Neville, Southgate, Matteo, Le Saux; Beckham, Barnes, McManaman: Shearer, Ravanelli, Ginola.
Player of the Year: Matteo.
Young Player of the Year: Matteo.
'Matteo is a good player. Good technique, good vision of the game, a good passer and a good defender.'

LEBOEUF. Team: James; Cunningham, Ehiogu, M Wright, Le Saux; Vieira, Keane, Barnes; McManaman, I Wright, Shearer.
Player of the Year: I Wright.
Young Player of the Year: Vieira.
'I find it hard to pick a team without Chelsea players. I played against Vieira when he was at Cannes and he was very good then.'

VIALLI. Team: Schmeichel; McAteer, Campbell, Adams, Le Saux; Beckham, Keane, Platt; Shearer, Ravanelli, Giggs.
Player of the Year: Beckham.
Young Player of the Year: Solskjaer.
'Quantity and quality from David Beckham, and I think he's an intelligent guy. He's a midfielder but he scores a lot.'

Zola's goals kept the tributes and awards flowing. Once again there was another pre-match presentation before the fans – this time it was the BBC's Goal of the Month.

Match of the Day announced his goal against Manchester United as the award winner for February. And Zola recalled just how he completely dismantled the champions' defence at the Bridge: 'After first dribbling, I look at the box and I didn't see anybody in there, so I decide to go on with more action. I think I was lucky, they waited for my decision and when they decided to contest me, it was too late.

It was too much hard for Schmeichel to save. I was too close to him. He couldn't do anything. I'm playing well because I am having fun.'

The Goal of the Month presentation took place on Wednesday 19 March prior to the game with Southampton.

And Zola did it again – yet another match-winning goal. A long clearance was chested down by Mark Hughes and Zola took control, just one stride before cracking one of his specialist long-range shots into the top corner, his eleventh goal in a mere twenty-two appearances. A player supposedly exhausted at that stage of a season filled with cup ties and international commitments, Zola, five minutes from the end, worked back into his own half to win the ball and run half the length of the field to take a return pass from Roberto Di Matteo, before his shot brought a full-length save.

He had scored yet another spectacular goal, but Zola generously praised the man who created the opening. Mark Hughes. Zola said: 'I have played with some very good forwards – Alessandro Del Piero, Fabrizio Ravanelli, Gigi Casiragni, and Alessandro Melli at Parma. They are all good players in different ways, but I rate Mark just as highly. He has different characteristics to Del Piero and Ravanelli, but he is very similar to Casiraghi, the man who partnered me at Wembley. They are both strong on the ground and in the air, and there are other big similarities between them.'

Hughes, known for his bulky physique and labelled 'Popeye' in the programme, has always been noted for his muscle rather than his mind. But Zola said: 'Off the pitch, Mark is a very serious man, very quiet. He reads a lot of books. It is easy to see that he is a very intelligent person, and that comes across on the pitch. Look at the goal I scored against Southampton. Yes, I was very pleased with my shot and I guess I got all the headlines. But without Mark, it just wouldn't have been possible. He conceived that goal in his head long before the ball got to me. He could see the possibilities and knew exactly where he was. I stayed a short distance from him, he won the battle with his marker in the way he does so well, and he delivered the ball just right in front of me to hit. He is the ideal partner for me, and I enjoy being alongside him. He allows us to keep the ball when we are in difficulty because he is so strong, and he allows me the freedom to play the way I want and work around him. Our manager Ruud Gullit seems very happy with the way the combination is working and so am I. We are playing well together and we both have a good feeling about the way things are going. We have already scored a lot of goals together and there is no doubt the partnership is working in the right direction.' That partnership had produced twenty goals in just eighteen games.

Saints manager Graeme Souness said: 'Credit Zola, it was a fantastic strike, a great goal for Chelsea.'

The Bridge was practically deserted by the time the popular Zola had finished his marathon interview stint. Franca Zola waited patiently in the press room until her husband obligingly completed his task with his usual humility and dignity at 11pm.

Zola was big box-office and the Italian mentality is to court the media. In Italy there are three daily sports papers with acres of space to fill. The players shoulder as much criticism as the top players attract from the tabloids over here, but the Italians' attitude is to co-operate in the hope of putting over their point of view.

It was an attitude towards the media that was sure to reap its reward when it came to the biggest individual prize of them all – the Football Writers' Footballer of the Year trophy at the end of the season.

Zola was also named by *Goal* magazine as No.1 in their poll of the top 100 foreign stars in the English game.

As the FA Cup build-up reached fever pitch, the circus was over-poweringly in evidence as the youngsters mobbed the players after training, anxious for an autograph on shirt, ball or any scrap of paper, while the *Sun*'s female football reporter and photographer were busy interviewing and snapping Zola as the newspaper's Player of the Year, as voted by their readers. Eager young hands grabbed at little Zola as he posed with his trophy. Zola said: 'I want to thank everyone who voted for me and all those who have believed in me. It is a great pleasure for me to receive this, and a big surprise. I have only been playing here a few months and really appreciate this support, particularly as I scored a goal against England and know this was not a good moment for fans here.'

Zola had read the newspaper coverage that he was in line for the football writers' Footballer of the Year award. He said: 'In England there are many great players and it will be hard to decide who is best.' But his immediate target was the FA Cup.

9

The Italian Job

'Make sure you feed Zola stodge all week,' was the message from England coach Glenn Hoddle to the Trimmings training ground cook Sian Bowles.

Hoddle knew that Zola was the Italian dangerman, the player most likely to halt England's passage to the World Cup Finals. The England coach was prepared, he had watched Zola personally on several occasions. But that didn't stop Zola inflicting enormous damage at Wembley with the winner in the vital World Cup tie.

Hoddle, of course, didn't have to travel to Italy to discover the potential threat of Zola. There was plenty of evidence in the Premiership. But, accompanied by his assistant John Gorman, he went on a spying mission to Italy's warm-up match before they took on England at Wembley.

The Italians met up in Rome on Tuesday 21 January 1997 before making their way to the warm sunshine of Palermo, in Sicily, in preparation for their first international under new coach Cesare Maldini. Zola said: 'One of our first objectives is to get the supporters closer to the national team. There has not been a peaceful climate between us and the players have felt it. First of all we must play for them, then for ourselves. We must make the people love the Italian side.'

The next day Hoddle watched Zola's eleventh strike in twenty-nine internationals. It came just eight minutes into the reign of Maldini against a makeshift Northern Ireland side. The smoke had hardly cleared over the La Favorita stadium after the firework display that greeted a new Italian era when Zola opened the scoring with one of his specialist strikes. As Pierluigi Casiraghi was buffeted by Taggart, Zola stole in behind the challenge, gaining possession. And although he looked to have been driven too wide, his little feet were power-packed.

There was no smokescreen as the Italians laid bare their tactical formation for Hoddle to see. Zola operated very much in the Cantona role as a second striker, difficult to pick up and lethal once he got into the penalty area. Premiership managers had wrestled with the decision whether to man-mark Zola. When the little maestro was shadowed relentlessly, he proved less effective, but Hoddle was loathe to assign a specialist man-marker for Zola at Wembley. It was to prove to be England's temporary downfall.

In Palermo, Zola went off on the hour to a hero's ovation and a hug from his new coach. Roberto Di Matteo also came off as the second half took on little more significance than the chance to give virtually everyone a game. Zola and Di Matteo would have been on their mobile phones immediately, to report back to Ruud Gullit or Gwyn Williams that they had come through injury-free for the Liverpool FA Cup tie.

Hoddle said: 'I've always thought that technically Zola is up there with the best in Europe. I also think he's very clever, very astute. We all know about international defenders who can read the game when the other side have the ball; Zola is an attacker who reads the game extremely well when his own team have the ball. If you give him space, he'll use it. I've always admired him, which is why I tried to buy him for Chelsea. He's a lovely footballer.'

So the question of whether to shadow Zola switched from the club arena to the international scene. Zola relished his role as a free spirit, and despite his insistence that he could cope with man-marking, he was not so at ease when closely shackled. Frank Leboeuf said: 'If you mark Gianfranco man-to-man, you must be very strong mentally. He is very intelligent. He can leave a lot of space for other players, that is why the decision to man-mark him is so difficult for other coaches.'

Zola dominated Hoddle's weekend. The England boss also went to Stamford Bridge when the tiny Italian changed to a Chelsea shirt.

Hoddle primarily wanted to know whether Steve McManaman could produce the sort of blistering running and goalscoring form that might prove an antidote to Zola.

As Hoddle prepared to announce his England squad, Zola himself picked out McManaman as the danger. Brilliant on the ball, a wonderful dribbler, virtually unstoppable, but what a woeful finish, as demonstrated in the FA Cup game watched by Hoddle. Zola said: 'England have a lot of talented players; Shearer, Ferdinand, McManaman, Ince. That's why it will be a difficult match. England are full of eleven international-class players. McManaman is excellent, he can turn a game round when it's "stalled".' Zola's English was rapidly improving, but he meant 'deadlocked'. The Italians feared the Liverpool star far more than Gazza.

Zola said: 'We shall have to watch McManaman at Wembley.' With his newly acquired English sense of humour, he added without any egotistical edge: 'From what I read in the press, they think they will have to watch me!'

With fifty requests for interviews with Chelsea's Italians and Gullit prior to the England–Italy match, a special 'second' conference was conducted at the training ground. On one side of the giant Gullit sat the diminutive Zola, with his old-fashioned craggy features; in the centre, the laid-back, philosopher Gullit; on the left, Di Matteo, a slight, elegant figure. They were introduced as 'the boss and his sons'. 'He is my grandfather,' Zola quipped.

Gullit was called on to help with translation, emphasize an answer, or encourage Zola not to commit himself about whether Maldini would be returning the Italian team to its old style.

Zola said the man-marking in the Premiership had given him problems, but he would not mind if England put a man on him. It was something he was used to, he said: 'I expect man-marking every game. This is no hard news. It's my job, I have to sort it out.' Gullit, interestingly, said that Zola had told him that he actually hoped they *would* man-mark him. 'They can mark me,' Zola said later, 'but there are other players on the pitch.' When asked who had marked him best in the Premiership, Zola grinned and would not be drawn. 'I don't remember the team,' he said, prompted by Di Matteo and Gullit. Wise said that he found man-marking Zola in training a tough task. He has 'happy feet', Wise said. 'He jinks one way and then the other and then it's "see you", isn't it?'

The question was raised again after Chelsea won 2–1 at White Hart Lane. Gullit did not recommend it to Hoddle, after Gerry Francis became the latest Premiership boss to attempt a 'stop Zola' strategy, with Dean Austin assigned the thankless task. Zola was contained to a degree, but still wriggled free to play havoc with Tottenham's defence. Gullit said: 'Everybody saw what happened, saw what he did today, and he was still marked. One moment he produced a very good first touch and it was nearly possible that Mark Hughes could score a goal, and also in the first half there was a cross when Mark Hughes was not alert enough. He did all these things when he was still man-marked. It's not important for me for a player to be all the time busy, I want him to be sharp for only two moments in the game. For example, Vialli, you might have thought, was not so good against Liverpool, but then in the second half he produced two moments and two goals. It's not important for a player to be working, crossing, busy all the time, and it may be he's not in the game for twenty minutes at a time, then he strikes; that's what's important. If you man-mark Zola then you have one player less. We played against ten men and the only thing they could do was boot it. He played very well, all the time available, and could have scored. He was not disturbed, he is used to playing that way in Italy, and he doesn't mind.'

Gullit's description of Tottenham's tactics would not please their fans, but it gave a clue to why there was so much emphasis on Spurs' tactical deployment of Austin. Without so many star players, Spurs often resorted to the long ball, particularly in the latter stages. Zola, despite Austin, again emphasized why he would be such a threat to England. Austin said: 'He is a great player, one of the best in Europe, absolute class. It takes a great deal of concentration and I felt in the first half I made him play with his back to goal. I went everywhere with him, but I thought it hurt us more than Chelsea. Glenn Hoddle will have his own ideas, but if England play three at the back I think you can get away without man-marking him, leave him to the nearest player. What they don't want is one of the three sticking to Zola. There were times when I had to go into tackles against other players and I was left desperately looking for him. It was very hard because I wasn't in the game. Chaperoning such a player, you only have to leave him for a split-second and you're dead. Suddenly the ball is in the net. Either he has put it there or laid it on for someone else. His movement off the ball is superb and his runs are devastating.' Austin once left Zola to tackle Hughes and no other Spurs defender reacted. If Zola hadn't slightly overrun it, he would have scored.

Zola's pedigree with the national side was impressive: Italy's second-top scorer among the current players with eight goals, behind fellow striker Casiraghi, who had scored eleven in thirty-eight games. Zola said: 'It will be a hard game for us – but for England also. I know there are many Italian people in London who will come along and support us, but most of the big crowd will be on England's side and that is something extra for us to fight against. We respect England and I have found much to admire in the game here, but we are confident in our football and we can win if we perform at our best.'

English football went Zola crazy. He was in line for a £100,000 payout to deliver a World Cup KO to England, promised the lucrative bonus by boot manufacturers Mizuno. The sportswear giants planned a major promotional campaign featuring Zola as part of a £3 million sponsorship deal. 'Gianfranco is guaranteed a substantial bonus for taking part in a global competition like the World Cup,' confirmed Mizuno promotions manager at the time Kathy Friar. 'He signed a new performance-related agreement with us shortly before Euro 96 which is linked to extra payments for success at club and international level.' Mizuno were delighted with Zola's impact. 'Gianfranco was obviously signed with the Italian market very much in mind,' Friar added. 'He was still playing for Parma at that time and we had no idea he would be coming to England. Our Italian distributor was quite upset when he joined Chelsea, but he has proved a fantastic addition to our team in England. He's been a revelation in the Premier League and the bonus for Mizuno is the fact that his performances are still making headline news back in Italy. It has been a pleasure to work with such a professional, and he has made great efforts to fit into the English way of life. We launched a Zola boot in the summer and there will be a Zola sports bag range on sale soon. Gianfranco already features in our advertising campaigns throughout the rest of Europe and also in Japan, where he is very popular. Now he will figure prominently in the promotional work we are planning for the English market in the new season.' A winner off the field, and also one on it.

Despite all the pre-match warnings, Zola clinched an Italian victory with a memorable goal to become the first Chelsea player to score against England and the first Chelsea player to score in an international at Wembley since Jimmy Greaves's hat-trick against Scotland in 1961. Di Matteo said: 'Only great players can score a goal like that and Gianfranco is a great player. Players like him can make the difference in a game, and he did just that.'

Zola's Wembley winner left English football deflated. Zola said: 'We are close to it, but now we have to carry on like this and not fall into the mistake that England made here. They were so convinced that they would win.' Hoddle had preached confidence, no fear of the opposition, without arrogance. But the Italians felt that the pre-match hype was that the game was a certainty for England. Another Zola wonder goal put paid to that: 'It was my dream goal. The control of the ball was everything. It put me in a position to shoot and it was a wonderful moment. To score a goal like this, especially against England at Wembley, is a dream for me. It is what I dreamed about as a small boy, scoring this kind of goal on this kind of occasion. I don't know if we will qualify, because England are a team we still respect and it will be another difficult game when we play them in Italy.

'I hope the Chelsea fans will understand why I feel so happy after scoring for my country. They have given me such a warm welcome in England and I hope they will not put this goal against me. Surely they know I had to do this important thing for my country.

'I want England to qualify for the World Cup because they are an important country in football terms. I can't think of a World Cup without Italy, England, Germany or Brazil, because they are the main countries in football and their involvement leads to a big interest. But until the next World Cup game, my efforts are concentrated on Chelsea.'

Goalkeepers usually hang their heads in shame when beaten on their near post, but England's Ian Walker, standing in for the injured David Seaman, insisted that he had no chance with the decisive nineteenth-minute strike. 'It was brilliant work by Zola, but I had his shot covered until it took a deflection off Sol Campbell's studs. I honestly believe I couldn't do a thing about it and I won't let it completely ruin what was a proud experience for me. It was fantastic going out there for my first full England game at Wembley and in such a huge match as well. Obviously the result sours it more than a little, but I don't think I have anything to be ashamed of.'

Zola was hailed as a hero in Italy. *Tuttosport*'s headline, '*Zola genio, Italia si*' needed no translation. 'It's Zola, It's Italy,' said the *Gazzetta dello Sport*, above a picture of a jubilant player twisting away from goal with a finger raised.

Zola added that England's footballing stock had not plummeted as a result of their defeat: 'It would be wrong to think that England are not at the same level of teams like Italy or Germany just because of one defeat,' he said. 'You cannot make judgments like that after just one match. The level of English football is growing all the time and I am sure the English team will be able to demonstrate it is a very good team. It is harder for them now to reach the World Cup finals because only one country goes through automatically. They have to win every game now because a bad result could mean their exclusion, but we have to as well.'

Not for the first time, Ken Bates reserved a barbed one-liner for the manager who had launched the Blues' revival then quit for England. Asked whether Zola would be given a hard time back at Chelsea's training ground, Bates replied: 'Of course not – why should he get one? He was the best player on the pitch, and it's not his fault England played kick and rush.'

Perhaps the Italians would be back at Wembley for the Cup Final? Di Matteo hoped so: 'I would love to play at Wembley again and also have the same success.'

Vialli was at the game, commenting for Italian television, and he interviewed Zola immediately after the match. Vialli: 'You must be very tired now, Gianfranco?' (Clearly, angling to take his place in the FA Cup!)

Zola: 'I knew it, I knew it! Yes, I'm tired, but very happy. I'm ready to dive back into English football, but I hope you can come back into the team as soon as possible at Chelsea. We need you.'

After a celebratory meal out with their families and the wives of Albertini and Costacurta, plus Williams and Byrne, Zola and Di Matteo cheekily turned up for training the next day wearing their Italian shirts!

The exhausted Zola was so much in demand that a press conference was held for the Italian media at the Royal Lancaster Hotel in the afternoon, with the English press turning up as well. Zola might have been excused for picking out the goal against England as his most memorable in recent weeks. Not so: 'No, I pick the goal that gave me my main satisfaction, it has been the goal that Vialli scored against Liverpool, our third goal.' I wondered whether that was really the case, or was Zola being diplomatic for English consumption? Zola was always eager to please, to say the correct thing and state that he is not big-headed.

Chelsea travelled to Milan the following week for a mid-season 'televised' fixture. Gullit's twenty-man squad departed from Gatwick, arriving at their Milan hotel at 5.30pm. Bates spotted Zola: 'You are the smallest person around here, you push the President's baggage trolley to the check-in desk.' Zola: 'Yes, El Presidente.' Bates tipped him with a £10 note! And he took it.

Zola was mobbed by fans and press on arrival at Milan airport as Italy continued to celebrate his winning goal against England. Zola: 'It is a big thing to be coming back to Italy. But it is very strange coming here with an English club. I have great memories of the last time I played at the San Siro, because it was when Parma beat Milan to win the European Super Cup against all the odds. That still ranks as my greatest memory in football.'

Half an hour after getting to the hotel, they were off in the rush-hour traffic to a training ground near the San Siro, attracting 200 fans. Vialli and Gullit were mobbed, Zola warmly applauded.

As a means of relaxation, the next day Zola went to the cinema to watch *Arise* starring Arnold Schwarzenegger – in English.

Zola was back in Italy at the end of March on far more serious business – a World Cup double header. Injuries to Casiraghi and Ravanelli left Maldini little option but to draft in the uncapped Juventus forward Christian Vieri as partner for Zola against Moldova. Zola or Vieri to score Italy's 1,000th international goal?

Zola had claimed Italy's 997th in 541 official matches with the winner against England.

Italy cruised to a 3–0 victory in Trieste, which was more bad news for England. The Italians had taken maximum points from their four matches, leaving them three points clear of England, who had played the same number of games. Coach Cesare Maldini's son Paolo grabbed a superb individualist first goal after twenty-four minutes, and Zola got the second a minute before the break. Vieri wrapped it up very early in the second half with the landmark 1,000th goal.

Zola was Italy's star again in the goalless draw in Poland on Wednesday 2 April, when England's hopes of avoiding the dreaded play-offs were given a much-needed boost by this result in Chorzow. The Italians had dropped their first points and now led by four having played a game more. Hoddle watched from the main stand of the packed Slaski stadium. Zola came closest, with a free-kick just curling over and a fierce shot saved. Generally, he was shackled by his shadow Skrzipek. Roberto Di Matteo was one of four Italians booked.

England got their revenge in the Tournoi di France in the summer. From being a dispirited, dejected team heading for the World Cup exit after the Wembley setback, England recovered to win a vital tie in Poland and then beat Italy in their opening Tournoi game, as goals from Ian Wright and young Paul Scholes gave them their first win over the Italians for twenty years. Italy's cause was not helped by the early loss of Di Matteo. After just nine minutes, a clever Di Matteo chip was met with a glancing header by Zola, but the chance went well wide. Then after twelve minutes, Zola's defence-splitting pass went straight into Di Matteo's stride inside the box and when he cut inside Martin Keown, he must have thought he would score until he felt the force of a Stuart Pearce tackle. Di Matteo hobbled around for five more minutes before he was replaced. Cesare Maldini was less than impressed with another crunching tackle, this time on Zola, leaping to his feet and pointing aggressively towards Hoddle in the opposite dugout. The Italian coach had to be restrained, but Hoddle ignored him and at the end they shook hands.

Pearce had been accused of elbowing and punching Zola by Maldini. Hardman Pearce, who has carried the nickname 'Psycho' throughout his career, had a one-word riposte for the Italians: 'Shame!' Maldini said: 'When Pearce challenged Zola I got angry, because he had been using his elbow and he used his elbow again.' Pearce showed no sign of remorse for upsetting either the Italian coach or the Chelsea stars. In fact, the England team were encouraged when Pearce made such a telling tackle on Di Matteo. David Beckham said: 'The first ten minutes was cagey, things were just not working; we didn't keep the ball as well, even though we went into the game taking it seriously. Once Stuart Pearce made that tackle, it made people think, "yeah, they'll be in a game." '

England had never made Italy look quite so vulnerable in defence or lacking inspiration in midfield, even blunting the menace of Zola. England went to the top of the table and ended up winners of a morale-boosting tournament.

Zola reflected: 'I was not happy losing so badly in Nantes to the representatives of a country who chose me as their season's best player. But I did warn my team-mates that the English know how to battle and stay strong on every occasion.'

Gullit believed Zola owed his place in the Italian team to his move to England. But Zola added: 'I only half-agree with Ruud when he says I had lost my credibility in the Italian team after missing a penalty against Germany in the European Championships. Sure, Chelsea have helped me, because I have to admit I have played well for Italy since coming to England, but I hadn't really fallen as low as Ruud thought.

'I'm just pleased no-one in England holds my World Cup goal against me. Maradona had to leave Italy after eliminating the national team in the semi-finals of the 1990 World Cup, but in England I am applauded.

'The idea of England not qualifying for the World Cup upsets me, but I will still have to give my best when we meet again in Rome in the autumn.'

10

Footballer of the Year

Spectacular goals, a warm smile and willingness to take part in seemingly endless interviews, plus his match-winning ability that took Chelsea to the FA Cup Final, swayed the country's soccer writers in favour of Gianfranco Zola.

He was the first Chelsea player ever to win the award; not even Jimmy Greaves had won the fifty-year-old trophy.

Zola was named Footballer of the Year on Friday 2 May 1997. Gwyn Williams arranged for Zola to ring Dennis Signy, a prolific worker for the Football Writers' Association, to comment on the award. The interview would be passed on by Signy to the Press Association for use by all the national and provincial press, radio and TV. Zola said: 'Every footballer wants to win a prize like this and it is big honour for me. I feel very lucky. It is hard for me to explain with words what I am feeling. It is not easy to be voted Footballer of the Year, because there are many good players in England.'

Gullit, one time World Footballer of the Year, had come second to Eric Cantona a year earlier in his first season in the Premiership. He recognised Zola's phenomenal success: 'I'm pleased for Franco and pleased for the club. Let's hope he gets a Cup winner's medal to go with the trophy.'

Zola polled twice as many votes as joint second-placed Juninho and Mark Hughes put together. The top-placed Englishman was Beckham in fourth place.

Ironically, the votes were announced shortly after Gullit had demanded talks with soccer's authorities – and even Tony Blair's new Labour government: 'Nobody is buying English players anymore because nobody can afford them. I want to sign British players, but every time I make an enquiry I'm quoted £8 million and that's far too much when I can get players from abroad for nothing. It's very frustrating. All the talk, all the rumours of new signings and they are all foreigners. Englishmen aren't even being mentioned. Even Manchester United are now going abroad. We are reaching the situation where the Premiership is being flooded with foreigners who are not as good as the English players. But that is not the fault of the foreigners, nor the club owners. It's the fault of the system, and we have to have a meeting to make English players cheaper. It's not a problem for me – I don't care if the British players are upset by all the foreigners and neither do the fans. As long as the team is winning, I am happy. But home-grown players are suffering because you have to pay a fee for them and not for European signings. They are at a disadvantage, and they must have the same rules for everyone. You have to adapt and become a part of Europe, even though many people in this country don't want to be. Maybe now you have a new government, you can change the system and sort this problem out. There is no point in moaning about too many foreigners – you have to do something about it. The problem is that the transfer money is no longer circulating within the game. It's disappearing into someone's pocket.'

Bryan Robson was amazed that Zola won the award ahead of Juninho, his Cup Final adversary: 'With respect to Gianfranco Zola, I don't see how a player can come into the league just before Christmas and still win the award. He is a class player, of course. But for me the vote had to be between Juninho and Roy Keane. I really don't know what fires Juninho, but he has showed quite amazing energy through these demanding games.' David Pleat didn't agree: 'Zola is a deserving winner of the Football Writers' award, having shown hard work to be a requisite not only of average players but gifted ones, too. You can see that Zola has worked hard at his game and has learned from the likes of Maradona, with whom he played at Napoli. He loves to run at defenders with speed to unbalance them, but it is his imagination and touch in the last third which will pose Middlesbrough the greatest threat.'

Zola was presented with the award at the Royal Lancaster Hotel at the lavish soccer writers' dinner, two days before the FA Cup Final, an occasion made all the more special by the presence of his father Ignazio. He came to England for the first time in his life from his Sardinian home to watch his son play in the Cup Final and receive the prestigious award. Zola insisted that he accompany him to the Royal Lancaster: 'He deserves the satisfaction of being there with me. It's my first award and I will be very proud to have him beside me tonight.'

Zola was presented with the fiftieth anniversary FWA award by the first recipient, Sir Stanley Matthews in season 1947–48. With Gullit sitting close to him, a nervous Zola made a lengthy speech – the guest comedian remarked later: 'I understood him better than I do Gascoigne!'

Zola thanked those who had voted for him, but humbly said: 'I think the jury must have been a bit drunk.' He captured the hearts of the audience by stumbling through his acceptance speech in broken English. Zola said: 'I must thank my team-mates, my coach and the Chelsea supporters who helped me settle down very quickly. It's very great to receive an honour like this. Every player would like to receive it. And looking at the past winners, it's very easy to imagine what I feel. I have a little emotion.'

Ken Bates and his partner Suzannah were on the *Daily Mirror* table with myself and *Mirror* editor Piers Morgan, and Franco's father came over to greet the Chelsea chairman. Bates recalled: 'He was sitting in my office and I told him I knew Sardinia well. When he told me where he lived, I said: "Isn't that the place where all the kidnaps take place?" He said it was and I told him I was holding him to ransom because his son could afford to pay it. I think the joke got a little lost in translation, but he understood and laughed.'

Ignazio said: 'I will be very proud at Wembley Stadium. But Franco takes everything very calmly. He has always been a very modest boy and people at home in our village will tell you he is even more modest now. They do not treat him as a hero exactly, but they are very satisfied with how he has become famous. When he comes home to visit, he is just like one of them.

'It is my first time in London and wonderful to see my grandchildren, Franco's son and daughter Andrea and Martina. I don't know if the boy will be a famous footballer, too, but we knew Franco would be a great player when he was only seven.

'Since then, Franco has given us many proud moments playing for Napoli and Italy, and it has been my pleasure to support him. Of course, I consider myself a Chelsea supporter now.'

Sir Stanley Matthews felt Zola a worthy winner: 'He plays well. He is crafty, he finds gaps and he is very quick off the mark. You have got to be quick. All the great players have had pace.'

The first winner of the award in 1948 had never imagined an Italian becoming the fiftieth. He could scarcely have imagined Jurgen Klinsmann, Eric Cantona and now Zola would win in the last three years the same silver trophy that was to boast such choice examples of born-British stars as Billy Wright, Nat Lofthouse, Tom Finney and Bobby Moore. 'Going back half a century, who would think that a foreign player would receive the Footballer of the Year award? Who ever would? You would not. I never thought it,' Matthews said. 'There were no foreigners playing here then. Once upon a time, you used to give them two goals' start!'

But Sir Stan believed that Zola, and players of his ability, deserved such recognition: 'Foreigners are more skilful than we are. There is no doubt about that. They control the ball better. They can give and receive a six-yard pass far better than we can. You have got to admire them. They can get out of tight situations. We are not comfortable with short passes. I really don't know why that is. Today, everyone wants a winning side. Where can you go and get an outstanding, skilful player in England? Nowhere. So all the clubs go abroad now. I think it is bad for the development of English players but good for the fans. I think one day that the players' union will say enough is enough. No more than two per team. It could be a good thing.'

The eighty-two-year-old added: 'Is it possible that foreigners enjoy it over here and play better because they are not as closely marked as overseas? I have a feeling that we have lost the art of tackling. It may have something to do with all the yellow cards, but we do not defend well.'

There was one English player who impressed him: 'Alan Shearer. I like him because he behaves himself off the field and he's always scoring goals. He is always in the right position.'

Zola would treasure the Footballer of the Year award, probably his most prized possession alongside his FA Cup winner's medal.

Dennis Signy has been responsible for notifying the winner of the award since 1968; he has never come across anyone so possessive towards the famous statuette.

Signy takes up the story: 'I made the usual arrangements through the club to notify the winner, and Zola rang me back: "It's Zola here." I explained that he had won the award, and made sure that he understood everything about it, including how heavy the trophy is. "By the way, it's a very heavy award," I told him.

'On the big night, he came to the dinner accompanied with his father, lawyer, and Gary Staker, his interpreter at the club. Gwyn Williams and Colin Hutchinson delivered him safely. I said to him, "Before we go any further, have a look at the trophy." I was worried that he might drop it or do himself an injury – and miss the FA Cup Final. I said to him, "Just feel it."

'In the next room were several photographers waiting to take his picture. They asked him to pose this way and that, the usual procedure, but I told them they only had five minutes because the TV crews were also waiting. I said, "That's all, thank you very much, gentlemen." Then I turned to Zola and said, "Shall I take it for a minute?" "No, it's mine," he said.

'And he wouldn't let it go! The dinner was about to start.

' "Can I have it?"

' "No," he repeated.

' "I am only going to take it and put it on the table in front of you and you can have it back after dinner." '

Zola was a runaway winner, although he came through on the rails. There were a number of significant stages in his rise to the very top in English football. I would pick out two. The goal against Manchester United at the Bridge, which made him an overnight candidate to challenge David Beckham, and then his wonder goal against Wimbledon in the FA Cup semi-final, which saw off the late challenge of Mark Hughes, whose outstanding form had ensured that Luca Vialli was destined to stay on the substitutes' bench. Those two goals, plus the enormous impact his goal against England had in English football, brought him the Footballer of the Year votes.

Zola reckoned his match-winning effort in the vital World Cup qualifier against England went a big way towards him clinching that honour. 'I think that goal was very important for me; after that, everybody knew me better. That goal was a very good step for me for getting this prize, because all the country was watching that game, and it was a very, very important game. So if you win and you score, you can get good popularity. But yes, it was a big surprise for me to win it because it's a very important prize for a player. I'm playing in a top championship where there are some excellent players, and I came here a couple of months after the season started. I thought it might be hard for me to settle in the beginning, but everything has gone in the right way. And for that I have to thank my friends and Chelsea team-mates, they've helped me to be confident. I thought Shearer, Bergkamp or Juninho, or even Mark Hughes, could have won it – they've all had great seasons.'

Gullit had the perfect opportunity to assess two of the candidates for Footballer of the Year when Manchester United drew 1–1 at the Bridge towards the end of February. Such was Zola's immediate impact that by then he was already one of the favourites alongside David Beckham ... so would it be one of England's budding young talents or the pick of the recruits from *Serie A*? Each scored another spectacular goal; Beckham's brilliant volley and Zola's trickery illuminated a contest Manchester United couldn't afford to lose and Chelsea had to win. Gullit said: 'The Premiership now has world-class players and that is well known now in England and Europe. Both Zola and Beckham's goal also illustrated the kind of players who could offer something extra. England can be proud of its Premier League. I've played abroad and I know that the Premier League is now an example for the rest of Europe, notably in its organization. When we were in Milan last week, the directors asked me more about the Premiership, about how it's organized, how it divides the money, and on the field it's getting better and better all the time, not just because of the foreigners.'

Sunday 13 April 1997. The date was another significant milestone in Zola clinching the Footballer of the Year vote. The High Noon FA

Cup semi-final at Highbury was the match that catapulted Zola and
his team to the FA Cup Final. Chelsea annihilated Wimbledon 3–0
and Zola's goal was a dream.

For Gullit it was a moment to savour, a special achievement even
in his distinguished playing career: 'I have just been told that I am the
first foreign coach to take a team to Wembley in an FA Cup Final and
am very proud of that. But it is important we win it, as first place is
the only thing that matters in any competition.' Zola and Hughes
enjoyed the glory goals, but Gullit proved he had a tactical brain
underneath those famous dreadlocks, masterminding success over
the team Chelsea dreaded the most by dismantling his wing-back
system in favour of a hybrid English-style back four, to counter the
Wimbledon bombardment that had crushed Chelsea at Stamford
Bridge in the league.

Kimble launched a high tackle on Zola after just seventeen
minutes, with the little Italian taking the full brunt in the face, but the
dangerous clash went unpunished. When Zola was caught offside a
minute later, he showed his frustration by throwing the ball back, not
away, and it seemed a harsh decision for him to be booked for that.
Chelsea gradually gained more space, Wise bursting through from the
half-way line to launch a shot that Sullivan was right behind; and
again the keeper was well-positioned to save from Zola after a clever
turn and angled drive. Chelsea gained a touch of luck for the opening
goal a couple of minutes before the interval, but it began with a glorious long-range crossfield pass from Frank Leboeuf at the back.
Zola's perfect first-time control, then reverse pass to Wise, gave the
midfield player the space to cross with his left foot to where Burley
was lurking at the far post. Kimble intercepted but the ball bounced
off Hughes's chest and he couldn't fail from close range.

Kinnear threw on striker Dean Holdsworth for full-back Ardley
after sixty-three minutes, but there was no time for the all-out attacking formation to settle down before Zola's decisive strike. His superb,
swift switch of direction was enough to open up the space for one of
his typical whiplash shots into the corner. It was his twelfth goal, and
another gem.

When Hughes scored his second goal in injury time, the twenty-
sixth FA Cup goal of his career, Gullit, who until then had been

sitting serenely, leapt from the bench and punched the air. As for the feud with Vialli, the two men embraced three times at the end. Di Matteo threw his shirt to the crowd as the players did a lap of honour as the two sides of the stadium where a sea of Chelsea's fans were decked out in Cup hats, scarves, flags and shirts. Wise wore his lucky Cup vest: 'Cheer up Luca, we love you.' Vialli never kicked a ball in anger, but his sheer joy at Chelsea's victory and his part in the celebrations confirmed his willingness to stay part of the set-up under Gullit's guidance. Wise said: 'I thought we showed a lot of people that when it comes to the big event, we're up for it. We showed a lot of class. I think we shocked people outside Chelsea, the way we played.'

Zola was heading back to Wembley to fulfil a promise he made to himself after his winning strike against England in the World Cup. He sat next to his giant boss, smiling proudly when Gullit talked about him in glowing terms. More at ease with the language, Zola probably didn't catch the meaning of every complimentary adjective, but he got the drift.

Zola was much slower than the Dutchman in the delivery of his words: 'I like Wembley. When I left Wembley after scoring for Italy, I vowed to come back and do the same with Chelsea. The atmosphere that night was unbelievable, and now I have an opportunity to put on another performance. I have a month to prepare for the Cup Final and I will do all I can to give the Chelsea supporters the trophy they have waited so long for. I haven't been playing very well in recent league games and I badly wanted to give my best against Wimbledon. Now I want to join all our supporters in celebrating this success and to take it a step further by winning the Cup.

'All my family and friends have been waiting for this moment back home in Italy; they know how important the FA Cup is and how much it means. My goal was special for me personally, but it was just as special for them, too.' Two-goal Hughes led the tributes to Zola: 'He wasn't bad today, was he? If he keeps playing like that, he's got a chance! To be honest, I didn't get a good view of his goal, because I was running about trying to make a few angles. But I will settle down with a few beers in front of the telly tonight and enjoy watching it over and over again on the action replays.'

Relaxed after a shower in the changing-rooms at Harlingdon,

before the team flew off to Newcastle Zola reflected on his FA Cup
dream: 'The atmosphere was maybe even better than Liverpool.
Against Liverpool we were at home, there were more people for
Chelsea. But again the atmosphere was very, very unbelievable. The
crowd was so excited that you could feel that. So I got like them.' As
for his goal, 'I knew what I was doing. I knew the defender was
behind me and I had to try to pass him. I thought that way could be
the right way. It was a very good goal because the goal was good to
see and important at that time of the game.' Zola knew Wimbledon
had been outsmarted: 'They tried to play their football, we stopped
their football. I know if we let them play like they wanted, it would
be more difficult for us.'

Zola was baffled by the possibility of facing Chesterfield in the
Final. It was the first time he had heard of them. 'But I think they're
a big surprise not only for me, but for everyone,' he said. 'Sometimes
a team from the second division in Italy get good results and get to
the final. It happened a couple of years ago, but is very, very hard. But
not a team from the third division, not ever.' He wasn't fussed who
won the other semi-final, though: 'It doesn't matter. We must think to
play how we play. We can get the Cup only when playing our best
football. If we play our best, we must be confident. We must be sure
we can do it. If we don't play our best, we will lose, against
Chesterfield or Middlesbrough, it doesn't matter which.'

Frank Sinclair purred when he recalled Zola's semi-final goal:
'He's just a pleasure to watch. When he got the ball and turned, it was
unbelievable, there was going to be only one conclusion, it was going
in the net. I didn't know how, whether he'd blast it in the roof or what,
but I just knew he was going to score. It was brilliant, and it made the
game comfortable for us.'

Zola wrote about his innermost feelings in a book, *Golden Heroes,*
which chronicles the fifty winners of the Footballer of the Year
award: 'My first season in English football was just unbelievable and
the memories of it will live with me forever. I felt humble when I
looked at the names of the great players who had won it before me,
and when I realized that I had won the vote ahead of such exceptional players as Juninho, Ravanelli and Alan Shearer. I was singled
out, but I must say I could not have achieved so much in my first

season without the great team effort by everybody at Stamford Bridge.

'The beautiful statuette, which I will cherish all my life, was presented to me by Mister Football himself, Sir Stanley Matthews. He is a god in the game and I was almost speechless not only to meet him in person but also to find myself sitting alongside him. We had a long talk about football past and present, and I found that he was completely up to date with everything that is happening in our great game.

'I was overjoyed to have my father at the awards ceremony. It was his first visit to England and like me he could not believe that the legendary Stanley Matthews was there to make the presentation. It is something that I will never forget.'

Zola, his father Ignazio, his lawyer, Gary his interpreter, and Gullit all made an early exit from the Royal Lancaster to continue their preparation for the Cup Final. Suddenly Ken Bates appeared. 'Follow me,' he said. The chairman led them out through the fans to offer his limousine to take Zola home and return afterwards to pick him up. Bates even opened the door and let them all in. They sat there waiting for the driver. They waited, and waited. Suddenly the chauffeur opened the door, looked in and shouted: 'Oi! What're you lot doin' in 'ere?' They all climbed out. There was Bates laughing, and they were all laughing too – as they clambered into a waiting taxi. Practical jokes, it appeared, were not confined to the dressing room at Chelsea!

11

Cup Final Fever

Gullit wanted to book a European place before the Cup Final, but Chelsea had slipped to seventh place in the Premiership. After three successive defeats in the league, a good result at St James's Park would have put them back in the frame for a UEFA Cup spot, but Chelsea crashed again, 3–1 at Newcastle. Three down at half-time, they put up a better fight in the second half with Zola whipping in a cross that Burley planted into the net in the sixty-second minute, bringing ironic cries from the Chelsea faithful of: 'One-nil in the second half.'

Zola was concerned at how the team had slipped up in their quest to qualify for Europe via the league: 'We don't know if we can win the Cup, so we have to improve in the championship. If we play well in the league, we can get to the final at Wembley in the right condition. That is the important point.'

Although there were still four league games to go, it had become increasingly more difficult for Gullit to get his team to concentrate on anything other than the FA Cup Final.

Cup Final fever was clearly evident at the training ground on Friday 18 April as the chosen suppliers of Wembley suits had a variety of cuts and cloths on show. Players' pool agent Paul Stretford was there, meeting first with Dennis Wise and Steve Clarke, and then the rest of the squad after training. Several bids were made to supply the Cup Final song, but the Warner offer involving Suggs was the winner.

Luca Vialli needed to produce something special in the few matches that remained, or Zola or Hughes had to be injured, for him to have any chance of starting at Wembley. 'To play would be fantastic,' he said. 'To be at Wembley would be fantastic as well. I have played football for sixteen years and I know sometimes something can go wrong, something is not like you would like it to be. I know you can go up and down, then suddenly something changes and you have to be ready. Now I'd like to play as soon as possible, but that is not up to me, that is up to the manager. I don't decide, the manager decides. What I've said was something different, it wasn't about football or about the manager's decision.'

On whether Vialli would win a Cup Final place, Gullit said: 'It all depends how everyone is doing. There is Zola and Mark Hughes who have played so well, and they are the facts.'

Gullit's message to his Cup Final team was to enjoy the experience, play their football, but be tuned in, focused, concentrated, and above all else produce their optimum and win: 'We have experienced players like Mark Hughes who are suited to the Cup Final, the same with Zola. Everyone has pleased me in their own way. No exceptions. Especially the young players like Jody Morris and Paul Hughes.'

Chelsea beat Leicester 2–1 at the Bridge and the ever-modest Zola admitted that his move had gone better than he could ever have imagined, after a small yet significant role in a welcome win over the recent Coca-Cola Cup winners. 'It has been like a dream for me, and it would have been impossible to imagine the satisfaction that I have had since coming to Chelsea,' he said. 'I have been very pleased with the way it has gone so far, and now I want to finish the season by winning the Cup.'

Zola added: 'We are a strange team, who can beat Manchester United and then lose to the bottom side. We have to concentrate more all the time. Ruud told us that it is not possible to play your best football all the time, and that sometimes you have to be solid and not give the opposition any chances. That is what Italy did against England. It is not just an Italian mentality – I saw Manchester United play like that at Liverpool. Chelsea have demonstrated that we can beat those sort of teams, but we need to make some improvements if we are to be a top side. But we are not far from it.

'I was on the bench because Ruud said I needed a rest. I am OK but sometimes you need a break, we have so many games. I like to play all the time but I know it is not possible. It would be very bad if I got an injury now, especially because of the FA Cup.'

New boots, but the same Mark Hughes, making the first goal and scoring the winner before limping off with fifteen minutes to go. Off on the 6.45pm shuttle to Manchester nursing the blisters that came from breaking in his smart new blue footwear, but again showing why he is so important with his fourteenth goal of the season, shaking off a persistent Leicester only when he was reunited with Zola, himself a late substitute. By then it was clear why Gullit was right again about Vialli; his only meaningful contribution was to be involved in the first goal. At times, both Hughes and Vialli hunted the same ball, and when Pontus Kaamark moved inside to pick him up, Vialli found himself stifled by the specialist man-marker, something he might have been used to in Italy.

After seventy-two minutes, with the game delicately balanced, Zola began warming up to a profusion of flags proclaiming 'Zola Power'. They sang his personalized song. Zola stepped into the action, attracting the attention of Kaamark. Still Vialli contributed little, but Hughes got free to head home Danny Granville's cross as Chelsea suddenly found some space. The young full-back was Gullit's man-of-the-match. At the final whistle, Vialli was off and out of the Bridge in a chauffeur-driven limo, knowing he had blown another chance to force Gullit to think again. Gullit said abruptly that he didn't want to talk about the situation between him and Vialli. The future for Vialli was either on the subs' bench, or the door marked exit.

Buoyant after regaining some semblance of form, the next day most of the squad joined pop star and Chelsea fan Suggs to record their Cup Final song in a west London recording studio. 'Blue Is The Colour' was a football classic of the 70s; now it was 'Blue Day' under the name Team Chelsea. Zola enjoyed the experience and was featured in the cover shots for the CD.

The 1997 version, written by Chelsea season-ticket holder Mike

Connaris, was to become an emotional hymn of praise for the Chelsea faithful at Wembley.

> *The only place to be*
> *Every other Saturday*
> *Is strollin' down the Fulham Road*
> *Meet your mates and have a drink*
> *Have a moan and start to think*
> *Will there ever be a Blue tomorrow?*
>
> *We've waited so long*
> *But we'd wait for ever*
> *Our blood is Blue and*
> *We would leave you never*
> *And when we make it*
> *It'll be together, oh oh oh*
>
> *Chelsea Chelsea*
> *We're gonna make this a Blue Day*
> *Chelsea Chelsea*
> *We're gonna make this a Blue Day*
>
> *We've got some memories,*
> *Albeit from the seventies,*
> *When Ossie and Co restored our pride.*
> *Now we've got hope, and a team and suddenly it's not a*
> *dream.*
> *We'll keep the Blue Flag flying high*
> *Now even heaven*
> *Is Blue today, you should*
> *Hear the Chelsea roar*
> *Hear the Chelsea roar....*

'Blue Day' went into recording even before the players had agreed to do it; Suggs performed the lead vocal days before, and the players went to the studios to join in the chorus and record the video. For the video, the players came to the mike at random to sing in time to the music. When Luca strolled up for a solo, he took a deep breath, hands clapping to the rhythm . . . . and the tape ran out! Amidst the laughter, David Lee shouted: 'Ruud's turned it off!' Hysterics followed, and it can be heard on the CD featuring a special Karaoke Mix.

Actually, Ruud wasn't there – he preferred to stay out of the limelight. Suggs said: 'I wouldn't hear a bad word said against him, but for some reason he wasn't that keen to join in with the record. He was probably more concerned with working on tactics for the big day.' Also missing were Mark Hughes, who had flown home to Manchester for the weekend the day before, and Roberto Di Matteo, who flew home to Switzerland at the same time.

They all moved on to a photographic studio to shoot the cover for the CD. There was a piano there; Zola couldn't be persuaded to play, but Luca had a go.

The record was released twelve days before the Final, and Dennis Wise said: '"Blue Day" really catches the team spirit. We had a great laugh recording it – but it's a good job we play football and don't sing for a living!'

Cup Final rivals Boro teamed up with comedian Bob Mortimer and pop legend Chris Rea to record a version of 'Let's Dance' . . . . There was only going to be one Wembley singalong winner!

The next assignment was a rerun of the semi-final, at Selhurst Park, where Chelsea again beat the Dons, 1–0. Leboeuf was captain for the first time, and Zola gave Wimbledon another footballing masterclass. But there was also the obligatory Cup Final injury scare.

Zola pulled up in pain in the final seconds, running for a loose ball, and was hastily replaced by young Sherrin. Zola gingerly trudged off with a limp and immediately departed for treatment, clutching a hamstring, but Gullit was confident he would be fit for the Final: 'He has a little muscle problem but it's not that bad. His thigh muscle has gone into spasm; we will not know the full extent of the damage for twenty-four hours. But I am not too worried about him for the Cup Final because it is too early to say, and anyway, we have other players who can replace him. They do not have the same kind of skill but can certainly do a job for the team. He will go with the national team but I don't think he will be able to play; but I will allow him to travel with the squad. We didn't take any chance and he was having treatment as soon as he came off. While away, he will be able to get treatment from the Italian doctor every day, and that should help him.' The injury made Zola a big doubt for Italy in their World Cup qualifier against Poland in Naples, on the same day that England faced Georgia at Wembley.

Zola was determined to make the Cup Final: 'I was running for the ball a minute from the end and felt a twinge. The muscle just went tight. I know exactly what these things are like, so I didn't do anything silly. We'd already won the game and I thought the best thing was to get off the pitch as soon as I could. I'm not in any pain, it's just a matter of wait and see what the medical people tell me. I'm desperate to play for Italy because it's a very important game for us. But I will not be taking any chances. That's because the FA Cup Final is less than four weeks away and I definitely want to be ready for it. I'm travelling to Italy and will have treatment every day. Hopefully, I will be fit for the Poland match, but I shall not take risks. I love Wembley and want to go there and score again.' Zola would have medical tests in Florence to determine the exact nature and severity of the problem.

Despite what Gullit said, there was no getting away from it: no Zola, no chance in the Final. In terms of ability and invention, he was irreplaceable. Gullit admitted: 'He gives the team something extra.' Once again his performance had underlined that fact. An admiring Joe Kinnear reckoned Zola had been the foreign import of the season: 'Everybody would like a Zola in their side. I think he's been the pick of the foreign players this season. Zola can unlock sides when it's stalemate and win a game with one piece of skill. And when you think he's only been here since November, he has settled in brilliantly.'

Chelsea made seven changes from the semi-final but were still too classy for Wimbledon. Sullivan made a string of fine saves, from Vialli and Nicholls in particular, to keep the score down. The solitary goal came after a quarter of an hour. Zola's exquisite pass sent Petrescu through alone on goal and he beat Sullivan. When Zola beautifully beat Perry out on the left and found Vialli with remarkable sleight of foot, Vialli's high shot was caught by Sullivan. Later, when Zola gave Petrescu another chance, Sullivan repelled the incursion, as he did when Nicholls forced him to turn the ball round for a corner. And in the ninetieth minute, Vialli, though all alone and clearly desperate to score, was thwarted by the resilient keeper.

The injury scare seemed to subside when Zola was declared fit to take on Poland; bad news for England, good news for Chelsea. 'As soon as I arrived in Italy and had all the tests with the Italian team medical staff, they all proved negative,' Zola explained. 'I needed a couple of days of rest and now I'm ready to play.' The Italians called up Roberto Baggio from his long international exile as cover, and Zola added: 'It was nice to see Roberto back in the squad, it must have been hard for a great player like him to be left out all this time. For me, it was great motivation to be playing when I knew somebody like him was waiting in the wings.'

Vialli, meanwhile, was in Barcelona playing for an all-star Europe team that lost 4–3 to the Rest of the World. 'It's a novelty for me to get a game,' he said. 'Chelsea give me so few chances to play. Now I'm looking ahead to the FA Cup Final, when some from among myself, Zola, Di Matteo, Festa and Ravanelli will become the first Italians to win a trophy in England. But it's no surprise to me – the reason English clubs have brought us in is to help them win things.'

In the build-up to the Poland game, Zola hinted that he favoured finishing his career in Italy. He was quoted in the Italian press: 'I will be at Chelsea next season – that is a 100 per cent certainty. But after that, we will have to see. I am no longer a little kid – in fact, I will be thirty-four by the turn of the century. I would like to finish my playing career in Italy, and I will do it for sure. I have made up my mind where I want to go, although I can't yet say where. I've got a plan and I know what I would like to do. I've already decided but I'm not going to say. It would bring me bad luck.' Napoli was believed to be his target. 'Napoli made me into the player I am today,' he said. 'I was nobody when I joined them, but I had the chance to learn from Maradona. There was a real atmosphere about the place, and it was the most important stage of my career.' But moving to Chelsea had helped him recapture his best form: 'I am very glad I moved to England. It has helped me a great deal. I have improved as a player because nowadays I am more self-confident and I have more freedom to play my own type of game.'

Ken Bates stressed, in his matchday programme notes, that Zola was not leaving halfway through his four-year contract: 'Zola is with us until the next century and can't be responsible for every Italian phrase taken out of context or misquoted.'

Zola cleared up any doubts: 'I hope I can stay here for a long time. I have a long contract and I hope to respect it. My family and my children have settled very well here. London is a fantastic city and I enjoy myself living here.' Zola clarified the situation by stating that he wanted to end his playing days with his local side Cagliari.

Back home, the players' pool was in full swing. A number of agents had vied for the lucrative pot, and a players' committee had the final choice. Successful applicant Paul Stretford's task was to 'sell' the Cup Final team for as much money as possible in the short space of time. Newspapers were one source of revenue. Stretford contacted the papers with player interviews for sale. He had a three-tier price range. 'The big hitters' were on offer for between £7,000 and £12,000 each – Gullit, Wise, Leboeuf, Mark Hughes and the three Italians. Category B was Petrescu, Clarke, Sinclair, Burley, Morris and Myers at £3,000 to £7,000. 'The supporting cast' were valued at upwards of £1,000: Rix, Forrest, Kharine, Grodas, Granville, Paul Hughes, Minto, Parker, Rocastle and Lee.

Gullit was unaware of his own involvement, and after being told a few days later by his agent Jon Smith, he opted out. Smith, who contacted Stretford to explain Gullit's policy, said: 'He felt the whole business of charging the media for interviews "silly". He has never done it and didn't want to start now.' Zola was in talks about signing for Smith and he, too, would be taken out of the interview 'pot'.

Meanwhile in Naples, Zola started in attack alongside Ravanelli, and Di Matteo grabbed Italy's twenty-third minute opener in the 3–0 defeat of Poland, his first international goal. Paolo Maldini notched the second and Roberto Baggio scored a glorious third as Italy took control of a game that kept them top of World Cup qualifying group 2. Baggio came on for Zola, who had struck the bar with a venomous shot in the first half and been thwarted by the keeper when put through. Zola limped off after fifty-one minutes, but his early exit was 'precautionary'. He was doubtful, though, for Chelsea's final home game with Leeds.

In fact, Zola wouldn't play again until the Final after returning with a slight hamstring strain. He underwent a scan, but Gullit stressed that the problem was not serious; Zola had been given the all-clear after the scan. Gullit said: 'It's good news. No damage, it's only a matter of muscle fatigue. A week's rest will do the job.'

Gullit summed up the season in his final address to the fans in his programme notes for the Leeds match, a goalless draw. 'It has been a rollercoaster year,' he said.

Gullit was amazed at how much Di Matteo and Zola had improved: 'Zola is now having the best spell of his career with the Italian national team. Before he came here, he was never an automatic choice. He was known as the man who missed that Euro 96 penalty against Germany. Now he is their playmaker, the most important man in their team. And I am proud of that. Di Matteo, too, has made so much progress. He never scored for Lazio. He was almost punished if he went too far forward. Now he is playing with greater freedom and posing much more of a threat. And that is all down to the way he is being used at Chelsea.'

Zola was again rested as the curtain came down on the Premiership season at Everton. He missed the game to ensure his participation in the Cup Final, but in an ominous message to Boro he assessed his form and fitness: 'Since I came here, I think I'm playing the best football of my life. I'm now more consistent every time I play, so my game has got better in every match. All the things I've needed to play my football well have happened. I'm perfectly content on the pitch, and off it with my family as well. It doesn't matter what job you do or what profession you're in, when you're relaxed, confident and happy, you perform well – and that's certainly the case with me.'

With Zola given another day-off, Vialli was offered the chance to stake his Wembley claim; it was depressingly snatched off him after only twenty minutes when Grodas was sent off. Ferguson, looking suspiciously offside, raced onto Watson's long clearance. The big striker, three yards outside the penalty area, lifted the ball past the onrushing Grodas but in trying to go after it was pulled down by the keeper. Referee Peter Jones brandished a red card after speaking to his assistant. Gullit had no option but to bring off someone for substitute keeper Hitchcock. It just had to be Vialli!

Vialli sprinted straight past Gullit, who was standing on the touch-line reorganizing his formation, without a sideways glance – and without breaking stride, he headed straight back to the dressing-room.

Hughes, a Chelsea fan since childhood, had great sympathy for Vialli's plight: 'I actually feel sorry for Luca. He is a world-class player and I know that if I don't produce my best, he is waiting there to take my place. That's what has inspired me to play so well. Luca has actually been unlucky. He suffered some injuries early on, so when Gianfranco Zola arrived it was me who partnered him. It could easily have been the other way around. Luca is a lovely guy. A really nice bloke. Dennis Wise wears his "We love you Luca" T-shirt not for effect but because he means it. Luca is great. He understands the situation and there has never been a problem between us. We talk all the time about football, about golf – he even asks me for help with his English.'

Hughes knew the Cup Final spotlight would inevitably fall on mighty midgets Zola and Juninho: 'It's just what you would expect. The focus was always going to be on these two little fellows because they are two of the few players around in the game who can influence it dramatically with their marvellous talent. In fact, I'll be surprised if neither Zola nor Juninho doesn't play a significant part in the outcome. I think they will certainly have their chances, because the way both sides play I can't see any specialized man-marking being done on them. Sometimes Cup Finals are a let-down when people expect so much, but with these two players, there's got to be a good chance it will be a very good, open game.'

Among the numerous 'experts' asked for their views on the Final was former England manager Bobby Robson, who gave his name-sake the edge in purchasing foreign stars (although with hindsight he might change his mind.): 'I think Bryan comes out a little bit in front, despite his team's league position. Festa and Leboeuf have similar qualities as defenders, but Ravanelli's thirty-one goals make him a better signing than Vialli. Zola is fantastic, full of feints and move-ment, with a marvellous football intelligence. But Juninho's vision around the box is just as sharp, and I'd go for him because he is so much younger. He might have won the Footballer of the Year award this season instead of Zola if he had been with a more fashionable club.'

Charlie Cooke, meanwhile, reminisced about the good old days down the King's Road when Chelsea were the most fashionable club in town and he was the darling of the fans. Now the King's Road was swaying to a new rhythm: doing the Continental, and the one-time wizard of the wing was delighted that Chelsea were on the threshold of success for the first time since the seventies. At the age of fifty-four, Charlie was enjoying his new life in Cincinnati, USA, anxious for any news about his old club back on the glory trail: 'Out here it's not easy to find soccer on the telly, even though there are millions of channels. But I'll be searching to find the Cup Final, that's a game I don't want to miss. The little I've seen of Zola has been brilliant, he's like greased lightning.' When I told Charlie that Zola was the Footballer of the Year, he enthused: 'Great! Is he? That's fantastic, I'm really pleased.' Charlie was stunned that no other Chelsea player had won it before. Of Zola he said: 'I've seen him play for Italy quite a bit and, cor, what a quick, quick player. He's so fast with his stops and starts. It's wonderful that Chelsea have players like that at the club, with so much ability. I just wish I could see more of the team. It's such a shame that I can't.'

Zola was hailed as the new Charlie Cooke, but with everything in sport it's faster, better and with far greater financial rewards. Charlie and the heroes of '70 and '71 earned a couple of hundred pounds for winning the FA Cup. 'In our day the internationalism of the league was happening, but nowhere near the way it is now,' he said. 'It's good to see it coming off for Chelsea, justifying the money they've spent, and I don't begrudge the players the money they're earning now. I don't agree with players in the past who feel that the wages now are obscene, it's just the nature of the business. I feel it sounds embarrassing, it sounds bitter and twisted – give me a break! I enjoy my memories of that Chelsea team in the seventies and it's sad when you hear people worrying about how much players earn now compared to the old days. The club were good to me when I came over three years ago, they invited me to the Savoy for their after-Cup Final dinner. But, I didn't think it would happen, but when I got there, I felt it was wrong to be there. It was their day and I felt a wee bit "Why the hell am I here?"'

Howard Wilkinson, the FA's new technical director, also assessed Zola in comparison to Juninho.

First impressions of Zola: 'I'm sure he's surprised a lot of people in Italy, because he's done a lot better over here than his performances over there would have suggested. He settled well and quickly into the Premiership.'

Tactical differences: 'If you drew a line across the middle of the Chelsea team, Zola would operate nearer the front player, or between the midfield players and the front ones. He is not seen so often doing the sort of deep defensive work that Juninho seems to enjoy.'

Special strengths: 'Both players have touch, vision and change of pace. There is also power and accuracy of shot and sense of opportunity at free-kicks. I don't know whether it's natural or whether he's worked on it, but Zola's positional play is very good. He seems to know where to go to make life difficult for his opponents. He says to himself, "Well, I'll go and take him into an area where he's not used to playing and see how he likes that.' He's able to find the spaces and look at the formation of another team and the way they're playing, and pop himself into the place where he can most conveniently get the ball. But he doesn't usually hold it as long as Juninho. I wouldn't say that either of them has electric speed, but they do have a tremendous change of pace. That change of pace could make all the difference in the Cup Final. I sometimes wonder whether, whereas Zola seems to think things out, Juninho, because of his energy, doesn't have time to think. He finds himself where he is because that energy has taken him there. It's a bit like the film of the Jack Russell terrier chasing around the pitch with the ball and never losing it. You don't take the ball from Juninho, he loans it to you and wants it back – even from his own players.'

Weaknesses: 'Next question.'

How would Zola play at Wembley? 'He's played there before, though not as recently as Juninho. He has said that even before he came here, one of his dreams was to play at Wembley, and the game is on Italian TV. He's used to playing in important games. He's also a very intelligent player who is going to think things out and create opportunities by knowing where to be at the right moment.'

Could they be tamed? 'It will be interesting to see whether Ruud Gullit and Bryan Robson decide to do something specific to counter the threat of the two players. I've always taken the view that at this level, when you ain't got the ball, you've got to stop them and win a football match. If I thought one of the opponents was so important to the opposing team as to be almost indispensable, I always wondered whether *we* could dispense with him (fairly, of course). But it's not going to be easy. In a game I saw recently, Juninho was involved once a minute. On nine out of ten occasions, what he did with the ball had a positive outcome. If he enjoys that sort of freedom, and that sort of success rate, then Chelsea have got a problem. You have to remember that when you talk about his success rate, you're not talking about an easy ten-yard pass, but a dribble, a one-two or a defence-splitting pass. But with Zola, he does need to have people give him the ball, whereas Juninho tends to go and get it. Zola has the advantage of having Mark Hughes's strength ahead of him, knocking the ball back, but you have to remember that Ravanelli, if he plays, is no shrinking violet.'

David Pleat, of course, had first-hand knowledge about whether to man-mark Zola or not. He said: 'That is the question which has faced numerous managers in the Premiership this season, myself included, when confronted with the menace of Gianfranco Zola. When I took my Sheffield Wednesday side to play Chelsea at Stamford Bridge in December, we discussed at some length the question of whether or not to mark the little Italian. In the opening twenty minutes, Zola destroyed us. Our intention was that a central midfielder would pick him up when he dropped deep, and for the very quick Des Walker to take care of him when he pushed further forward. But he timed his diagonal runs to perfection and even shook Walker with his pace. Such was the fluidity of Chelsea's all-round movement that we suddenly found ourselves two goals down and fighting for breath. After half-time we reorganized and Peter Atherton tracked Zola wherever he went, and we managed to come away with a 2–2 draw. Apart from the stifling effect which the close marking had, we found that Zola tended to receive less of the ball. In England, players are reluctant to pass the ball to a player who is tightly marked, even though Zola, from his time in Italy, has learned to thrive in such circumstances. Like Glenn Hoddle at his best, he has the ability to disengage his marker with quick movement or by taking a return pass played behind the marker.

'I feel that Robson, like Hoddle against Italy, will decide not to shadow Zola at Wembley. Against England, of course, he proved to be the match-winner, although I think defensive error rather than mistaken tactics were to blame on that occasion, since he did not otherwise dominate the game.'

John Charles played in two Italian Cup finals for Juventus but never an FA Cup Final. The 'Gentle Giant', now sixty-five, joined Juventus from Leeds for what was then a world record £65,000 fee in May 1957. He is still revered in Turin forty years on. He said: 'The FA Cup Final is unique. It has a magic all of its own. I don't think the foreign stars realize what an occasion it will be. In Italy the Cup didn't count for much. The final was played over two legs in my day. Players and fans were only really concerned about the championship. But talk about English football and people always mention the FA Cup Final and Wembley in May. It is part of our way of life. I cannot ever remember an FA Cup Final with so many foreign players, Italians and Brazilians, taking part. They are very lucky when you consider the number of good players who have never played at Wembley. When you look at the talent on both sides, it should be a spectacular match, and I'm looking forward to watching it on TV. I hope Fabrizio Ravanelli plays. He has scored some wonderful goals for Middlesbrough this season, and it would be a shame if he was to miss out through injury.

'Perhaps little Zola will make the most impact. I thought he might struggle here because of his height. But all credit to him, he has settled in quickly at Chelsea. He works really hard, is physically strong and has formed a good partnership with Mark Hughes, who is vastly underrated. Chelsea and Middlesbrough are two good footballing sides, and I think the fans are in for a treat.'

Joe Kinnear, who took Wimbledon to two semi-finals, tipped Gullit's team: 'Chelsea rely heavily on the brilliance of their little Italian Zola and the muscle, might and experience of Mark Hughes. If these two continue their perfect striking partnership, then I see Boro's defence being cut to shreds. The big battle of the little men . . .

It's tempting to suggest whoever shines most between Zola and Juninho will sway the final outcome.'

Trevor Brooking took Chelsea to win by 3–1 or 4–2. In his *Evening Standard* column, he picked out Zola to 'give us a memorable Cup Final after the years of mediocrity'. He added: 'All too often the air of optimism and expectancy surrounding the Wembley showpiece quickly turns to tedium for the watching millions. But the Italian produces moments of skill and vision which no other player comes near, and is the main reason why I believe we could have a Final to savour. If I had to choose one player from all the overseas stars in the Premiership to turn it on at Wembley, Zola would be at the top of my list. His wonderful turn and finish against Wimbledon in the semi-final was a typical example of the exceptional balance and speed of thought which makes him so elusive. Zola and Mark Hughes have blended into a superb striking partnership which possesses everything a manager desires. Hughes complements his partner perfectly and is the ideal focal point for Chelsea to launch their attacks. His ability to hold up play and allow others to join is legendary, and I cannot detect any reduction in his influence since leaving Manchester United somewhat prematurely two years ago. He is a man for the big occasion and his tussle with Nigel Pearson will be a key factor in the outcome. Chelsea are not solely reliant on Hughes and Zola because the passing and movement in midfield is excellent, with Roberto Di Matteo, Dennis Wise, Eddie Newton and Craig Burley all contributing significantly to this Cup run.'

Juninho promised a devastating performance after the bitter disappointment of the Coca-Cola Cup Final battering from Leicester. The Brazilian man of the match in the emphatic replay defeat of brave Chesterfield, wanted his boyhood heroes Pele and Zico to come to Wembley.

He knew, also, how important it was for Boro to ensure European football at the Riverside if the club were to have any chance of keeping Ravanelli and Emerson: 'I have already played twice at Wembley and now I am so happy to be going back there. It's a brilliant pitch and a fabulous atmosphere, which brings the best out of you. I can see why the English players think the FA Cup is the best competition in the world. Now it is important for us to bring a trophy back for the supporters.

'I came to England to win things and now that is starting to happen. We had a chance in the Coca-Cola Cup and it didn't happen, but now we have another chance. I think Chelsea will suit our style more than Leicester did. Like us, they always look to bring the ball down, pass and play. That can only be good for us, and for the crowd. I think I will get more space this time. But I have watched a lot of Italian football, and I know that Zola is an excellent player – different class. I think that the English supporters prefer Italian football to the South American game, but I have had a wonderful welcome in this country. Wherever I go, people call my name and ask for my autograph. Not just Middlesbrough supporters, but all fans. I am very proud to be going back to Wembley, but what is even more important is that we stay in the Premier League.' They didn't, failing to win at Leeds on the last day of the season while Coventry were winning at Spurs.

One of the most bizarre moments in the countdown to Wembley was the idea that Zola and Cantona might play for England!

Labour's new sports minister Tony Banks, quickly making an impact, was responsible. He believed foreign players living in this country should be made eligible to be chosen for Hoddle's squad, and he also wanted the home nations merged into one United Kingdom team: 'The more we're involved in Europe, we ought to think about if you play in this country for one of the league teams, you can play for the country as well – in other words, the right to play is not one of birth but one of residence. Think about it, freedom of movement within the European Union, able to vote; let's start thinking the unthinkable – if people are playing over here and want to play for England and Scotland, why not play?'

The totally unworkable idea came to Banks when he watched England slump to defeat in the World Cup qualifier against Italy – when Zola scored the only goal. Banks argued: 'There were a lot of Chelsea players looking at that Italy match and saying, "Do well, Zola, do well!" Wouldn't it be better instead of sitting there and saying "Do well, Zola" when he actually puts your international team out, instead saying, "Zola, you're over here, we're paying your wages. Why don't you play for England?" It's not government policy, but let's discuss it. Why don't we talk about it – we're in Europe, we're involved. Tony Blair said to me, "Get in there and liven it up," and I'm going to do precisely that. These are things worth discussing; it's no good saying it's rubbish, we can't do it. Why shouldn't we discuss it? My role here is to be a bit challenging and controversial and to act as a catalyst.' Nice one, Tony. But on to the next idea!

'Team Chelsea' switched to the Bridge press room with Vialli leading in Zola, Newton and Morris. The background was a sponsors list: BBC Sport, Yves St Laurent, Cerruti, Coors, Umbro, and the Great Ormond Street Hospital. Vialli wore a 'Make the tear disappear' T-shirt; the boys were decked out in YSL.

Morris, on the far left, never had to utter a word; he wasn't asked a question. Newton was asked about Juninho and one or two other questions, but the Italians were bombarded.

A headline, 'Zola for England', was held up.

Zola looked puzzled, leaning across to seek advice from Gary, the ever-present interpreter, and Vialli before bursting into laughter.

'You want to embarrass me,' said Zola.

Vialli said: 'I'm available!'

That brought the biggest laugh of the day – Vialli had spent the previous ten minutes explaining his heartbreak at missing out on the start of the Final and was still unsettled over his future. Perhaps England would take him!

Zola gave the best possible Wembley news. He had had a full week's rest and was now gradually stepping up his training: 'I rest for one week. I'm improving my condition. I started training three days ago, I don't have a problem; day by day, I am improving.'

He had not spoken to Ravanelli: 'I prefer to speak to him after the match.'

Zola weighed up whether it was good or bad for Chelsea that Boro had been relegated: 'It's not a good thing, this Cup becomes more important for them. It is going to be a very hard game for us. We must play our best football that we can, that's all.'

He didn't accept it would be a catastrophic setback if Chelsea were not in Europe. He explained: 'We would like to play in Europe to give a good impression of Chelsea. A place in Europe is important for all the team, not just me. I shall try to do my best for all reasons. But it doesn't matter for me; if we don't succeed, it doesn't matter, we will do good next year. Everything at Chelsea is in front of me.'

Most important for Zola was to win the Cup. He sensed the importance of the occasion; 'Yeah, the feeling for this game is special,
absolutely special. You can feel the atmosphere around you, everywhere you go, in the newspapers, all the people talk about it. I hope
Chelsea play special game for all our supporters.'

As he worried about his acceptance speech for the Footballer of
the Year award the next day, he explained how playing in the
Premiership had made him a better player: 'Playing here has
increased my skill, I have become more complete than when I played
for Parma.' He did not accept that English defences were weaker
than in Italy: 'It is different situation. In England there is a different
mentality. In Italy they think defensively, in England it's the opposite
and that's a point for me. I've played good seasons against good
defenders. What is important is that you have to be confident and
have to be right – I am confident and I am right.'

He expected to be closely watched at Wembley: 'They are going to
try to stop me playing, it's normal. I have to think about it and to find
the way to put myself in confidence in the game. This season has
given me great satisfaction. I never thought I could play like that. I
have to thank all my team-mates who have helped me give of my
best. I have to thank Chelsea and all our supporters, they have been
fantastic for me. I hope to deserve all their satisfaction; I hope to give
them all my best in the next games.'

Vialli had resigned himself to a place on the Wembley bench. He
was still smiling, but only on the outside; inside, he hurt: 'I have
learned to become a good actor. I have discovered that I must always
be in control of my emotions and to be patient when I am not playing. I must always be nice with my girlfriend when I go home! I have
to smile even if inside I feel very disappointed. Ruud is the manager
and I am a player. That is our relationship. We are both professionals
trying to do our best for the team. But it is a difficult situation for me
because the manager only needs me if the team is playing badly or
they are not winning. Do I hope to come on or not? Perhaps for the
last five minutes after Gianfranco has scored a hat-trick!'

Luca felt like he was cast in a play – clearly not in a leading role,
more of a bit-part actor. 'The Final is like a movie,' he said. 'Gullit will
be our director, Zola the superstar main character and the other play-

ers will be the support actors. But you need all those people to make a movie. Even Gianfranco can't play on his own. And if I am not playing, it is important I still help everyone as much as I can. I hope I get at least five minutes at Wembley, but the most important thing is to see Dennis Wise lift the Cup.'

Bryan Robson stressed that the Final was not simply a battle between the two smallest men on the pitch, as most pundits declared. The Boro manager, a Cup Final winner three times with Manchester United, agreed that the two players were integral to their teams, but he pointed out that it was simplistic to look at the game in that way: 'They are both top players, both of the highest quality, but there are lots of good players on both sides. I have seen Mark Hughes win Cup ties and Cup Finals with his sheer presence, as he did for Chelsea at Portsmouth in the quarter-final this year. He was the main man. He played with passion, scored a great goal and made it comfortable for Chelsea. On Saturday we've hopefully got Fabrizio Ravanelli, who could also make a real difference. That's not to say that Zola and Juninho won't make a difference. I just hope that Zola doesn't have a good game and Juninho does, as simple as that. I hope so for us, but we've got ten other players as well as Chelsea, and it's how the whole team performs.'

Tony Banks was back in the news, making the most important pronouncement of his short reign so far as the new Sports Minister: 'It's Chelsea to win 3–2.' Banks also predicted Zola would score the first goal – after dreaming about the result. He bet £1,000 at odds of 75–1 at William Hill's Stamford Bridge branch. If his dream came true, he would win £75,000 – but Banks pledged the money to the charity SCOPE, formerly the Spastics Society. William Hill spokesman Graham Sharpe said: 'Mr Banks apparently dreamed the correct results of Chelsea's early round FA Cup matches. It would be a dream result for SCOPE if his prediction is correct – and even if Mr Banks has backed a loser, we'll hand his stake over to the charity.'

Banks had always been a Chelsea fan, despite living in West Ham land. His view of Zola: 'Deserves all the superlatives that have been heaped upon him. This man is the match-winner. He is crucial to Chelsea. When he gets the ball, a buzz goes round the ground. The last time I remember the same thing happening was when Jimmy

Greaves got the ball – you always felt that there was a goal in the making. Zola has settled down so fast and achieved god-like proportions as far as the supporters are concerned.'

The cut-off point to the outside world arrived. Two days before the Final was the players' and management's final press conference.

More than 120 journalists from all over the world crammed into the upstairs canteen area for a mega-audience with the players and Gullit – an FA-organized event for all sections of the media, with the manager and every single member of the Chelsea squad available for interview.

Dennis Wise dealt with the foreign culture-shock issue: 'I've had no problems because I speak a foreign language as well – fluent Cockney. But the quality the foreign guys have brought to the club is amazing. They turn bad moves into good ones, and you have to get better yourself just by being on the same pitch as them. I don't captain guys like Zola, Di Matteo, Luca and Frank Leboeuf, I just let them get on with it. And with the team we now have, we're capable of achieving a lot of success in the next few years. We need to get over the obstacle of the first trophy and then we'll really take off.'

Zola wanted his parents to have a winner's medal from English football: 'If I could give them a Cup winner's medal and a place in Europe, that'd be a dream. I will try to do that; I know it's not going to be easy, but I will do my best to make that happen.'

Zola had been an inspirational purchase and even Gullit was surprised by the extent of his success, so quickly: 'I knew he was a great player, and for me to get him was a great opportunity. Of course, I didn't imagine he'd have success like this – you can only dream about that. But I'm quite happy about it and I think we did well to sign him – and for that fee, yes, he looks a bargain.'

Zola himself said: 'I have become more skilful and confident. I now know before each game exactly what I am capable of. It is a great feeling. I have played against all of the best defenders in the world, but here in England I have taught myself different things – to be quicker, mentally stronger. The first thing I must do in every game is escape what the opposition has in store for me. English football has made that easier, because here the game is so much quicker and your mind has to be even more alert.'

Thinking of Wembley, he added: 'I never thought I would get the opportunity to go back so soon, especially in a match of this proportion. I know the Chelsea fans will be expecting so much of me and I will do everything I can to give them and everyone watching pleasure. It will mean a lot to me for Chelsea to play well and win. I don't feel the pressure, even though I know that a lot of eyes will be upon me. I have confidence and my mental condition has never been stronger than it is since I played here.'

Zola had scored twelve goals, including four in the FA Cup. He put much of his success down to Gullit: 'When you come to play in a foreign country it is vital that people have belief in you. Ruud Gullit gave me complete backing. He gave me this big opportunity, and there will be more exciting times ahead for this club. He wants great things for Chelsea. People tell me this club has waited a long time to win something big. I find that hard to believe, because of the football we have played and the kind of atmosphere that is generated at Stamford Bridge. The big occasion is important for all clubs. You have to find that something special. The English game has been so good to me. I would like to give something back in return and that would be a goal and then a trophy for this club.

'I would like to give the Cup to the Chelsea supporters, because they deserve it.'

There was sadness once more from Zola for his good friend Vialli: 'It is a very difficult situation for me. It will be very hard to see him on the bench on such a big occasion. When I came here, there were three big strikers. The club decided to make a change and Luca does not play. There is nothing more I can say about that. It must be hard for him. But we have to respect the coach.'

Gianluca Festa, who hails from the same town as Zola, was Boro's mid-season signing from Inter Milan. He was convinced he could contain Chelsea's dangerman. He said: 'Zola is world-class. He was one of the best players in Italy and is one of the best here in England. It will be a great challenge for me on an important occasion. If we can keep him under control, we have a good chance of winning. I have played against him many, many times, but I have marked him only once. My job in Italy was usually to mark the main striker, and of course Zola plays deeper. The time I did mark him, he didn't score but I am not claiming it was because of me! I just hope he doesn't score against us at Wembley.'

Festa was not the only Zola fan among the Boro Cup Final squad. Juninho had voted for the Italian in the PFA Player of the Year award.

Hughes felt that while the magic of an FA Cup Final atmosphere was still to be discovered by the foreign imports, two of the Chelsea line-up had benefited from their taste of Wembley on a high-profile occasion. 'Both Gianfranco Zola and Roberto Di Matteo played for Italy when they beat England in that World Cup group match a few months back,' said Hughes. 'They will have learned a lot that night about what it is like when there is a full house at Wembley. It won't be such a surprise to them.'

Juninho prepared to bid adieu to this country at Wembley, with Spanish giants Atletico Madrid, money no object, the destination of the twenty-four-year-old. The Brazilian hoped to say his final farewells to the Boro faithful by giving them one last sight of him in full flow, in what he believed would be an open game: 'Chelsea have some great players, but I'm happy that we're playing them. It will be a great game to watch because Chelsea like to play football. They play beautiful football and when we play teams who play like that, we tend to play well ourselves.' Gullit did not believe in man-marking and that thought brightened Juninho, recalling the two Coca-Cola Cup Final matches against Leicester when Pontus Kaamark did not leave his side. 'I hope not!' laughed the man from Sao Paulo. 'You have to let the players play. Chelsea have players like Zola, Di Matteo and Hughes, and you have to let them show their football. If they are all man-marked, it would be an ugly game.'

Ravanelli was desperate to silence his special pal Vialli: 'It's very important I come out on top over Vialli because we are still very close, and I'll never hear the last of it if we don't win the Cup! It's really important that I have something to show for my time spent in England. I was really upset I could not do it for myself and the club against Leicester. I've been fortunate to win several big cups with Juventus. But the thought of being the first Italian along with Gianluca Festa to hold the FA Cup would give me so much pleasure. It is so important we have something to show for our time in the

Premiership and now we have another chance. It's funny that previously no Italians have picked up a medal. Now it's either us or Zola and co – and I am going to make sure it is us. It'd be marvellous to do it. We have played some great games to get this far, and we deserve the Cup just on some of those showings.'

12

The FA Cup Final

Saturday 17 May
CHELSEA 2, MIDDLESBROUGH 0

Franco Zola ecstatically danced around trying on a profusion of hats as his smile lit up Wembley. A huge blue-and-white striped hat that nearly submerged him completely, then a giant 'Z' that slipped off too often. He finally kicked it away, as the fans threw him yet more of their colours. But the 'hat' he loved best of all was the top of the precious piece of English silverware, the FA Cup.

After Zola and his team-mates collected their winners' medals, he looked at the prize as if it was as valuable as any he had won in *Serie A* with Napoli and Parma. When the BBC interviewer pressed a microphone close to his face for an instant reaction, all those lessons, all his hard work to master the language deserted him. He was so overwhelmed he could just about repeat the word 'fantastic' a few times as he searched for more meaningful vocabulary. He said: 'Thank you very much for all your support. This has been fantastic. It gave me a great satisfaction.'

As predicted in the Suggs 'Chelsea, Chelsea' Cup Final song, it was certainly a Blue Day at Wembley. And Zola was singing along with the rest of the players: 'We waited so long, but we'd wait forever.' The twenty-seven-year wait was over.

When it came to a rendition of 'Blue is the Colour' from the seventies, Zola and a few of the other foreign stars looked a little lost for the right words!

For those fans who were there, those will be memories to savour for the rest of their lives; it was the longest-running carnival I can ever recall for a Wembley Cup Final. There was a real family atmosphere as Ruud Gullit insisted his players made the fans part of their celebrations. His 'lovely boys' had won the Cup. No-one was lovelier than the craggy-featured Zola.

The spiritual presence of Matthew Harding was felt by Gullit and the fans. His widow Ruth, dressed in emerald green, kissed Suzannah, Ken Bates's partner, as the Cup was finally won. Ruth was one of the official party of twenty-nine FA guests, the list provided by the club. Ruth also joined the all-night party at London's Waldorf Hotel. She said: 'The Final would have been the best day in Matthew's life, and it was the best day of mine. I felt he was upstairs looking down on the occasion.' Harding's girlfriend Vicky was not on the official guest list, but she was also at the Final. She decorated the outside of her leafy London home with a Chelsea flag and balloons before leaving to watch Matthew's team at Wembley. She heard the Chelsea faithful pay him a moving and emotional tribute as they chanted, 'Matthew Harding's blue and white army.' She said: 'They are the ones we mustn't forget, the fans who queued up to get tickets for the match, who queued up to be there. Matthew was a fan, but he was a great believer in other people.'

The team coach departed their hideaway hotel, the West Lodge Park near Barnet, at 12.30pm, and was parked outside the dressing-rooms at 1.08. A relaxed, shirt-sleeved Gullit sat in the front with Rix, feverishly chewing gum, as his players stepped off the bus and were soon on the pitch. Vialli stood there taking in the scene with a white handkerchief in his pocket instead of the button-holes of his team-mates and manager. Dressed in a baseball cap, Vialli blew bubbles with his gum. The Boro bus arrived a little later and their players headed straight for the pitch, where Vialli and Ravanelli greeted each other warmly. The silver-haired Ravanelli grabbed his little Italian team-mate Zola in a head lock.

Ninety minutes before the kick-off, Gullit wrote out the names of his team on the blackboard. Vialli was on the bench – he wished his team-mates the luck to win the Cup.

Chelsea fan Lord Attenborough defined the Gullit formula that had transformed Chelsea's Jurassic football into the slick Continental style of the club's space-age future, irrespective of the outcome, although Attenborough was convinced his team would win. He said: 'Ruud has performed a magical job, married the flair of Di Matteo or Zola and all these Continental styles with the wonderful commitment and desire of English football. That has produced a great team.'

Boro fans booed throughout the presentations, aggrieved at the Premier League's docking of their three points; Sir Cliff Richard led the community singing of 'Abide With Me'. The atmosphere was electric. Now they knew for the first time what an English FA Cup Final was all about.

In the Foreigners' Final, there was a distinct division between Robson's collection of Brazilian and Italian stars and the way Gullit integrated his overseas captures into a successful team strategy.

Gullit said: 'As a coach, you must improve and I'd like my players to improve, and what is important is they now know the feeling of winning, and we want to keep it going now that we have broken the chain. They had never tasted winning something; now they have, there is something to build on. I just did what I had to do. I knew that winning this Cup meant a lot to the club. It is also a boost qualifying for Europe, because the way we play, and also our players, are now famous around the world. This team didn't know its limits. If anything, I have taught them how to be a winner and my next aim is win even more.'

Could Chelsea be champions? Gullit said: 'I certainly want to do better, and how good we can be depends on next season. We have made mistakes, all of us, but it's still been a very good season. We have played very well against the big teams and played some good football, but you don't win the championship or finish in second place to qualify for the Champions' League unless you beat also the small teams.' Gullit would strive for greater consistency in the league, having already created a Continental passing team capable of making an impact in Europe.

The celebrations were better than the game! When Di Matteo struck that marvellous dipping thirty-yarder after just 42.4 seconds,

Chelsea looked certain to fulfil what had seemed to be their destiny ever since Harding's tragic death and the phenomenal comeback against Liverpool. Wise won possession, and his pass bypassed Zola to give Di Matteo plenty of space in a centre circle vacated by the opposition – Robson's midfield was on the missing list. Emerson was left in Di Matteo's slipstream, and with the defence backing off and Pearson preoccupied with Hughes, the Italian's wickedly dipping shot whipped over Roberts. That goal gave Di Matteo the confidence to strike up a man-of-the-match performance.

After twenty minutes, Juninho's glorious pass gave Ravanelli his first sight of goal. But the first time he had to break into a full stride, Ravanelli's hamstring gave way a split-second after Sinclair made a telling tackle. Without their thirty-one-goal striker, Boro looked tame in attack, with Beck replacing him. Juninho was their only hope, although just before the interval Festa headed into the corner from Stamp's cross but was caught marginally offside.

Just before that, Leboeuf was tripped and Zola made his first telling contribution with a thirty-yard free kick, tipped round the post. In the seventieth minute, a tantalizing Zola dribble past three defenders was finally ended with a ferocious shot which the keeper pushed out.

Finally, the irrepressible Zola helped create Chelsea's second goal, eight minutes from the end. Eddie Newton began the move and Petrescu's delicate chip to the far post seemed beyond Zola; but his delightful back-flick was finished off from close range by Newton.

With the game won, the chant for Vialli went out and after eighty-eight minutes and thirty-three seconds, he came on for Zola, who departed a hero and paid homage to Vialli as he came on. It was a touching moment. Zola insisted: 'I really hope Luca stays here. I realize he has not played much this year, but that is not his fault. And his behaviour has been fantastic. When he came to Chelsea he was one of the biggest players in Europe, but even when he didn't play, he just continued to train very hard and always be ready to play. That shows that he is a big man and I will try very hard to persuade him to stay. He has helped me a great deal to settle into English football and I need him around because he has a big heart . . . and because he is the only golfer at Chelsea who I can beat!' Di Matteo added: 'Of course

Luca is adored by the supporters, because he is a great player. It is a strange situation for him because he has not played as many games as he would like, but he is very popular in the dressing-room and all the players want him to stay. Zola and I will talk to him while we are on tour, but I think only Luca can decide what is best for his career.'

Mark Hughes became an FA Cup legend. As he collected his fourth winner's medal, he raised four fingers in front of the cameras. Chelsea were going places, according to Hughes: 'The opportunity to become the United of the South is there. We've got to grab it. Everything is now in place for Chelsea to become a major club, including the financial backing which maybe wasn't there in the past. If we're honest with ourselves, we've underachieved in the league this season. But now I really believe we're good enough to challenge for the championship. It was absolutely vital we beat Middlesbrough. We've made a lot of progress, but we needed to win a trophy and now we've done that. I knew how important it was when we won the league for the first time at United. That was the catalyst for everything that has followed, and now the same could happen at Chelsea. Everyone in the team now knows what it takes to win big games. And we can all use that experience to go from strength to strength. We had a great result at Old Trafford in the league at the start of November and were very encouraged by that. We won 2–1 and I think that helped our season, really, because from that day, we realized we could compete with anybody. United have been setting the standards for the last five to six years and that's what we've got to try and emulate – to churn out the results like they can.

'We were a good side last year but not a great one. But Ruud has added quality players to the side and there'll be even more next season. This success will also help the club attract the top youngsters. It will give us a real boost. United are ahead of everyone right now on the youth side of things. Their set-up is magnificent. But maybe further down the line, the likes of David Beckham won't leave London to go to Manchester anymore. They'll want to be part of what's going on at Chelsea and come straight here.'

Di Matteo and Zola were feted by the Italian press. The whole occasion was packaged as yet another successful Italian assault on the spiritual home of football, a continuation of the party which started when Zola's goal saw Italy beat England in the World Cup qualifier. Zola's assistance in Newton's goal stole much of the limelight. As far as the Italians were concerned, it was England nil, Italy three.

Di Matteo and Zola are 'Kings of Wembley', announced the *Corriere dello Sport*. 'They are the chief protagonists at Wembley yet again. Ex-Lazio star Di Matteo turned Middlesbrough to jelly after 42 seconds.' Only the Italian players received marks out of ten: Di Matteo 8, Zola 7, Ravanelli 6.5, Festa 6 . . . and Vialli wasn't on long enough to earn a number.

'Two Italian Blues won this Cup for Chelsea,' the big-selling *Gazzetta dello Sport* echoed. 'Di Matteo and Zola are kings. A stunning goal, an assist and a triumph.' Festa was given ample space to complain bitterly that there was nothing wrong with his disallowed goal: 'The Final could not have gone any worse. I am so disappointed. The goal didn't seem offside. They have seen the replays and everything back home in Sardinia, and they have told me everything was fine. The goal was good.'

Zola paid tribute to his Italian fitness guru for his appearance despite a thigh injury: 'I have to thank Mimmo Pezza, who yet again made sure I was able to play. I was scared that the injury would go at first, but later, when I really warmed up, I was able to relax.'

The celebrations continued into the small hours at the Waldorf Hotel. Gullit's speech praised his entire backroom staff. Bates gave an insight into that private dinner: 'It was wonderful. He picked out every single person individually, down to the groundsman, the kitman and "our girls at the training ground who cook for us". We had Pele as our guest and Jimmy Tarbuck as our host, who made a special presentation to Erland Johnsen, who is now leaving us. The game was repeated on TV screens without the sound and then the BBC had produced a special eight minutes' edited highlights of t;he final. Di Matteo scored ten times – and that was before he went to bed!'

Old Chelsea favourite Peter Osgood put this success in context: 'I actually wrote "May 17: Chelsea – Cup Final" in my diary months ago. That's how confident I was. I reckon the second half against Liverpool, when we came back from 2–0 down, was the best forty-five minutes seen at the Bridge since our great days. We contested five major finals in eight years, and I'd like to think these lads can do even better than that. Though to be honest, I think we're still two or three players short of having a championship-winning squad.' The seventies team went on to land the Cup-Winners' Cup, but were underachievers in the league. Osgood said: 'We were all so young, twenty-three or twenty-four, that it was hard to take in the fact we'd just beaten Real Madrid, the greatest name in world football. That's why I'm really pleased there are so many talented youngsters at the Bridge today. This team, like ours, will have the chance to grow together. Ruud Gullit can feel well pleased. An FA Cup victory and sixth in the league in his first season in charge isn't a bad start.'

Between 60,000 and 100,000 fans turned out at the Hammersmith and Fulham Town Hall to pay a colourful blue-and-white tribute to the players, with Gullit and their wives also aboard the open-top bus. Outside the town hall, the bus pulled up and Gullit told the fans: 'We're happy to make your dream come true. We love you all.'

A stream of blue lined the streets, the sun shone and their song rang out time and again, just as it had at Wembley. It was a Blue Day again. In scenes not seen for twenty-seven years, fans jammed every corner of the streets in west London, sitting on each other's shoulders, perching up in lampposts and even climbing up on rooftops to catch a glimpse of their heroes. The heat was muggy, the crowd overbearing and the hangovers still evident, but nothing could stop the massive cheers that went up as fans saw Wise lift the coveted silver trophy above his head yet again.

Bates said: 'This has been the greatest party in the history of English football. This is the carnival Cup, the happiest Cup. Euro 96 was the summer of love for the English game, but this has been electric. I can't believe that I've just seen the biggest street party since the Notting Hill Carnival. I thought I'd seen it with the greatest party on the pitch at Wembley. We've seen so much knocking over the years and this is the best answer to it all. We want to be in Europe every year. We had already signed three more internationals before we even played in the FA Cup Final. Winning the FA Cup has added at least £2.5 million into the club.'

Zola's smile was endless. 'It's beautiful, fantastic,' he said. Little

Andrea Zola took pictures like any Italian tourist as the wives were just as astonished.

The FA Cup Final will always live in his memory. Gianfranco looks back with deep affection. 'Oh yeah! Absolutely fantastic memories of that game. I remember everything – the tunnel, the noise, the crowd, the colour. Gianfranca was sitting to the right of the Royal Box but I did not see her until after the game. I was so tuned in. It is not easy to explain but I think each time I remember how lucky I am to know this day, to have played in such a game. That is why I must thank Chelsea, all those supporters. When you live to be a footballer, you do everything you can in the hope that one day you can experience a day like that. And I will remember it for always.'

13

The Future

It was imperative for Franco Zola to sort out any confusion about his commitment to the Chelsea cause, to clarify any misunderstandings about his future at the Bridge before the start of a new season, and the fresh start of a Premiership campaign for the Italian superstar.

'A lot has been said about me wanting to leave Chelsea to go back to Italy and this is a good opportunity to clear it all up,' he announced. 'I have said that I would like to end my career back in Sardinia with my home-town club Cagliari, but only when I am ready – and I am not at the end of my contract yet.

'I have never said that I will be playing for Cagliari next year. I have a contract at Chelsea and I want to respect it, because I love the team and I love the fans. You can never tell what the future holds, but I am very happy at Chelsea and I have no desire to go back to Italy at the moment. I still have a lot of ambitions in football; the moment I don't have any ambition left will be the time to quit football.'

He was livid with suggestions he was only counting the days until he would return home: 'I don't intend to go home next year, absolutely not. I want to see out my whole contract with Chelsea until 2000. Everyone seems to think I'm going to Cagliari next season because I said I'd like to finish my career in Sardinia. But I'm not on the point of finishing my career, it is still alive. I really believe we have a good enough side at Chelsea to win the championship this year. I have this contract which gives me two more seasons here whatever happens, and I will honour that. My contract runs out in 2000, but Chelsea intend to extend it because I'm so young and integral to their plans! But seriously, it's rather early to talk about an extension with Chelsea. I don't rule it out, though.

'So far, I have had a wonderful career. I'm very satisfied with what I have achieved and I couldn't be happier at Chelsea. The fans are the best I have ever known and the club is desperate to win trophies. This is going to be one hell of a season at Stamford Bridge and I am so glad to be part of it.

'This season is going to be great for Chelsea. First of all, I'm looking forward to battling for the Premier League title, and then, of course, we will be looking to do well in the Cups, especially the European Cup-Winners' Cup.

'Personally, it is a very big year for me, with the World Cup finals in France next summer. After the disappointment of the last World Cup, when I was sent off against Nigeria and the team went on to lose in the Final, I am determined to play a big part in next year's tournament. I feel very good at the moment and I am working hard in training to keep fit and sharp. I am hoping for great things with Chelsea this season.'

Zola knew his attacking qualities were conducive to the new philosophy of attacking football in England: 'It's a championship which offers privileges to players in attack most of all, because the mentality is more attacking. I'm very happy.'

The fans were full of fresh hope and anticipation at the start of a new season, with the FA Cup already in the trophy cabinet. Trophy cabinet! That used to be little more than an embarrassing contradiction in terms at the Bridge, without any meaningful silverware to adorn it. Opposition fans would taunt: 'Silverware, no silverware, you still have got no silverware.' No more.

Now Bates could welcome guests to 'The Trophy Room' with pride (and in his particular case, plenty of prejudice). He was sure there was every chance of something else to adorn the display cases. As it was, the FA Cup spent more time on display in the new Megastore, earning £24.99 a time for pictures with eager non-member fans, £19.99 for members. Every time I visited the Megastore, the queues for the 'actual reality' session with the glittering FA Cup were seemingly endless. At the first Premiership home game with Southampton, it was estimated that 10,000 fans visited the store before and after the game. The most popular items were the new shirt – Zola leading the field – the picture with the Cup and the club-approved books.

In comparison to the Red tat in the Old Trafford store, the new Chelsea Disney/Planet Hollywood-style chrome and glass was packed with Chelsea designer gear, even Italian-style scooters and badge-emblazoned bikes. The Ruud Wear designer line bearing the manager's logo was added in the autumn collection.

However, there was only quality, no tat, on the field at Old Trafford, and champions United were still the team to beat in the race for the coveted title and entry to the Champions' League, and Gullit's quest for the 'trophy with the big ears'. Sadly, Chelsea's history since their solitary League Championship triumph of 1955 was awash with potential rather than solid achievement. Plenty of style under Dave Sexton in the early seventies resulted in an epic FA Cup Final win over mighty Leeds, followed by a memorable Cup-Winners' Cup Final success over Real Madrid in Athens in 1971. In real terms, though, that was it. Yes, Chelsea reached the FA Cup Final under Glenn Hoddle in 1994 – where they were clinically taken apart by United – but they rarely looked capable of sustaining a challenge for the championship – until now.

Gullit's innovative style of management produced the FA Cup and glimpses of a potential championship team. Their big weakness was the inability to beat the lesser lights of the Premiership, and Gullit was still unhappy about the depth and quality of his squad, the team relying too heavily on Zola.

Gullit's formidable task was to coax a sustained title challenge out of one of the most exciting teams in the Premiership. But Bates believed the club to be in a stronger position now than at any time since he saved them from financial collapse fifteen years ago. He also insisted that Chelsea and Newcastle had joined Manchester United, Liverpool and Arsenal in the 'big five', ousting Everton and Tottenham from football's top table. Chelsea, though, had still to prove themselves worthy of Bates's boast. Another trophy, and again qualification for Europe, would be necessary to establish them as a credible, enduring force, rather than a one-season wonder.

The trophy that really mattered was the championship, which they would have to wrestle away from Manchester United, the title having almost become their exclusive property. What was unusual about United was their old-fashioned faith in English players. The signing of Teddy Sheringham gave them nine players from Glenn Hoddle's England squad – Pallister, May, Butt, Beckham, Scholes, Cole, and the Neville brothers were the others. Most of their serious rivals, predominantly Chelsea and Arsenal, looked abroad for squad reinforcements and it was now possible for Gullit to field an entire team without a single representative from the UK.

Gullit signed five more 'foreign' players: Tore Andre Flo (Norway), Bernard Lambourde (France), Ed de Goey (Holland), Celestine Babayaro (Nigeria) and Gustavo Poyet (Uruguay), before eventually buying an English international when Chelsea splashed out £5 million to bring Graeme Le Saux back to the Bridge from Blackburn – but that had as much to do with an unfortunate injury to Babayaro. The 1–1 draw in the Charity Shield, which United won on penalties, proved to Gullit that he couldn't cope in the opening stages of the season with only Danny Granville at left-back, after the free-transfer defection of Scott Minto to Benfica.

De Goey, the 6ft 6in goalkeeper signed from Feyenoord, was perhaps the most significant acquisition. A £2.25 million investment, his signing was designed to solve Chelsea's most persistent defensive problem.

But Poyet, the twenty-nine-year-old midfield player signed on a free transfer from Real Zaragoza, was the man Gullit hoped would provide Chelsea with their attacking momentum to supplement Zola, give him more space, and provide more goals from midfield.

Zola shared the supporters' optimism, convinced the Blues were a good bet for the Premiership title. Usually a season would begin with the fans resigned to a mid-table place. Now Chelsea were among the title favourites for the first time in decades. Zola insisted: 'My tips for the championship are Liverpool, Man United, Arsenal and ourselves. They have all made good summer signings – and now we have strengthened ourselves even further by bringing in Graeme Le Saux. My second year in the Premiership will be harder than the first. I am better known now, and I will be marked more tightly. But I would love to finish top scorer this season. Alan Shearer's injury will give me a chance, and it is an honour I have dreamt of throughout my career.'

Zola also warned the rest of the Premiership: 'I can only get better. Last season I learned a lot about English football in my first few months here, but this time I will be better and stronger from the start. I have been working hard to raise my performance levels, and I am in very good shape. But I will need to be, because this season will be harder for me and for Chelsea, now that we have won the Cup.' And Zola was convinced that Chelsea had as good a chance as anybody of winning the Premiership – if they could add consistency to their game. 'We played well against United in the Charity Shield,' he explained, 'and that showed us we can compete with them for the title. We have kept most of last season's squad and added six top-quality players, so we are very strong now; but we know where we have to improve. We need to be more consistent. We played well against United, Liverpool and Newcastle last year, but not so well against the lower teams. It is a problem that we need to address, but we are working on it and feel very confident about the season ahead.'

One of the mysteries of Zola's power is that someone of his height has such enormous strength. He tried to explain the anomaly: 'I look after myself. With players my size, you must not injure ankles and knees. You must be strong, you must be fit. I like to relax away from football, with my wife and kids. I don't need to go out all the time. I came to London because I wanted to experience living in such a huge city. It is amazing, but I don't want to go to nightclubs, I am a foot-baller. I go to the cinema or the theatre, but I can't understand it all, they speak too fast for me! So I just enjoy the living. It is a big city and I can walk around without people coming up to me; I go shop-ping, to the supermarket, they don't care about seeing someone like me. But anyway, I am a footballer and I love it, why would I want to make it bad for myself? I don't come here to drink beer.'

With Gullit signing a new striker in Norwegian Tore Andre Flo, there was increased speculation that Vialli would leave, with Crystal Palace heavily linked with him. Zola felt otherwise: 'Gianluca has been training hard for the new season, and he has stayed put because he enjoys living in London. But now there is an extra striker at the club, and he is definitely unhappy at not being able to play. I feel sorry for him when he is out of the side, and I desperately hope he stays.'

The debate about the influence and influx of foreign players was never far from the surface, particularly as the ranks of imports swelled in the summer to unprecedented levels.

The FA, fearful of a Premiership wholly dominated by foreign coaches and players, was taking steps to encourage domestic players to become coaches. Jimmy Armfield, the FA's technical consultant, would work with the Professional Footballers' Association to ensure that high-profile players followed the likes of Glenn Hoddle, Kenny Dalglish and Bryan Robson by staying in the game after they retired from the field. 'This is not an anti-foreigner thing,' Armfield, who would be in charge of the PFA's six regional coaches, emphasized. 'To say there should be no foreigners here would be nonsense, and if young goalkeepers watch Peter Schmeichel or forwards learn what Gianfranco Zola does, I'd be more than happy. But we need to ensure that the expertise of more players like Dalglish and Robson are not lost when they stop playing. The PFA coaches and myself will be going to clubs and talking to players. Today's professionals are where the coaches of the future will be.'

Armfield, who managed Leeds United to the European Cup final in 1975, felt that clubs were looking to short-term solutions of signing foreign players rather than spending money developing their own players. Better coaching, he believed, would produce better young players and reduce the need for imports. 'I went to a Premiership match last season where there were only seven players eligible to play for England,' Armfield said. 'That cannot be good for the domestic game. Arsenal looked abroad for a coach, as did Celtic, and Blackburn also went to Italy, even if Roy Hodgson is English. There is going to be more of that in the future and we have to be ready to meet that challenge. If it was any other business, they would already have done it. I feel very strongly that the development of our young players should be a priority for the Government and the Football Association. In the past, I've felt this has been left to somebody else, as if it takes care of itself; but it doesn't.'

When Glenn Hoddle became Chelsea's manager in 1993, he decided to change the club's youth set-up and appointed Graham Rix, the former Arsenal and England midfielder, as youth coach. Rix, now assistant manager to Hoddle's successor, featured in a television documentary following a year in the life of a group of YTS players at Chelsea. It was Rix who had to judge which players were likely to make the grade and which ones would fail, and he admitted that the drop-out rate was frightening. 'We would usually,' he said, 'have around thirty boys at twelve or thirteen years old, training with us as associate schoolboys, and out of that lot maybe ten would join us as first-year apprentices when they leave school at sixteen. If one signs professional at eighteen, you've done well. They've got to have good technical ability and a certain mental toughness, because although they might be the best player in their school or district, they are likely to come up against world-class players regularly if they progress in the game. They also need the intelligence to take on board some of the things coaches are telling them, and they need the right sort of personality to cope with life at a football club. The hardest thing to impress on young players is the fact that they have to deliver the goods week in, week out. There are so many kids who are up and down, not just from one game to the next but from second to second.

'Standards have risen dramatically here over the past three or four years. You now look at a young player and ask: "Can he play in the same side as Gianfranco Zola? Is he on the same wavelength as players like that?" The players have to be that much better now, and youngsters like Jody Morris and Mark Nicholls have shown that they can hold their own in the company of world-class players.'

Rix was upbeat, though, about the future of football in Britain: 'Despite all the other distractions for kids, there are still a lot of very talented youngsters who want to play football and can make it at the highest level. They just need encouraging and teaching the right things. We all had heroes when we were young, and today's kids are no different. But you have to get across to them the fact that great players are not born – they work hard to get where they are.

'Zola practises his free-kick technique three times a week after training – twenty-five from the right, twenty-five from the left. You could forgive him for thinking he's got it down to a fine art, but he doesn't think like that – he keeps working at it to get better and more consistent.

'I was watching him practise with a group of YTS lads and they soon got the message – you have to keep working at it, no matter how good you are.'

The influence of foreign players like Zola had had a major impact at Chelsea, according to Rix: 'We've got our fair share of foreigners, but there are still youngsters like Morris and Nicholls coming in. The difference is that standards have risen. We are not making do with moderate players in the first team or at youth level. Instead of look-ing for kids with the potential to play in a Chelsea team at the wrong end of the Premiership, we are looking at players who can handle playing in Europe every season and challenge for major trophies. We often have a few YTS boys join in the eight-a-side games to give them a taste of what it is like at a higher level. Ruud wants them to see how the senior players train and conduct themselves. The game has changed here now, so that it is more technical and players are encour-aged to pass the ball and use their skills more. We will never lose that British passion, but the game is becoming more Continental over here. It is interesting to see that all the big clubs are waking up to the importance of developing their own young players. Despite all the foreigners Ruud has signed, he would be the first to admit that he would love to have a team made up of kids who have come through the youth policy.'

Gullit was often criticized unjustly for blackballing English talent in favour of cheaper labour abroad, but he was fully aware of the dangers for the English game in becoming isolated because of inflated internal transfers, making it inevitable that clubs would seek to bring in more foreign stars. But Gullit also believed that importing the best players in the world, rather than just indiscriminately bring-ing in foreigners, would enhance the development of youngsters. Jody Morris, Mark Nicholls, Danny Granville and Paul Hughes had proved prime examples of the development of English players at the Bridge, and there were more coming through impressing Gullit.

Gullit also backed an Ajax-style football coaching scheme to teach English youngsters how to play the Dutch way. He called on clubs across the country to copy the Dutch methods in an effort to help

England produce world-class players. Gullit took time out from his pre-season preparations with Chelsea to visit the Football Technique centre in Portsmouth. He watched youngsters aged from ten to twelve being put through their paces by two senior Dutch FA youth coaches who specialized in nurturing the best young talent in Holland. And he said such centres were the only way the English game could make sure they developed the best young players into future international stars.

Gullit said: 'The principles of Football Technique are exactly right and they should be followed by everyone in this country. If a young player has ability, the most important thing to do is encourage him. But there are too many coaches in the game who teach a kick-and-rush style which is not suited to the play of good, skilful players.'

Zola's success in the Premiership tempted a host of top Italian stars to try their luck in English football. Attilio Lombardo joined Crystal Palace. He laughed when asked whether he would turn out to be, in terms of English football success stories, a Zola or a Ravanelli? 'I hope to be a Zola,' he said through his interpreter Dario. 'I don't want to be a Ravanelli because I don't want to end up playing in the First Division. Anyone as big as Ravanelli would be unhappy about playing there. It's been a lot easier for Zola because he plays for a good team. If I turn out to be as successful as Zola, then it would mean that Palace have had a good season.'

Ironically, Italy's football supremo Luciano Nizzola was voicing a fear that too many foreigners were ruining the game in *Serie A*! Nizzola made his comments in the wake of AC Milan president Silvio Berlusconi's statement that his side contained too many foreign players. Nizzola said: 'I think there are a few too many foreign players in Italy and this does not help national coach Maldini in his job. The recent Bosman ruling has led to a huge influx of European Union players, not all of whom are of the highest level.'

The Charity Shield was another wonderful day out at Wembley for Chelsea, but it was a bitter disappointment losing on penalties to Manchester United. Whose idea was it anyway to send out poor Frank Sinclair to face the wall of United fans and take the first penalty against Peter Schmeichel? But maybe it was just as well that Chelsea failed to add the Shield to the FA Cup. Perhaps expectations

were running just a little *too* high, and coming back down to earth
wasn't such a bad experience.

Chelsea's superstars also had their precious boots and kit stolen
after the Charity Shield. The club cancelled the next morning's
planned photocall. Police were called when the van carrying the gear
was stolen, and Ruud's stars were faced with the prospect of having
to wear in new boots in time for the Premiership kick-off. But twenty-
four hours after the theft, the boots mysteriously turned up in a hotel
near Heathrow – though the kit was still missing. Graham Rix said:
'We have found the skip, thankfully, with all the first-team boots. It is
not so much the boots, but the special insoles the players use to aid
with injuries to backs and hips. They take a long time to make and
cost a lot. But also, it was close to the start of the season to wear in
new boots.' In fact, two skips turned up, one with the boots, the other
containing towels and other accessories. But the skip with the shirts
was still missing.

The Premiership season kicked off with a 3–2 defeat at Coventry
after Chelsea were in total command, Dion Dublin helping himself to
a late hat-trick to renew all the doubts about whether the new
Chelsea still had the old problem of overcoming the so-called smaller
teams.

With a long break because of World Cup commitments to ponder
it, skipper Dennis Wise knew they must get that habit out of their
system straight away. He said: 'We let ourselves down against teams
we are expected to do well against. If we can put that right, then we
will be challenging. Lack of concentration and complacency creeps
in.'

The response was unbelievable, a record-breaking 6–0 win at
newly promoted Barnsley – and it was Vialli's big day. Four goals was
his answer to all his traumas of the previous season and this time it
was Mark Hughes's turn to be benched.

Fear of failure drove Vialli to the personal demolition of Barnsley
that threatened to set Chelsea's season on fire. But still he faced
intense competition for his place! Zola, Hughes, as well as newcomer
Flo, were all competing for striking roles.

Vialli said: 'It's very difficult to play for Chelsea because there are
four strikers. There is Mark, Gianfranco and Tore Andre, and they are

all good players. So when you get the chance, you have to play well and score as much as possible, because it's not easy to change the manager's mind. It's the first time I have scored four goals in a match and it was a bit strange because I was very worried before the game. I knew that this was my chance and that I had to perform.'

Vialli's agent, Andrea d'Amico, said: 'It was a great performance against Barnsley but then Gianluca is a great player. The most important thing for him is to play continuously, and last year he couldn't do it. He is a serious man, a good man and a great striker, and he doesn't like having any problems. He's never let anyone down and he just wants to do well all the time. The desire to perform at his best helps drive him on.'

The unflinching support from his team-mates and the Chelsea fans helped to keep up Vialli's spirits in the bad times. 'I'd like to say thank you to all my team-mates,' he said. 'They have always been very close to me, and when you score four goals it means the team have been working very hard for you. I am very happy for myself, of course, because I had such a bad time in my first season in London, because of my injuries and all the other bad luck. But now everything is getting better. I am fitter than I was at this time last season. I am working harder during training, so the manager knows I am ready to play my football. I'd like to think all my problems are firmly behind me now. But you never know what can happen in football. It's such a strange game. Things can change very quickly.'

Vialli knew that Gullit's policy of guaranteeing nobody a first-team spot meant he could even be back on the bench for the match at Wimbledon. He said: 'I know I have nothing to prove to anyone. I am thirty-three and I have been playing football for the last seventeen years – I think everyone knows what I can do on the pitch. Now I think it's going to be a good time for me at Chelsea.'

Vialli was not for sale at any price, insisted the Chelsea chairman, who declared him 'priceless'. Bates said: 'Despite all the speculation, few people wanted to take him in the summer and those who did, we told them to p*** off. It was all a load of nonsense that he was leaving, because they couldn't afford his wages.' Celtic, Rangers, Southampton, Crystal Palace and Torino had all been linked with moves for Vialli.

Instead, Vialli met the challenge head-on by stopping smoking and getting himself stronger and fitter for the new season. But he extinguished that cigarette theory as the sole reason for his sharpness, saying: 'It's not about me giving up smoking. It's about fitness, it's about luck and it's about confidence. If you are always confident in every capacity, then God does the rest.'

Vialli's goals at Barnsley made him the first Chelsea man to score four in a top division match since Peter Osgood did so against Crystal Palace twenty-eight years earlier.

Now, Hughes was on the bench – and Zola was substituted at Oakwell. Gullit explained: 'Players have to leave their professional pride behind. If you want to be an individual, then go and play tennis. The FA Cup was won by a team, not individuals. Players who were not happy with that last year left. In the end we had the silverware and they didn't. We want players to be aware that this is the policy that will work for us.'

Sure enough, at Wimbledon, for the first time since his arrival, Zola was left out. But Di Matteo blasted a wondrous thirty-yarder into the top corner, reminiscent of his long-distance strike at Wembley, as Gullit's team plundered two goals inside three minutes, with Di Matteo's blockbuster quickly followed by a second from Dan Petrescu. The biggest shock, though, was another team shake-up by the Dutch player-manager: Footballer of the Year Zola left on the bench, taking over the position held for so long by Vialli. Vialli kept his place after his four goals at Barnsley – how could he have been left out after that? – but Gullit opted for the 6ft 4in centre-forward Flo to partner him, with no place again for Hughes. Not many managers in world football would make a couple of changes two days after their team won 6–0, but Gullit also left out defender Andy Myers to give Michael Duberry a remarkable comeback game. Duberry had been out since January after a personal tragedy when, on the verge of an England call-up, he snapped an achilles tendon running all alone in a training session. Gullit's faith in Duberry was fully repaid as the powerful defender was Chelsea's man of the match. In the end, Joe Kinnear had to haul off his twin strikers Dean Holdsworth and Efan Ekoku after a masterly performance in central defence by Duberry.

Ten away goals in three successive games before they returned from their travels for their first home game of the season against Southampton was an impressive haul by anyone's standards. Wimbledon never looked as though they would avenge their FA Cup semi-final defeat by Chelsea – even with their tormentor-in-chief Zola a spectator.

Vialli fully justified his retention in attack, producing one glorious turn and shot that the keeper scrambled to save. And he was involved in a glorious move, combining with Frank Sinclair and Petrescu before producing a fierce header but straight at the keeper on the line.

A newspaper report suggested Chelsea planned to nurse Zola as he was suffering from a long-term groin injury, and that Zola didn't want his World Cup with Italy spoiled by the Premiership's demands. Rumours of Zola's injury spread like wildfire through Selhurst Park after an impressive victory, but the speculation was denied by Gullit.

Gullit wore a broad grin as he relaxed in the knowledge that he had finally got things exactly how he wanted them. He had wanted to implement a squad system ever since he took over as player-manager from Glenn Hoddle. He named himself in a nineteen-man squad for the game against Southampton. Gullit said: 'Now they understand. They realize now it's a squad thing. First you need a good example to prove to them it works, and I think Wimbledon was a good example. Everyone expected certain players to play, but they didn't – and it worked. Everyone understands how it works, but I still want players to be disappointed if they aren't playing. It's only human. It's not a game I'm playing. I don't want to try and be clever, and I'm not always wondering what the opposing manager is thinking. That's not the point. The point is that in certain games I need certain players. I work in a professional club and I want to make it as professional as possible. Manchester United have done this for a long time. It just takes time for everybody to get used to it.'

Chelsea played their first game at Stamford Bridge after three away games, their fixtures arranged this way to allow for construction work at the ground to be completed.

It was the fourth match of the season and yet another new line-up. Zola and Hughes were back leading the attack, Vialli and Flo on the bench. For an hour or so before the kick-off, Zola always likes to lie on a massage bed and read a book. Before this game it was an English paperback, *The Moonstone* by Wilkie Collins. His English was definitely improving.

But after going 4–1 up by half-time, Chelsea were finally made to sweat by Southampton and Gullit reacted by substituting Zola, bringing on top goalscorer Vialli. So far Gullit had changed his side in every game. Dennis Wise, once totally bemused by Gullit's philosophy, had now come to understand it. He said: 'When we arrived at the ground, a few of the lads wanted to get changed, they wanted to get out of their suits, but no-one knew who was playing. I asked Ruud if he could tell us who was in the sixteen. He said to me, "Okay, lovely boy, I'll put the sixteen names up." But he still waited to 1.30 before he came into the dressing-room and wrote the eleven names on the board. There's nothing wrong with it, but last year I didn't quite understand it. Now I understand it all. He didn't play me in a game, but we spoke about it and I understood what he was doing, and now I can see that he wants everybody together and if we want to achieve something, it can only be done with twenty players, not eleven. Everybody is on the same level, whether you're a £300,000 player or £5 million. He has explained to us all that not everyone can play all of the games. And if you don't play, it's not because you've been doing poorly. He wants us to do better than last year. Then, he wanted us in the top five, but we finished sixth and he was not too pleased with that. Fortunately, we won the Cup and qualified for Europe. He wants us to finish in the top five and anything else would be a bonus.'

Petrescu opened the scoring with a glorious chip after just seven minutes, but a defensive catastrophe for De Goey gave Kevin Davies the twenty-fifth minute equalizer. Then when Zola whipped over a cross from Chelsea's specialist short corner, Poyet's header was chested off the line but Leboeuf bravely headed Chelsea back into the lead. A far-post Hughes header from a Le Saux cross, and a simple tap-in from Wise after Zola bamboozled the Saints' defence, gave Chelsea their 4–1 interval advantage. A measure of the absurdity of Chelsea's dominance was that even Zola nearly scored with a header!

Chelsea old boy Ken Monkou scored in the fifty-ninth minute and

Zola, Dennis Wise, Suggs, Gianluca Vialli and Dan Petrescu together for 'Blue Day'.

Zola takes on the Wimbledon defence in the semi-final of the FA Cup and below, celebrating scoring his spectacular second goal of the game that took them to Wembley.

Dennis Wise and Zola in a hug of delight after the game.

Zola and Middlesbrough's Brazilian star Emerson in the FA Cup Final of 1997.

The FA Cup goes back to Stamford Bridge for the first time in over a quarter of a century.

Zola receives the 50th Footballer of the Year award.

Celebrating Chelsea's 4-0 win against Derby. (*Allsport*)

Zola leaps John Scales in Chelsea's 1-6 win at White Hart Lane. (*Allsport*)

Zola at full stretch in Chelsea's 2-0 win against Slovan. (*Allsport*)

Chelsea lived on the edge when they should have piled on even more goals, Hughes shooting straight at the keeper and Poyet hitting a post. When Frank Sinclair was shown the red card with twelve minutes to go, Gullit's side suddenly rediscovered their concentration and held out.

One thing was for sure: there's never a dull moment down at the Bridge.

I asked Gullit whether the rumours about Zola's injury were true. 'No! Rubbish!' Would he care to elaborate? 'One time last week I wasn't even in this world and the next I was Rambo.' Rumours had spread through the city that Gullit had died in a car crash and a couple of days later he was pictured outside a King's Road cinema carrying a distressed member of the public. Gullit gave little credence to rumours.

However, he did discuss the reasons for Zola's slow start: 'He didn't play so good today and that was the reason we changed him. Next time he can be better. Form is fluent, it comes and goes, and he is not at his best at the moment, but he contributes very much to the team. And it can give me an opportunity to try something else.

'But the most important thing is that he works very hard for the team, and that's what I want from him or from any player. There was also a phase in the game that he did enough to have an effect, and that was good to see.' Gullit felt his team was still 'growing'. He observed: 'The quality is there, we are working very hard to make it even better. We are humble, we don't think we have done the business.'

After just four games, Gullit had used seventeen different players and had still to play two of his summer signings recovering from injury. But Chelsea were handily placed in fourth position, having scored fourteen goals from a variety of sources.

The Premiership programme went on World Cup hold for a second time early in September, with Italy embarrassingly unable to score in Georgia and held to a draw, while England crushed Moldova on an emotional night at Wembley. Gullit decided to rest his entire Italian contingent the following Saturday at Selhurst Park. The tiring journey back from Tbilisi, where Di Matteo was booked and substituted along with Zola, was the reason for the pair joining a most expensive list of substitutes against Crystal Palace. Chelsea won comfortably 3–0 without needing any of them.

Steve Coppell pulled a crumpled team-sheet from his pocket and wearily muttered a mild expletive. Holding the paper in his hand, Coppell said: 'When I saw the names on the Chelsea subs' bench, I went, "Oh ...." ' He admitted: 'We are in the same league as Chelsea, but it is a handicap competition. Their players earn a lot of money in wages and cost a fortune to assemble. But we'll hang in there. What can we do about it? I can't walk away again.'

Gullit stressed that he would play the guessing game for the rest of the season, to keep his goal-crazy players on their toes. It all made for a 'delicious' uncertainty, according to Tore Andre Flo, who was as shocked as anyone to be given the nod ahead of Zola and Vialli: 'It's a very strange situation for me because in the past I've played every game for my club and always known who my strike partner will be. Now there's me, Gianfranco, Luca and Mark Hughes, and none of us knows which two are ever going to play. And it doesn't seem to make any difference because the team is scoring all the time. I was prepared for this situation when I arrived at Chelsea, and it's a lot better than being on the bench all the time.' Vialli put more effort into his fruitless second-half warm-up routine than any of his colleagues were having to on the pitch. He left Selhurst Park deep in conversation with his former Juventus pal Attilio Lombardo, clearly disappointed not to have been given any opportunity to cash in on Palace's dreadful defence. Palace supporters urged him to join them and guarantee himself regular first-team football; Vialli wasn't that desperate.

Chelsea's seventeen goals in the first five games had now been shared around by ten different players, with Graeme Le Saux the latest to get in on the act with his superb last-minute strike. Hughes observed: 'We're all aware that we may be at the start of something very special. It might all go pear-shaped, but I don't think it will. British players have got to change their attitude to being in the team. In the past, a regular first-team player expected to get forty games a season. But those days are gone here.'

Gullit added: 'I was pleased with our performance. We made a lot of changes and young lads like Mark Nicholls and Paul Hughes played as though they'd been in the team all the time. There's no such thing as one team. That way, some players do not feel part of it.' Gullit simply shrugged his shoulders when it was pointed out that he had more than £9 million worth of talent sitting on the bench at Palace. The result alone more than justified his decisions. Like Alex Ferguson at Manchester United, he had a squad of twenty inter-changeable players to pick and choose from as the occasion demanded.

Palace's £2 million defender Neil Emblen admitted: 'When we looked at their line-up and the players they'd left on the bench, we thought Chelsea were taking the mickey. But they've got such a great squad that they'll be able to rest their best players all season.'

Gullit was encouraged by the sequence of wins: 'The players are starting to realize just how good they can be. Motivating them for European games is the easy part. It's the games against the small sides which are most difficult, as Newcastle found out against Wimbledon.' The Geordies had lost 3–1 at home to Joe Kinnear's team that day.

Ruud and his girlfriend Estelle Cruyff attended the prestigious, celebrity-laden LWT recording of a 'A Night in the Company of Elton John'. But not Zola or Di Matteo. Elton wanted Zola to play the piano with him and join a huge sporting cast on stage when he played 'Saturday Night's Alright for Fighting'. But Zola was concerned about his piano playing, because he hadn't practised seri-ously for a year, and now planned to buy a piano for his new home. He said: 'My fame as a pianist is exaggerated. I haven't played for over a year, since I came to England. When I do things, I like to do them seriously. Just at the moment, I'm not ready for a duet with Elton. I must concentrate on my football.' I was at the LWT Studios with my Chelsea-supporting girlfriend Linda as Ruud was chosen as one of the stars from the audience to ask Elton a question. Ruud asked him, 'If you could be any footballer, which footballer would you like to be?' 'George Best,' Elton replied. When the mammoth show was edited, Ruud's question had been cut. That might have annoyed Vialli!

As Chelsea prepared to begin their Cup-Winners' Cup campaign, Hughes warned his team-mates not to get carried away by the bookies' odds making Chelsea favourites for Euro glory. 'That's all a bit premature,' he said. 'European football is all about who makes the least mistakes. And if we can keep them to a minimum, we've got a chance. But we've got to be aware at all times of what the opposition can do to us.'

Gullit believed Chelsea's greatest obstacle to European glory would be the quality of refereeing the Blues encountered on their travels. Chelsea, who reached the semi-finals of the Cup-Winners' Cup in 1995, had been drawn against Slovan Bratislava with the first leg at Stamford Bridge. Gullit confessed at the time that he knew nothing about Chelsea's opponents and would be studying them closely on video. But he insisted that unfamiliarity with the methods of European referees, rather than the Slovakians, would be their biggest problem. He said: 'The main difference in Europe is the referees. The referees won't allow you to play the physical game you play here. You have to rely more on tactical and technical players. If you don't have those tactical and technical players, you will struggle. Last year I saw a lot of British clubs in Europe were frustrated because every time there was a challenge it was a free-kick. Only Manchester United could cope for a long time, and Liverpool had the players but were a bit unlucky in some of the games they played. If you touch the goalkeeper it's a free-kick, and players in Europe always react, rolling over, and it's showtime. In England you can't get away with that. The crowd turn against you for acting, while in Europe the crowd turn against the referee for giving the free-kick.' The European campaign, therefore, looked tailor-made for the Italians.

Zola was back to something close to his best form in the 2–0 win over Slovan on a Thursday night, the match screened live on Channel 5. His wicked long-range angled free-kick clipped the top of the bar on a night Gullit sent out all three of his Italian stars – maybe the manager had spotted that the officials were Italian. Vialli was outstanding even though he failed to score on the pitch, although he was scoring off it – a diet of sex was keeping him fit. The self-styled Italian stallion boasted: 'It's because I am busy making love as much as possible.'

Vialli added: 'I feel extremely fit. In the summer I worked a lot, swimming, bicycle work, running and making love as much as possible.

The only trouble is, it's not too good for my back.' He was delighted with life off the pitch with beautiful long-term girlfriend Giovanna.

Gullit could not believe it when he heard of Vialli's unorthodox 'extra loving' fitness-training method. 'Is that what he said?' he exclaimed. Then, laughing loudly, the Dutchman added: 'As long as he's happy.'

Revitalized and refreshed after sorting out problems on and off the pitch, Vialli said: 'I came back already quite fit, and, of course, I stopped smoking. I wasn't a heavy smoker, only about five or six a day – but I decided to stop and it had helped.

'Yes, I think I have to finish my career at Chelsea because I'm already thirty-three. And then after that, possibly I could become a manager in England. Which club? Maybe Chelsea. But now isn't the right time for me to ask for a new contract, because I still have one and a half years on my current one. And both Chelsea and I have to understand that when I'm thirty-five if I'll be good enough to play for them. You never know, when you're thirty-four you can play very well, but the next month it can all turn sour – so I think it's better to wait and see what happens at the end of my contract. Last season, quite often I was as sick as a parrot. I arrived from Italy and I got into trouble, I was not fit and I didn't play too often. I had problems on and off the pitch, I didn't find my place until February. There were a lot of little things all together and I couldn't perform very well. This season, I'm as fit as a fiddle. I worked very hard on my fitness in the summer and I was lucky I didn't get injured pre-season. I feel better and I'm ready to do everything the manager wants me to do. And I try to do my best every time I'm in the team. I know this situation about the manager changing the team, because a lot of clubs in Italy used to do it, too. You could be in the side on Saturday and on the bench on Wednesday, and not because you're not good enough but because the manager wants to change things tactically, or whatever. Our job is to be always ready, and ready to do our best every time the manager picks us. I feel my happiest and most settled since I've been here. I've got my place, I get on very well with my team-mates – we have a great spirit here – and the supporters, so everything is right for me now. So, if I don't perform well now, it's because of me – I can't blame anyone else. And it's very nice when the manager speaks well about you, because you know you've done well; even at thirty-three it's nice to hear compliments. Last year I was always in the newspapers because of some controversy and that was not very welcome. I'd much rather prefer to be in the papers because I've scored or played well. And yes, I'm still in love with football, otherwise I couldn't play football. That's because I'm wealthy enough to do something else. If I play, it's because I enjoy it very much. And I'm still ambitious. Last year was wonderful to win the FA Cup. And it'd be wonderful to win the Premier League and then the Champions' League for a second time. I know this is a dream, but why not think positively?'

Vialli did enough to persuade the manager to play all three Italians again against Arsenal in the battle to go second to Manchester United. He said: 'This will be a good test for us. We believe we are one of the best teams in the Premier League. But you can only find that out when you play and beat teams like Arsenal, Manchester United, Newcastle and Liverpool.'

Chelsea v Arsenal was billed as the clash of the foreign stars, but it was Coventry-born Nigel Winterburn, imported from as far away as Wimbledon, who settled the contest with a late screamer. Eleven foreign players started and there were five more on the bench (total cost: £36 million), plus two foreign coaches. Dennis Bergkamp was virtually unstoppable: two goals and two fouls on him by Frank Leboeuf and the Frenchman was heading back to the dressing-room, and with him the last semblance of Chelsea's resistance.

When Zola tapped in his first goal of the season for 2–2, seconds after Bergkamp had put Arsenal into the lead for the first time, this fiercely contested London derby was still in the balance with all four goals having come from the foreign legion. With Chelsea reduced to ten men and switching around their team, Gullit's tactics seemed to be keeping one of their main championship rivals at bay until Winterburn let fly from twenty-five yards into the top corner. At the end, Arsene Wenger was leaping off his bench to begin north London's celebrations in a significant win against west London's challenge for the title.

Zola said: 'I wanted my first goal of the season to be better than that, but it's OK, it's good to get my first and now I hope the next will be the winner at Old Trafford.'

These were the first points dropped by Chelsea since their opening-day aberration at Coventry and it brought to an end a sequence of five straight wins. The Arsenal game, live on Sky, was an early season indicator of the capital's pursuit of Manchester United's crown, and even in defeat Chelsea showed sufficient resilience and character to complement their talents.

A mark of Gullit's ambition to win this match was his third substitution, bringing on giant centre-forward Flo in place of Di Matteo with the scores level. Zola dropped behind the front two in a formation designed to go for the next goal. But just five minutes later, Bergkamp burst through again, Leboeuf overstretched and brought him down and Chelsea were condemned to the next twenty-two minutes of trying to hold out. Poyet dropped back to centre-half, Hughes into midfield, and Zola went back up front to play off Flo.

In the forty-two seasons since Ted Drake's Chelsea claimed Stamford Bridge's sole success, the championship had been won by a London club just four times. Wenger and Gullit knew that more than a quarter of their league games were derby clashes. The analytical Frenchman agreed that the sheer intensity of those encounters would prove a huge disadvantage to both his team and Gullit's talented squad: 'It's a handicap having to play so many derbies. Normally when you come out of a derby match with a draw, everybody is happy. When you look abroad, the derby matches always seem to end in draws; Inter versus Milan, Juventus against Torino – these games are always draws. But that means you're always dropping two points, and you can't afford to do that.

'If I didn't think a London side could win the championship, I wouldn't be here. But West Ham have started very well and have a very strong team; Tottenham can come back. All the teams here can win. You've just got to be stronger. It is a fact that we have ten derby games to play – maybe we ought to move outside of London!'

Gullit expressed less concern about the proliferation of cross-capital clashes, noting: 'Palace and Wimbledon weren't particularly physical, although the matches against Arsenal, Spurs and West Ham might be. I don't know if it is harder for a London side to win the title. I don't believe in that. The statistics might say so – I hope we can prove the opposite.'

The Dutchman and Wenger agreed that the nature of the fixture list lessened the chances of every top club fulfilling their potential. 'If, as a nation, you say you want to do better in Europe, you have to make a plan for that,' said Gullit. 'I'm not going to say what that should be, but the season is too relentless.' Wenger added: 'I don't understand why all the teams in Europe have to play big matches in the midweek between the European legs. That's not normal and it could mean some bad surprises for English clubs in the second games. For teams like United, Liverpool and us, we could have some bad surprises.' Wenger's fears were proved correct when Arsenal unexpectedly went out of Europe ten days later.

Manchester United's David Beckham and Chelsea's Zola now went head-to-head again at Old Trafford ahead of the vital World Cup clash in Rome. The showdown offered the Blues the chance to exact revenge for the penalty shoot-out defeat in the Charity Shield, but the rivalry extended far beyond the domestic arena.

Tottenham skipper Gary Mabbutt has played against both men. He said: 'They are two players who I would gladly pay money to see – two of the biggest names in English football and match-winners.' The former England international believed Zola was making the same influential inroads into the English game as Jurgen Klinsmann had at Spurs: 'Zola has made a dramatic impact on our game – as great as when Jurgen Klinsmann came to Tottenham. Both have been tremendous ambassadors for their respective countries. Zola is a great character, always smiling, and he looks as if he really enjoys the game. He works very hard at his game and I have got a lot of respect for him. You know that he is not over here just to enjoy a bumper payday. You can see how hard he is working, and I hear that his attitude is exemplary – he has certainly raised team spirit at Chelsea.'

Mabbutt felt Zola had an easier time from the British public than Klinsmann when he came to England: 'I think Jurgen had to work harder to get accepted because when he first arrived he was labelled a diver. But Zola seems to have people on his side, which is a big help. They are similar characters, with effervescent natures, and both are quality players. Zola is one of the best finishers in the game and particularly lethal from dead-ball situations. The little man has gained the respect of the English football supporter, despite scoring the goal which dented England's World Cup hopes in February. Having some-one like Zola over here is a benefit to our game. He is real quality, and an inspiration to all young players.'

Mabbutt is also one of Beckham's biggest fans: 'David is one of the best prospects in our game and will be very important to both Manchester United and England in the next few years. His finishing is incredible, particularly from set-pieces and long distance. He also works very hard for the team. He is one of the most all-round play-ers in the game, and can produce something out of nothing. If he continues to mature the way he has been doing, he will be incredible.'

Zola had scored his first goal of the season against David Seaman but did not go along with all the hype about striking psychological blows leading up to England's showdown in Rome.

'This is a Premier League game, a completely different situation from Rome and I will be giving my best for Chelsea, that is all,' he said with his trademark beaming grin.

But a strike against Beckham, Paul Scholes, Nicky Butt and partic-ularly defenders Gary Pallister and the Neville brothers would go down well back home: 'I know everyone is looking for all little signs for Rome. But I am thinking only of Chelsea – it is the only way to prepare.

'I can feel the build-up beginning and it is strange to be in the enemy camp. It is no surprise everyone is getting excited, because it is a huge game for both countries. So everyone is wanting. But as a professional you have to keep it all in balance. I cannot think too far ahead, otherwise I will approach the game in the wrong way.'

Zola could have been public enemy No. 1 in this country after hitting Italy's Wembley winner. Instead, he was voted Footballer of the Year! And he was confident he would not be pilloried if he condemned England to the lottery of the World Cup play-offs: 'I don't think people will turn against me. They know I am just a player doing my job. I love the way people have taken to me here.'

At Old Trafford the pressure was on Chelsea, the Premiership's top scorers (nineteen goals in six games), as they had slipped five points adrift of the leaders. 'This was a big game without losing to Arsenal, but that defeat was a good lesson for us,' added Zola. 'It was our first big game of the season and we now know we have to improve. Sometimes it is good to have a cold shower! Arsenal were better organized than us. When you play against the top teams, the first thing you must be is organized, to use all your weapons to best effect. We made some big mistakes and we paid for them. We cannot afford to do the same at United.'

Alex Ferguson relished Manchester United's biggest challenge of the season. He openly admits that one of his biggest regrets is that he once rejected the chance to give Gullit the opportunity to parade his skills at United. But Ferguson was full of admiration for the way the Dutchman had transformed the fortunes of Chelsea – and was looking forward to seeing his men compete with Zola and company: 'This is the hardest game we have faced so far. But these are the games that we really enjoy and look forward to, because Chelsea have done ever so well and it all adds up to a very good match. Ruud has done very well at Chelsea. He has brought a greater ambition to Chelsea and set their standards a lot higher. I said at the start of the season that I saw Chelsea as genuine title contenders, and have seen no reason why I should change my way of thinking.'

Bates had constantly said that his dream was to turn the Blues into a force capable of knocking United off the Premiership summit, in terms of silverware, support and pure financial muscle. But they faced a team unbeaten in eight matches.

For once, Gullit lost his cool; normally so laid-back, he leapt from the bench to join his team in an angry, finger-jabbing confrontation with referee Gary Willard over United's controversial first-half equalizer. The arm-waving fury ended with Gullit being ordered back to the dugout as this red-blooded clash threatened to thunder out of control. In the tunnel at half-time there was a fracas witnessed by police.

In the second half, Mark Hughes's first goal back at Old Trafford put Chelsea 2–1 up, but Ferguson's side completed their comeback when substitute Ole Gunnar Solskjaer scored on his first appearance of the season. Once the dust had settled, Arsenal had been handed top spot in the table and the meanest defence in the Premiership had conceded two goals for the first time and conceded a point at Old Trafford – only West Ham's John Hartson had managed to score against United before Chelsea. And, the significance of a single point

– even though there should have been two – would become clearer as the season progressed, as Old Trafford became a fortress where a point was a major accomplishment.

In a contest that spilled over with excitement, the major talking point was Paul Scholes's thirty-fifth-minute goal. Frank Leboeuf and his defence stepped forward as Gary Pallister played his pass and the entire Chelsea side stopped in their tracks as Andy Cole raced on to square the ball for Scholes to finish off. Gullit left his dugout seat to join in the protests to the referee and linesman.

Chelsea regained the initiative with Zola mesmerizing the United defence and setting up a chance for Dan Petrescu. Only an outstanding save by Schmeichel prevented Chelsea regaining the lead. Then a searching cross from Petrescu directed at Zola caused more panic, with Schmeichel losing the flight as it broke past Zola to Hughes at the far post, where he completed the simplest of tasks with the goal at his mercy.

Chelsea should have won. Frenchman Bernard Lambourde, making a delayed Premiership debut after injury, burst clear after a swift one-two with Poyet, but the French defender overran the ball, allowing Schmeichel to dive at his feet. And just four minutes from the end, as Chelsea appeared to be withstanding United's last attempt, David Beckham's cross eluded Leboeuf and gave Solskjaer his chance. The Norwegian curled his shot into the top corner to salvage United's unbeaten run.

Zola pledged that Chelsea would not be evicted out of the title race. Class had been augmented by solid steel, with Zola insisting: 'We can handle ourselves now in the big matches when the going gets tough. We feel we are a stronger side this year, tactically, physically and mentally. We have shown some good things in our last two games against Arsenal and United, two very good teams. We matched Arsenal physically, only losing to a late goal, then, just three days later, we showed what we can do by almost winning at United. We have many different players, but every one is capable and strong enough of doing a good job. We're better equipped now to cope with the physical challenge of other teams – we've increased a lot this season. Last year we were a good team who had good skills, good possibilities, but didn't believe too much in itself. We sold one player, bought half-a-dozen very good international players and increased our strength. And another important thing is now we believe – we've seen we are able to do good things in comparison to the other big teams. The confidence is growing from that; now we have to go on and finish the job – but all the signals look good. But it's true teams are trying harder to beat us now because we are the Cup winners – we are a name now. The game against Newcastle is very important because they are one of the four to five teams who can win the title, including ourselves. We need to win, especially after only taking one point this week, and because we are playing at home.'

Zola wanted to repeat the previous season's inspirational form but was finding it difficult: 'I'm getting more attention now from defenders. They know me, and it's harder for me to find space, to find the freedom that I found last year. But if I'm a great player, I have to sort it out. It's good, because it makes the game more interesting. I know I'm not playing at the same level as last year in parts, but I've improved a lot in the last two matches. I'm quite happy with what I've done, but it doesn't mean I'm completely satisfied. You have to trust yourself and think you're doing well and keep going during this spell, and I'm confident I'll reach a higher level and start scoring soon.'

Gullit, whose last senior outing had been at Derby in March, was happy to remain on the sidelines: 'If I wasn't the manager, I would play, and I haven't lost the desire. But things are going well and developing well, and I have different responsibilities now. If it's necessary, I will play, but I'm not that vain about it. The team must come first. If you put yourself first, then you can't do the other parts of the job.'

Zola was back to his best against Newcastle – apart from the goals. He struck a rich vein of form that was enough to send a shiver of apprehension throughout English football. Uruguayan Gustavo Poyet conjured a set-piece headed winner, but Zola spoke as eloquently off the field as his 'happy feet' were back to their very best on it. If his English was improving, his performances, too, were on an upward curve.

I caught up with Zola, as usual with Gary Staker by his side, in the corridors outside the dressing-room. He only asked for guidance on one question and had some trouble with his 'finishing', as his pronunciation of 'finish' came out as 'finalize'.

But he was happy with the steady improvement, as he told me: 'I'm quite close to the top, but I'm not at the top. I am pleased to have so many chances but I need to score more goals. The way I'm playing, it won't be long before I do. When I play good football, a goal is a consequence of that. The only thing wrong is the fact that I'm not scoring my goals, but the way I'm playing is quite good now.' I suggested to Zola that his gradual return to the best form of his career was part of his master plan to peak in a World Cup showdown in Rome. He flashed that disarming smile and professed: 'No!' With all sincerity, he said: 'I started the season late, so I wasn't really ready; but now I have played more games, my form is getting better. Maybe it's because the last three games have not been easy ones.'

Like everyone else, Zola knew that any drop in his standards would mean a spell on the bench. But since being left out, he had emerged once more as a key factor in Chelsea's championship challenge. Gullit referred to the work ethic when he said: 'The so-called stars worked hard today and really set a good example. When it gets tough, these players work hard, like Zola, Poyet and Dennis Wise. The rest will follow their example.' Zola agreed: 'I've always said that you have to work hard for the team, and winning is all-important whether you win 1–0 or 2–1.'

Poyet spoke precious little English but I spotted him conversing in fluent French with Frank Leboeuf; and Gullit, with his array of language skills, gets his message across in Spanish or French.

The spectre of Zola still hung over England; yet despite the menace he posed for the national team, his popularity at Stamford Bridge was undiminished. As Poyet left the ground to cheers from the fans waiting for him, it was nothing compared to the way Zola was mobbed. The little fellow stopped to sign as many autographs as he could and even kissed one female fan as he struggled to enter his awaiting car.

Zola produced some amazing sequences, comprised of mesmerizing dribbles and thirty-yard shots, in the 1–0 win over Newcastle that reaffirmed Chelsea's title chances. Gullit described him as 'outstanding'. Kenny Dalglish was magnanimous enough to praise his opponents for being the better side. It was unfortunate for Dalglish that without England captain Alan Shearer, and having sold Les Ferdinand and David Ginola to Spurs, he was also deprived of Faustino Asprilla with a stomach bug. The pragmatic Scot deployed an ultra-defensive formation and that was as much a compliment to Chelsea and their potential. Dalglish said: 'They are a threat not only from their general play but also because their delivery of the ball is that good, from Zola from set-pieces. In their previous two matches against Arsenal and Manchester United they didn't have the luck, so perhaps they deserve this now.'

Gullit concluded: 'This is a different Chelsea. In the past we would have drawn, or given away a bad goal in the last minute.'

On his journey to the Slovakian capital for the second stage of the Cup-Winners' Cup mission, Gullit reflected on the progression of Zola: 'I'm happy with what he gives now. He can peak at the end of the season. I don't want them to be in great form too early; I want them to vie 100 per cent at the end of the season.'

It was also a different Vialli; Lucky Luca was back – literally. A goal off his backside killed the tie in Bratislava, and his glorious pass for Roberto Di Matteo to collect the second meant a 2–0 win on the night and 4–0 overall against Slovan. Zola and Hughes were rested on the bench and not even needed. The plan was for them to recharge their batteries fully for the next Premiership date at Liverpool.

Vialli admitted: 'It was a strange goal, but it doesn't matter how you score them – it's always a great feeling when they hit the back of the net. My goal made the tie very easy for us. Now we can look forward to the draw with confidence. I'm very happy at Chelsea; I'm fitter than I was last season, and certainly more lucky!' Gullit enthused: 'Luca's goal was a pleasant surprise, but the point is he deserved it because he did everything but score in the first leg. All strikers are entitled to a bit of luck – even Luca! It wasn't a good match because of the pitch and the wind, but it was a really professional performance by us. I was really amazed and disappointed that Luca didn't score at Stamford Bridge – everybody felt sorry for him because he played so well and didn't get the luck he deserved. But tonight he got the luck and got the goal. It doesn't matter how you score, as long as they go in. We got a bit sloppy in the last ten minutes, but the game was won by then.'

At Anfield, Paul Ince planned to deepen Italian depression by ensuring Zola went to Rome on a downer. The Liverpool captain wanted to do his bit in the psychological battles England were winning. And Ince, a key figure in England's 2–0 win over Cesare Maldini's team in Le Tournoi during the summer which gave Hoddle's team such a huge lift, was happy to see his former Manchester United team-mates adding to Italy's sense of insecurity with their brilliant Champions' League triumph over Juventus. Ince said: 'United's result against Juventus was tremendous, especially for the England lads in their team. It will give them tremendous confidence as they prepare for Rome. Beating Italy in France in the summer was probably more important as far as the nation is concerned, but it was still nice to see Juventus get beaten. In Italy they will have made more of it than we will, because Juventus are regarded as the cream of Italian football. Normally they can never do anything wrong, but for them to come over here and get beaten by the top team in England is good news for everybody here.'

Now Ince hoped to follow United's example by putting Chelsea's Italian trio – Zola, Di Matteo and Vialli – in their place. It was the first time he had faced Zola in club football: 'I never played against him during my time at Inter Milan, because in my first season in Italy he was not in the Parma team and in my second year he moved on to Chelsea. In the build-up to Rome, everyone will be asking me what players like Zola and Maldini are like. But everyone has seen them, everyone knows how good they are, so I can't say any more. Zola along with Di Matteo and Vialli have improved Chelsea because they are world-class players. I watched Chelsea on television the other night and they have so many good players who are comfortable on the ball. They are now a team capable of winning the championship.'

Zola expected that the impression Ince would make would not be overly physical, and certainly not with a mind on the big test in Rome the following weekend. 'We are playing an important game in the championship and we can only focus on this match,' he said. 'So I won't be worried if Paul Ince comes up behind me. I'm not worried about him doing anything he shouldn't – I trust him. I really don't believe any player would think about harming an opponent because of another game that's coming up. If Paul Ince hurts me, it will be for Liverpool, not for England!

'Anyhow, it's not easy to tackle me – he'll have to catch me first. And while he can hurt me, Roberto Di Matteo can hurt him!'

All said with the easy smile. But the serious side to his game was starting to dominate his thinking as well. 'Next week is very, very important,' he agreed. 'It is life, it is everything, and we know we must win.'

Liverpool had a big score to settle with Gullit's team. Roy Evans admitted that their 4–2 FA Cup defeat at Stamford Bridge in January had been one of his lowest moments in football. The manner in which they surrendered a 2–0 half-time lead that day helped convince him he needed someone like Ince to beef up the team. Evans said: 'It's fair to say the Cup defeat knocked the stuffing out of us for a while. We had got ourselves into a position where we should have won the game, and when we got bounced out it was like a kick in the teeth. After that game we had to dig deep to get ourselves back into things. We played Chelsea three times last season and really only had one bad half against them. We beat them 5–1 at home in the league and lost 1–0 down there when we should have got something from it. But it's the Cup game that everyone remembers, and we should have been home and dry at half-time in that. We've not yet shown the real quality in our play. This is a good time to start. It's a big game and it's one we need to win to keep ourselves in a reasonable position.'

Zola waltzed around David James for a superb equalizer at Anfield, but wasn't much longer on the pitch as Gullit was forced to reshape his team after an extraordinary early sending-off. Zola looked completely desolate and despondent as he took his place on the bench alongside Vialli.

For the third time in six Premiership games, Chelsea finished short of manpower, their dream of sustaining a title challenge in danger of evaporating in a rash of red cards. Sinclair, Leboeuf and now Bernard Lambourde had failed to last the ninety minutes as Chelsea sacrificed valuable ground in the championship race.

The Liverpool experience would do little to purge Chelsea of their simmering resentment towards FIFA official David Elleray, the 1994 FA Cup Final referee. Hard-line Harrow schoolmaster Elleray was on their case before a ball was kicked at Anfield, ordering Dennis Wise to remove one of those essential soccer fashion accessories, an ear-ring stud, during the pre-match warm-up. Lambourde was dismissed after just twenty-five minutes. His cameo appearance consisted of a blatant trip on Karl-Heinz Riedle and a gormless body-check on Steve McManaman in the space of eleven minutes. Gullit instantly sacrificed Zola to shore up Chelsea's defence himself, but Liverpool were to make the extra man pay to devastating effect.

Paul Ince's ball over the top caught Le Saux napping and Patrik Berger nipped in to lift an exquisite lob over the hesitant Ed de Goey. Liverpool's lead lasted only two minutes. Bjorn Kvarme crashed into Hughes, as Zola raced clear to receive Poyet's slide-rule pass. Like everyone else, Zola glanced over his shoulder as Elleray's whistle remained silent. He skipped round James to pot a hotly disputed equalizer.

With Chelsea down to ten men and Zola substituted, Berger then converted Bjornebye's cross after the Norwegian's slick exchange of passes down the left with McManaman to restore Liverpool's lead. Then came the 'no penalty' incident on which, according to Gullit, the game turned, as Jones flattened Poyet. Elleray was unmoved. With Chelsea left to chase the game, Berger was left unmolested twelve minutes after the break to convert the excellent McManaman's pass and make it 3–1. There was no way back for Chelsea after that, and six minutes later Fowler's deflected left-footer threatened to make it a rout. Gullit refused to settle for damage limitation. He slipped when he was clean through and looked a sure bet to bury Wise's pass. Elleray finally located the penalty spot seven minutes from time when Flo was bundled over by Jason McAteer. Poyet scored with a minimum of fuss.

Gullit was naturally furious after Chelsea's 4–2 defeat. Evans joined in the condemnation by accusing Elleray of a 'diabolical non-decision' which had allowed Zola the equalizer. Gullit raged: 'The game was undoubtedly influenced by the penalty which wasn't given when Gustavo Poyet was knocked over. That would have made it 2–2 and, even with ten men, it would have been a totally different game. We've only lost because we played for most of the match with a man short. It's a bit frustrating because I never thought we could lose here with eleven. I must give credit to the way we played because, even with ten, we created chances. Earlier this season, there have been games where a member of the opposition deserved to be sent off and the referee has realized he's already given that player a yellow card. I hope referees have second thoughts like that with us in future.' Elleray was under fire from both sides. Evans said: 'It always seems to end up niggly when we play Chelsea. It was always going to be a difficult game, especially if control of the match wasn't good. After Chelsea's equalizer it was time to calm everyone down and make sure we held the aces. I wouldn't agree with Ruud that the penalty decision changed everything, because Chelsea's equalizer for me was a diabolical non-decision. That he didn't see Mark Hughes barge Bjorn Kvarme out of the way could have changed the game for us.'

Gullit was booed by the 36,000 crowd after bringing himself on for Zola after less than half an hour, a tactical switch which some people might have wrongly interpreted as keeping the Italian striker fresh for the World Cup D-Day in Rome. Gullit said: 'We needed a player up front who could keep the ball and be a focal point for our attacks, and that would have been difficult for Gianfranco because of his height. Maybe they booed me because they were afraid that something might happen whenever I had the ball!'

Gullit felt the influx of foreign players and coaches had broadened English football's horizons. The former kingpin of AC Milan's all-conquering side at the start of the decade said: 'Even a month ago, some Italians were still saying their football was still superior, but I'm not so sure that is the case any longer. The gap has been closed not only because of foreign players joining Premiership clubs but because the English are now willing to learn. There are now several teams in the Premiership who have the right mix of foreigners and home-grown players.' Gullit believed the psychological war of nerves between rival camps in the media in the lead-up to Rome also played an important part: 'There's so much pressure created by the build-up. It's nothing short of psychological warfare. Look at the way the media hyped up the confrontation between Gianfranco Zola and Paul Ince for our game at Liverpool. The Italians are under pressure and this game may have come at just the right time for England. I don't want to get involved in talking about the leading personalities, or who will win, or what the score will be. I'm not even doing any work as an analyst for TV this weekend. What I will say, though, is that the match will be decided by a small detail like a set-piece, a corner or a small defensive mistake. And it won't all hinge on one individual performance but the collective strength of a team.'

But the Chelsea boss was happy enough to make one forecast: 'It will be a *bellissimo* match! A game that will take the attention of the whole football world.'

14

The Showdown

Zola was again earmarked to be the thorn in many opposing defences – not least England's in the World Cup qualifying tie in Rome in October.

The Italians were delighted that Glenn Hoddle was experiencing 'local' difficulties with getting his team together for the confrontation in which the World Cup qualification group would be finally sorted out.

But for Zola it was a difficult position. It was hardly appropriate for him to gloat. Instead, he offered sympathy to crocked England rival Alan Shearer: 'I really feel for Alan. Any kind of injury is a blow, but to be out for so long is a shame for both Newcastle, England and football fans.' Shearer was out of the Italy-England clash with a devastating ankle injury and cracked bone. Zola believed it would be a tight battle. 'It will be a good game, but my priority of course is Italy,' he said. 'I hope England also reach France next summer, but I am a professional and I have a job to do.'

Zola led Italy's attack in Georgia as the Italians sought the win that would leave them needing only a draw against England to qualify for the World Cup. Coach Cesare Maldini was wary of Georgia, who had been unfortunate not to force a draw in Perugia when a narrow 1–0 win for Italy hastened the departure of Maldini's predecessor Arrigo Sacchi. Maldini only made his team selection after a final training session. Zola partnered Pierluigi Casiraghi. Roberto Baggio returned and Antonio Conte also made his international comeback, nearly a year after being injured in the first game against Georgia.

Zola feared that England would snatch the sole automatic qualification spot from Italy. He felt England were emerging as favourites to qualify ahead of his country, despite having lost 1–0 to Italy at Wembley back in February. 'You just have to admire the English,' he insisted. 'They may lack the technical ability of Italy, but their determination to win has seen them bounce back from their defeat against us and continue their drive towards the World Cup. When they beat us in France in the summer, it was obvious they had come a long way since we beat them, and they must not be underestimated at any cost. There is no doubt they will beat Moldova at Wembley, while we have a very difficult tie against Georgia. Who knows – England could even go into the game needing just a draw to finish top of the group.'

Zola was adamant the foreign invasion had played a major part in the national team's revival: 'In the past it has been difficult for England because, unlike Italy, Germany and Spain, they have faced their own players week in, week out. But that has changed. English players are growing accustomed to the ways of European football because there are so many foreign players in this country. That is giving them renewed confidence at national level and has helped bridge the gap from domestic to international football.'

So much so, in fact, that Zola believed many English players were now capable of earning a living in *Serie A*, something that would have been unthinkable a few years before. 'It was very difficult for players in this country to adjust to a league as technical as Italy's,' he argued. 'What is going on in England now was commonplace in Italy a few years ago. All the top players wanted to play in Italy. Now, because there is so much money in the game, you are seeing a great deal of foreign players going to England or Spain. English players are now good enough to compete in Italy because they are becoming more accustomed to the ways of European football and are becoming more tactically aware. Having said that, it's difficult to see top-class players leaving this country to go to Italy. Why should they? *Serie A* is a good level of football, but the Premiership has reached a good standard, too.'

While many fretted endlessly that England's World Cup progress had already been undermined by the injury to Shearer, Zola disagreed. He believed England had the players to fill the void left by their captain's absence: 'They played without him and beat us in France. Obviously it's a blow to both Newcastle and England. You simply cannot replace a player like Shearer, who has consistently scored goals for both his club and his country. But England are spoilt for choice up front. They have Ian Wright, Teddy Sheringham, Les Ferdinand and Robbie Fowler, who can all come in and do a very good job.'

Despite his reservations, though, Zola still felt that the previous two encounters between England and Italy would have no bearing on the game at the Olympic Stadium: 'Those games are gone, forgotten. The match in Rome is another game with different conditions and a different feeling altogether. Everybody knows how important this game is to both sides; neither wants to finish second and face the possibility of a play-off game to reach the World Cup. I am already focused on this game, I know how important it is to work hard and play well leading up to the match. The Italian players trust their strength, but we know it's going to be a very difficult game against England. We know we can win 1–0, like we did at Wembley – or we can lose 2–0, like we did in France. Obviously home advantage will count for something, but you don't like to say too much after what happened at Wembley.'

Tottenham's Sol Campbell had been taught something about the harsh realities of professional football by Zola. The goal against England at Wembley instantly changed Campbell's perspective and, by his own admission, he 'woke up' to what was required at the highest level. The powerfully built central defender owned up to his part in what should have been 'collective responsibility' for a combination of defensive frailties. Campbell certainly learnt his lesson. The enormity of that goal, which severely dented England's World Cup aspirations at the time, was his introduction to the intense scrutiny of international football.

He said: 'I was just a young player in his second England game and I thought I played all right; in fact, if anything, my passing game was much better. But that situation around the goal was highlighted like I never experienced before. It tells you what international football is all about – the response to that game was unbelievable.'

His Spurs team-mate Ian Walker, in goal for England that night, also suffered. Club manager Gerry Francis sat them both down, went through the goal and proceeded to attempt to rebuild their damaged confidence. 'I told them that you don't become a good player or a bad player overnight,' said Francis. 'I also said that when you get good publicity, not to let it affect you because one day you will get criticism and you must be ready for that. I knew what playing for England was all about from my time as captain, and I wanted to help them at a difficult time.'

It worked, though for Campbell the memory lingers on: 'Something like that wakes you up. I reckon I learned more from that sort of game than some of the others.'

Campbell had clearly matured in the seven months since that night against the Italians. It was proof of one of football's oldest and most trusted maxims – that you learn more in defeat than in victory. While he had immediately owned up to his share of the blame for the goal, other, more experienced men on the pitch kept their own counsel. 'Maybe, in three or four years, I will be one of those keeping quiet!' he said.

Campbell's contribution to the England cause during Le Tournoi had been noted. His performances there were powerful and he said: 'I think that tournament was a good point in my career, and now I have to take it on. There are still lots of ways in which I can improve, and I am trying to do that. If you stop, people overtake.'

In Georgia, Zola won his thirty-fourth cap and hit the bar after twenty-three seconds. He was substituted ten minutes from the end, while Di Matteo, winning his twenty-seventh cap, was booked and suspended for the England match. It was a depressing goalless draw, while England rolled over Moldova 4–0 at an emotional Wembley, with the nation still mourning the loss of Princess Diana.

The Georgians proved to be something of a bogey team for Italy, and Cesare Maldini pulled off Zola and the rest of his forward-line in a desperate hunt for a late goal. Roberto Baggio, a second-half substitute, said: 'We did everything we could to score, but obviously we found it very hard. But a 0–0 draw here in Georgia is no big drama. It's a difficult place to win. We're just going to give everything against

England next month.' A visibly frustrated Zola found himself back defending at times. The Chelsea striker and partner Christian Vieri had difficulty finding each other to capitalize on a far from watertight Georgian defence. Vieri was replaced by Casiraghi halfway through the second half but the Lazio striker had no better luck. Baggio came on for Attilio Lombardo after seventy-one minutes and Inzaghi took over from Zola five minutes later. But none could find the net despite pushing forward in numbers in the final minutes.

Italy were still quoted as odds-on favourites to win group 2, with England at even money. Zola came back fighting, and predicting that Italy would shatter England's World Cup dream. He warned that England would face a different Italian side. Zola said: 'Italy never makes mistakes on the big occasions. The destiny of the Italian team is to perform miracles and we are resigned to that reality. At Wembley we managed a miracle and we will have to repeat that feat in Rome. We can do it. We suffered in the first half against the Georgians and we admit they put us in difficulty. But in the second half it was one-way stuff and we dominated. I have always said that September is a difficult month for Italians, and this team deserves faith from others because it has always responded well at difficult times. When we play England, we will be in much better physical condition. English morale will be up in the stars, but we can count on home advantage. I am telling everyone to be optimistic – even those who are upset at the moment.' Vieri confirmed that the Italians believed they were destined to win the big one. He said: 'I think we are just favourites to win the group – I think we have a fifty-one per cent chance of beating England. In decisive games, the Italian national team has never let anyone down.'

But Zola also warned his international team-mates not to be complacent about England, as he watched in admiration Manchester United's 3–2 Champions' League triumph over Juventus just a week away from Rome: 'We've got to get one thing clear in our minds – it is time for the entire Italian camp to start worrying about the English. I don't want to sound alarmist, but it is a fact that playing English sides is no longer as straightforward as it used to be, as the match at Old Trafford proved. They are making up for lost time, and catching up the deficit in victories that they have against us. They are learning fast and even the smaller English clubs have made great progress – especially with their tactics. It will be harder for us to face up to this situation, and there is only one way, by applying ourselves and working harder than ever. Complacency on our part would be fatal when we go into next week's match in Rome. We must approach the game calmly and aware of what we can do, and woe betide us if we play in fear. The key is to have a healthy respect for England, and confidence in ourselves.

'Everybody in Italy, the players and the fans, has to realize that we must be worried about the English team. Don't get me wrong, I'm not saying we have to start being afraid, but it is a fact that Manchester United confirmed that it is no longer easy to play against English teams. Our fans might think it will be easy, but if we are complacent it will be fatal for us in Rome. I've been saying for a while now that English football is growing. Now, at the last minute, our fans are beginning to realize that only an Italian team at its very best can do the job. The United game against Juve was very important because it showed that English football has grown. The English players in that match will now be very confident, and we know the danger is there.

'But it will be a very different sort of match in Rome. This time it will be the Italian side who are at home, but the way United played showed things we have to be careful of. Italy have won in the past, but now it's another game, another occasion. We can't afford to think that we won a game twenty years ago so we'll win this time. It's completely different. We are playing another game entirely and we know that England are now far more difficult to beat than they used to be. We must play an intelligent game, but also a careful one.'

The explosion of foreign imports to the Premiership affected the England manager more than anyone, limiting his options. Glenn Hoddle backed quality foreign signings, but was concerned over the quantity. He argued: 'We want the best in this country; the Zolas, the Bergkamps and the Cantonas have been great. But when I came around to picking the squad for the Italian match, only fifty per cent of my options were English. It will be a concern if that percentage gets less. We want the best, not the cheapest. It is no good if our talent ends up blocked because there is no place for them to play.'

Italian soccer's top managers warned that Zola was still the big danger to England. Lazio coach Sven Goran Eriksson, who had snubbed the chance to manage Blackburn, said: 'Zola knows all about English defending, and he can give Italy that something extra. He gets goals all the time for Chelsea, and he was the man who scored Italy's goal at Wembley. He is a striker of genius and imagination, and English sides have often been punished by players who are a bit out of the ordinary. There will be 80,000 fans in the Olympic Stadium, and the game is so vital in terms of money, pride and tradition. England are strong but not unbeatable, but Italy will need to pay attention to Ian Wright and Paul Ince. Their best bet will be to attack England right from the word go.' Luigi Simoni, boss of *Serie A* leaders Inter Milan, insisted: 'I am banking on Zola. Our national side have seldom failed to live up to expectations in important games, and we should be involved in the World Cup finals. The English are very strong at home, but far less competitive on their travels. I can't see Manchester United repeating their recent win over Juventus in Turin. But Cesare Maldini has lost some key players, including Roberto Di Matteo, and his midfield is in a state of crisis.'

Francesco Baiano of Derby observed: 'I'm backing Gianfranco Zola to give Italy the edge and take them to France as group winners. He was the difference between the teams at Wembley and is still in the same eye-catching form. He is a natural match-winner. But Italy will not have things all their own way, and that is why I would also single out Ciro Ferrara as another key figure. He is a tough-tackling, no-nonsense defender who will have to be at his best to keep England out. He will have to keep a particularly close watch on Ian Wright to make sure Italy edge through 1–0 or 2–1.'

Ray Wilkins, with his Italian experience, said: 'If Italy have a key player, it has to be Gianfranco Zola. The Italians press forward a lot more than they used to, and I believe they won't play with their normal cautious approach. They'll play it around at the back and they will be composed – but once they get into our half we will see them really up the tempo. I like to think that we've got the players to cope with that in the likes of Gary Pallister and Tony Adams or Sol Campbell, who really has speed to match anything they have up front. But Zola, so influential, so tricky and smart, is a vital element

who could cause us a lot of trouble. All the England lads will know
him because he's turned them all over at some time – they've all
suffered a bit of his magic. And I'm certain Glenn will make sure they
give him the utmost respect and attention. It's important never to go
to the floor against him. You've got to stand on your feet and force
him to beat you, to try and go by. They mustn't lay down by diving
into tackles to allow him an easy path. If they do, he will just skip
right by them and, as we all know, when he gets into the penalty area
it spells big trouble. Just look at the goal he scored against Liverpool
last weekend. One minute, as he's going through and stumbling, he's
looking over his shoulder to see if the ref had awarded a foul; then
the next split-second he was past David James, who's six foot five, and
in a flash the ball was in the back of the net. And Gary Pallister will
remember with some pain how at Stamford Bridge last year Zola
dodged around him. Zola may be not so quick but his trickery is
exceptional, and because he has a low centre of gravity and he's so
close to the ground, he can stop on a five-penny piece and change
direction so easily to wrong-foot the bigger blokes.'

Graeme Le Saux also warned his World Cup team-mates about the
smiling assassin. Chelsea's new recruit had seen the ruthlessness and
sheer professionalism of Zola at close quarters: 'I've really got to
know Franco in the past six weeks since I joined Chelsea, and we've
been having some interesting conversations. He told me that he
wouldn't speak to me for two weeks before the game . . . and a week
before would start kicking me! We've been having a few laughs about
this game and he's been walking around the training ground with a
John le Carré novel and an Anglo-Italian phrasebook recently.
Maybe he's trying to get inside the English mentality – more likely he
just needs the books to stand on!

'We all know what Franco's capable of and we have got to respect
his fantastic ability as a player. But beyond what he does on the pitch,
he's a lovely person as well. The team we have at Chelsea gels
together well because there are so many different cultures and
nationalities that there is a real openness about the place. Because of
the communication problems, there's a necessity to make people feel
welcome, and nobody does that better than Gianfranco because he's
very friendly, very cheeky and a great personality. He certainly enjoys

playing in English football. He likes our attitude towards the game and appreciates that the outside pressures are nothing like he used to get in Italy. I don't want to build him up to the stage where we're saying he's amazing, because despite all his ability, he's still very humble. There are no airs or graces about him. He's very down to earth. Add all that to his playing ability and it makes him a very well-rounded person, the sort of guy we can all learn from.'

He refuted suggestions that Zola was out of sorts: 'It's not been easy for the strikers to get going at Chelsea, because the boss has been rotating them all season. But they've all responded well and they've all been scoring. Franco certainly hasn't been quiet. Every time he's played, he's looked sharp and dangerous. There are two ways to stop him – man-mark him and try to snuff him out of it, or just play your own game and always be aware of him. Either way can be just as effective, but only if you are completely focused and concentrating on what he is up to. His biggest asset is his movement, as he proved at Wembley. He comes in behind you and suddenly disappears, and if you're not totally alert, he'll catch you out. As defenders, we've got to keep talking to each other, always letting each other know what he's up to. But we've got players with equal ability, and right now I'm trying to appreciate the atmosphere we're on and the excitement and sheer size of the whole occasion.'

The pundits had had their say: Zola was again the danger man. But after all the pre-match hype about how Zola could destroy England again, this time the glory went to Hoddle's team. Revenge was sweet for them, but for Zola it was a bitter experience. There in the Olympic Stadium, I watched his heartbreak as he was substituted after sixty-two minutes by Del Piero, to a great cheer from the England fans.

England held out for a goalless draw to end a sequence of fifteen straight World Cup wins in Rome for Italy and qualify top of the group, leaving the Italians in the dreaded play-offs.

Coach Maldini, to his credit, paid tribute to the way the England team had negated the menace of Zola: 'England are a very good team, especially in the middle where their players had personalities. Zola played too wide, wider than we intended, but I don't blame him for that. To England's credit, he was forced to go wide.'

Zola was involved in an extraordinary disagreement with Maldini before and after the game. Had he risked his international future by contradicting his coach? Although he accepted his share of responsibility, Zola hardly took the heat off Maldini afterwards. He suggested he should not have played if Maldini only wanted to play him out of position.

Zola started diplomatically enough: 'I'll take my share of responsibility for the result.' Then came the 'but', and it was a huge one: 'But Maldini asked me if I could play behind the two strikers to make up for losing Roberto Di Matteo. I was honest with Maldini when we talked of the possibility of me playing on the left of midfield instead of as a striker. I said the game was too important and we could run into difficulties. I have played on the left with Chelsea but as a third striker, not like this. In this role, it is better to have someone else. I even told him to leave me out if he didn't think I was in form. It was too important. I accepted his instructions in the end, but pointed out that to give my best I had to play up front. The game started and the English took control of midfield, so I had to come back and provide extra manpower alongside Demetrio Albertini and Dino Baggio. So I ended up running around like a madman behind David Batty. I wasted a lot of precious energy in this way. Let's be honest, I was no longer fish or meat – I was neither one thing nor the other. I didn't know what to do anymore. Under these circumstances, it would have been better for another player to be out there, not me.'

Zola was a disappointed figure. He felt he was given an impossible role. 'I don't make magic,' he said. 'I work and always try to do well. I succeed when we are all good. At the Olympic Stadium, I and all the rest were less good. I would have given my finger to win this game. I played as Maldini wanted. We spoke and I told him going back into midfield I'd have difficulty – and so it was. In that position, I do less. At the start, I tried to stay up to put them in trouble, but we suffered in midfield and I had to drop back. My performance was limited by this. There are no excuses, it is just the truth. I couldn't really play my normal game. But I made mistakes, too, and I have to take responsibility.'

Corriere dello Sport interpreted these remarks with a screaming headline: 'Like this I won't play anymore.' Zola was more diplomatic than that. But if he was to be played out of position, it might lead to confrontations with his coach. He could only hope that his simple honesty had not offended Maldini unduly and that his strange role – caught between the centre and the left of midfield – was a one-off nightmare.

But Maldini must have infuriated Zola with his own interpretation. Zola had complained about playing on the left, but Maldini claimed he should never have been there in the first place: 'Zola should have been more in the centre. But the English were very good at closing down spaces in that department, too. So I can't really lay any blame at his door in that sense.'

Zola also paid tribute to England: 'They've proved themselves to be a great side.'

Skipper Dennis Wise could now get his own back on the Stamford Bridge Italian mob. Roberto, Gianfranco and Gianluca had been quick to rub salt in England's wounds back in February after Italy's 1–0 victory at Wembley by turning up for Chelsea training wearing Italian team shirts. The draw in Rome which sent England to the World Cup finals gave Wise a chance for revenge. He explained: 'When the Italian guys arrived at training, we were standing there wearing our England shirts with "England – France 98" on the front and "Italy?" on the back. We weren't going to let Saturday pass without getting our own back. They've just about got used to our sense of humour and took it all right.'

Wise still hoped Italy would beat Russia in the play-offs to make the finals: 'It's probably the toughest draw they could get but I tip them to win it. After all, the World Cup would not be the same without them.'

Wise was determined to be there as well even though he had been totally overlooked since Hoddle left Chelsea to take charge of England, and said: 'It's a big motivating factor that we have qualified. I still think I have more to offer as an international.'

Paul Ince was sure Italy would beat Russia, but he was also convinced they would not win France 98 while they relied so heavily on Zola. Ince said: 'Zola is a great player, make no mistake – but he can't do it every game and it is unfair to expect it. The Italians rely on him to produce the goods all the time, and that's a serious problem at international level. All week it was Zola this, and Zola that, in

England and Italy. Maybe the pressure got to him. I still think Italy will qualify, but they all need to take greater responsibility.'

Zola returned to the Bridge to be rested from the midweek Coca-Cola Cup tie with Blackburn, with Gullit making eight changes. Zola wasn't even among the three subs. Di Matteo scored an equalizer. Vialli was sent off in extra-time for the first time in English football, and Chelsea won the penalty shoot-out comfortably, 4–1.

Vialli, ruled out of the home tie against Southampton in the next round, said: 'I don't want to get involved except to say I'm sorry. But I deserved the red card; I used my elbow.'

Worse was the news about Gustavo Poyet – out for the rest of the season after suffering torn cruciate ligaments during training. Poyet had scored four goals in twelve games and made a major impact in midfield. Gullit said: 'He just tried to turn but his knee stayed there and snapped. He has made a great start to the season, so it's a big loss. Although it is a big loss, we have a big squad and we have enough options. The same time last year I bought Zola, but I'm not looking to sign a replacement at the moment.'

Then came another shock injury setback – England star Graeme Le Saux out for two months. The £5 million left-back dislocated an elbow early in the 1–0 Premiership home win over Leicester, Zola's first game after the Italy match. It was Le Saux's twenty-ninth birth-day the day before.

Frank Leboeuf scored the winner with the most beautiful goal of his career, a thirty-yard scorcher two minutes from the end, leaving Chelsea on the tail of the Premiership leaders and Leboeuf hoping his spectacular strike would be shown enough in France to push his claim for an international recall. He said: 'It was boring at Chelsea when all the international players went and there was only six or seven of us left. I want to be part of the World Cup; I don't want to spend another boring fortnight like that.'

No longer could Chelsea be categorized as merely a sound bet for the Cup. As for the title, Leboeuf felt it was a question of how the team coped without the likes of Poyet and Le Saux.

Martin O'Neill, denied by another late goal at the Bridge, felt there was an insurmountable psychological advantage when Chelsea could parade a galaxy of international superstars on the bench:

Gullit, Lambourde, Vialli and Hughes. In his typical no-nonsense fashion, O'Neill said: 'Anybody who can afford to leave Mark Hughes out of a Premiership game they badly want to win augurs very, very well for their squad. Perhaps they'd loan me two of them! Vialli has a couple of European Cup medals and Mark Hughes would start in anybody's team.'

There were times against Leicester when Chelsea's possession football was reminiscent of Liverpool in the eighties and Leeds in the seventies. The second half was played out virtually in Leicester's half and it was incredible the number of chances that fell to Tore Andre Flo, as well as Celestine Babayaro striking the underside of the bar and Vialli the post.

Zola was almost back to his best, his shooting and passing exquisite at times, but he still hadn't regained his goalscoring knack. He escaped a yellow card early in the game for overemphasizing a fall in the penalty area when he might easily have been booked for diving – the little Italian's sincere apology to referee Uriah Rennie saved him. His best moment came four minutes into injury time in a move that ended when Vialli struck the post, but by then the Chelsea fans were already celebrating victory after Leboeuf's long-distance strike.

With Arsenal and Manchester United dropping points, the title again looked a possibility for Chelsea. But Gullit refused to become excited. Instead he insisted: 'We still have a lot of things to learn and a lot of things to do, and every week we keep on learning and improving. We have this new policy of a bigger squad and now everybody can understand it. We have so many possibilities and so much quality, but everybody accepts that sometimes they play and sometimes they don't, and that also applies to myself. I just want them to work hard. If we don't win a game but they give 100 per cent, that's all I can ask. Every game I demand 100 per cent and the players are giving it. Not only are they playing with their hearts but also with their heads. This game needed patience and that's what I mean by playing with your head. For forty minutes they had eleven men, in the second half, behind the ball, and we had to play with cleverness and patience. For me that was our best game, the way we interrupted the game. That makes a coach proud, digging in very deep, more concentrated, rather than even winning 6–0. Last year, maybe I was demanding too much.

We won the Cup, but I also wanted us to do well in the Premiership and maybe that was too much. But now we are more focused in every game. We're not thinking of the end result, the FA Cup or Wembley, no more. Now every week is important.'

Gullit's belief is that winning matches against teams like Leicester will bring the title, more so than victories against the likes of Arsenal and Manchester United. He explained: 'Matches against Leicester, Derby and Leeds are more difficult than the big games. Matches against Arsenal and Liverpool are difficult, but you have to concentrate in games like this.'

Chelsea looked an exotic mixture of Dutch total football and the Italian possession style that Gullit became well-acquainted with at Milan. The Leicester fans chanted 'England, England', in recognition of Glenn Hoddle's team making it to the World Cup finals ahead of Italy. But it never fazed Zola. The Chelsea fans simply responded with applause and chants for one of their favourite stars.

O'Neill made Arsenal his choice as the best team in the Premiership. After crossing swords with both of the capital's championship challengers, his preference was for north rather than west London: 'On the day, Arsenal were the best side we have faced. When we drew 3–3 with them, they were really fantastic. But Chelsea are a top-quality side and with that amount of class at the club, they must come into consideration. Zola is class, but thankfully he didn't show that much of it last Saturday!'

15

Zola Power Returns with a Vengeance

No-one could ignore the first anniversary of Franco Zola's arrival at the Bridge.

Two brilliant free-kicks in successive matches lit up his season after a slow start. First, against Tromso in the Cup-Winners' Cup, a vital part of the 7–1 demolition of the Norwegians; and three days later, a repeat against West Ham as Chelsea moved within striking distance of the top of the Premiership on the same day that Manchester United lost 3–2 at Highbury.

But the club also took the extraordinary decision to ignore the first anniversary of Matthew Harding's death. They refused to sell a new book on Harding in the Megastore. Ken Bates appeared prominently in a Channel 5 television documentary screened immediately after the live coverage of the first leg defeat in Tromso. In the fifty-minute programme, Bates poured out his feelings about Harding, admitting that he refused to 'grieve, because I'm not a hypocrite'. For that reason, there was no official recognition of the Harding anniversary.

The depth of the feud that had existed between Harding and Bates came over powerfully and formidably in the documentary, *It's All Over Now – The Matthew Harding Story*. In it, Bates explained why he would never have allowed Harding to take control of Chelsea. He said: 'He never had a chance once he revealed himself in his true colours. I don't believe evil should triumph, and he was an evil man. What's more important, after fifteen to sixteen years of blood, sweat and tears at this place, I was not going to hand it over to him. I did not trust him to run it the way it should be run. It would have been back to where it was when I inherited it – a mess. This is a much happier ship at Chelsea now he's no longer around.' The Chelsea Independent Supporters Association attacked Bates over the issue, and while I would have thought it wiser for the Chelsea chairman to have opted out of the documentary, as did Ruth Harding, Bates explained to me that he felt the truth, as he saw it, had to be told.

But with the bloodletting in the boardroom a distant memory, feats on the field were taking precedence at the Bridge, notably the quest for European glory and the pursuit of the title.

Gullit greeted news of the Cup-Winners' Cup second round draw by asking, 'Do we have any moonboots?' His misgivings about the ice-age tie just 350 miles from the North Pole were confirmed when Tromso's Alfheim Stadium was covered in two inches of snow. But as the pitch was protected by undersoil heating, the Norwegians were confident of the match going ahead. Chelsea took no chances, investing in £1,000 worth of thermals, gloves and woolly hats to combat the sub-zero temperatures; enough to keep even the Italians warm by the Arctic Circle. Flo, who scored eighteen goals in twenty-six games for Tromso in 1995, said: 'It can be bitterly cold at this time of year, with lots of snow. During the summer it's the land of the midnight sun, but in winter it's dark virtually all day. It's a place for real men. Tromso are a strong team: physically fit, very muscular, and they can fight hard if they need to. It will be a tough place to visit and we will be facing a tough team to beat.' Gullit sent Gwyn Williams on a week-end spying mission. Williams said: 'It will be difficult to adjust from warm sunshine against Leicester to sub-zero temperatures in the space of five days. But we will prepare for cold conditions, and if the pitch turns out to be a bit tricky under foot, at least it will be the same for both teams.'

Chelsea were met by conditions so extreme that they didn't know until shortly before the game whether they would be able to play – eighteen inches of snow had fallen on the area in the previous four days. Around 500 villagers from the tiny outpost swept the snow from the terraces. Jurgen Werner, the UEFA observer, arrived on the morning of the game to examine conditions. But a sell-out 6,500 fans were already there, and there were instructions that UEFA intended the game to go ahead come what may. Gullit inspected the ground and said: 'I cannot see how the game will be played if the ball cannot move, but we must await an official decision and if the game goes on, we will have to get on with it. Whatever happens, we are ready, our attitude is right.'

Zola had scored six times for Parma as they reached the final of this same competition in 1994, only to lose 1–0 to Arsenal in Copenhagen. He said: 'That hurt very much. Everybody said we were the favourites, especially as Arsenal had so many injuries. For me, losing was a body-blow and now I have a second chance to do something about it in this competition with Chelsea.'

Chelsea wanted the tie settled, with the competition then going to bed until March. Gullit added: 'I listen to nobody; I hear the stories that it will be a walkover for Chelsea. For me, that is impossible and my priority is to get our attitude right. Never mind the cold, the snow, or the conditions. It is how we play that is most important and what this tie is about.' Zola chipped in: 'No matter who we play, no matter what the conditions, how cold it is, I am ready, Chelsea are ready. We take nothing for granted and we are determined that this will not be a shock result.'

The tie had to take place in Tromso or not at all, despite suggestions of a last-minute venue switch to Oslo. It went ahead, live on Channel 5. When the snow came down it was hard to tell the difference – it normally snows all the time on Channel 5!

Gullit let rip after Chelsea skidded to a 3–2 defeat in a snowstorm. The Polish referee twice had to suspend play in the second half in conditions frightful enough to have made Captain Scott stay in his tent. The match was completed on a two-inch carpet of snow. Gullit raged: 'As a match it was a dead loss. The conditions made a mockery of the game. It should never have been played, but we were aware that UEFA officials were prepared to finish it in any conditions. The pitch was only just playable in the first half, but in the second the snow was driving straight into the eyes of my players and they couldn't see what they were doing. What you saw out there had nothing to do with football. They seem prepared to put limbs and livelihoods at risk. It is plain that the match should not have started. You have to see something green on the pitch.'

Gullit lost his rag twice in the blizzard-hit second half, which was twice halted while groundstaff teams swept snow to clear the pitch markings. He said: 'We were very disappointed because, in one instance, Tromso scored while we were trying to make a substitution. We weren't allowed to because the UEFA official did not have his board ready. On another occasion, I asked the referee what he was going to do because we couldn't see the lines, but I knew there was no way they would abandon the game.'

Fortunately, Vialli struck in the last five minutes when Chelsea trailed 2–0 and then 3–1. He said: 'They were important goals, probably on a par with the two I got against Liverpool last season in the FA Cup. But they will not mean anything if we do not go through. The referee spoke English and he understood what we were saying to him, that it was too difficult to play. In the second half, it was just a question of rolling up our sleeves.' Gullit added: 'I must salute the courage of my team in fighting back.' Vialli moaned: 'The next time I see snow, I hope it is when I go on a skiing holiday.'

It was plain that the game should never have started and plainer still from half-time onwards, when the snow came down, that the referee should have abandoned proceedings. 'I asked the UEFA man,' Gullit said, 'what did he think about it. He said: "I can understand your point of view, but the game has to go on because of the busy schedule of UEFA."

'After the game I told the ref it was not his fault. The instruction came from higher up. He had wanted to postpone the game but had not been allowed to. This should not have been treated like a Mickey Mouse game. It is a real competition and it would have been disgraceful had we gone out in those conditions. I have only ever trained in such conditions, never played in snow like that. You could not play football, the snow was in the players' faces and in the second half I just told them to lump the ball forward.'

Chelsea declined to make a formal protest, nor would Gullit complain about the UEFA cock-up over the substitution of Leboeuf. Gullit added: 'The ref waited while the pitch was swept but would not stop the game for us to make a substitution. I was more angry about that than about the conditions.' Leboeuf was wanting to leave the pitch because of a back injury when Tromso broke through for their third goal.

There was a significant moment in the second half when Babayaro slipped after making a challenge and fell awkwardly on the snow. There was every possibility that he had hurt himself badly. After all, the worst injuries, as Alan Shearer knows only too well, often occur in the most banal circumstances. In the event, Babayaro was able to get up and play on. 'Like I said, I am a guy who likes to play football, but to play football in normal circumstances,' Gullit said. 'It's very difficult to get into the right mood. We were sixty per cent in possession of the ball; the only thing was that it was difficult to get through.'

Tromso did not find it difficult at all. They may have scored their third goal while Chelsea were trying to replace Leboeuf with Myers, leaving them a man short in defence, but, against that, the Norwegians made a myriad of chances.

Zola had one chance late on, but from an angle he would normally find not too testing he shot wide, and was clearly furious with himself. But the shocking state of the pitch scarcely encouraged artists of the likes of him. Vialli, by contrast, having done little, came suddenly and vibrantly to life in the closing minutes. Each of his goals came after a gem of a solo run, but with characteristic modesty he said that he had been helped by the mud, which had restricted the movement of the defenders.

Bjorn Johansen, coach of the Norwegian part-timers, reckoned the second-half blizzard had stopped his side scoring six! He said: 'English football is supposed to be hard, but Chelsea's tempo in the first half was rubbish. We just watched them play in front of us. It was Chelsea who should be thanking the snow, not us. It levelled the game off. It saved Chelsea. We would have got five or six had the snow not fallen. In the second half there was a lot of whingeing from the Chelsea bench. Their players were also telling the referee it was crazy to continue. It should have been us complaining.'

Zola suspected that he might not start the impending World Cup play-off in Russia, but together with Di Matteo he made his way to Italy for another trip into bitterly cold Russia, as Chelsea reluctantly travelled to Bolton – without them.

Gullit asked the Premier League to postpone the game at bottom club Bolton by a further twenty-four hours or switch it to Stamford Bridge, but both requests were denied. They arrived back from Tromso only forty-six hours before Sunday's scheduled kick-off. Gullit said: 'We wanted the game postponed but the League said no. The demands are great and we just have to get on with it. We thought they could do something for us, but they have their reasons to block us.' Chelsea were not just missing Zola and Di Matteo. Vialli, Lambourde and Wise were suspended, Poyet, Le Saux and Duberry injured. More worrying for Gullit was the general fatigue: 'I will just have to see how the players recover and cope from the demands. This is a big game for us.'

At the new Reebok Stadium, Chelsea went down 1–0. Again Gullit, who threw himself into the action for the last fourteen minutes, was upset. He kicked the ball away at the final whistle to show his feelings about his side's performance. No snow this time, just frozen out in front of goal. His reshuffled, reshaped side still had enough class and experience to create the chances – but squandered them.

Cesare Maldini, meanwhile, expected hard winter conditions in Russia, but scoffed at suggestions that Zola was too small to play in difficult conditions. He said: 'I don't measure strikers in metres. Smaller players can be more incisive on a heavy pitch.' Zola declared: 'Where is it written that little players like me can't play on this type of ground?'

But the conditions still favoured the selection chances of Fabrizio Ravanelli, recalled to the squad following his move from Middlesbrough to Marseille, in place of Zola. Ravanelli reckoned his time in the north east of England meant he could cope with the harshest of conditions – including a Russian winter. 'Sub-zero temperatures and ice are normal in England. Our training sessions at Middlesbrough regularly took place in polar conditions, storms of water or snow. The weather in Russia will make relatively little difference to me,' he argued. Ravanelli duly spearheaded the attack with the powerful Christian Vieri.

The squad trained in sub-zero temperatures at Moscow's Dynamo stadium. Maldini declared that Zola was not fully fit and would be on the bench with Alessandro del Piero, in case Ravanelli and Vieri failed to crack open the Russian defence. It would not be easy – no Italian had ever scored for his country in Russia.

Anything less than victory over the two legs would be a national disaster, as Italy had made every World Cup finals since 1958. But the Russians were far from resigned. 'The weather will be our ally,' coach Boris Ignatyev said the day before the game, aware that Russia's winter had thwarted foes before and relishing thoughts of an inglorious Italian retreat from Moscow. Undersoil heating meant that despite the temperature, the Dynamo pitch was soggy, though the Italians had also brought special boots in case of an icy surface.

The Italians took no chances. Their training programme included muscle rubs, massages and eating high-energy sweets. Of more concern to them was the fact they had not scored for 220 minutes, and Maldini faced the axe if he failed to qualify for the World Cup.

In a blizzard and on a snowbound surface, Italy battled through for a 1–1 draw. Vieri scored the precious away goal, and Italy needed a scoreless draw or the narrowest of victories in the return in Naples to reach the finals. 'Don't bury us yet,' Ignatyev said after a messy game he felt his side should have won. He forecast a cautious counter-attacking approach in the second leg. Akhrik Tsveiba, who had just come on in the centre of the Russian defence for concussed captain Viktor Onopko, slipped to let Vieri open the scoring after forty-nine minutes. Within two minutes, in the best move of a game ruined by the weather, Dmitry Khokhlov beat Paolo Maldini with a surging run to supply the short cross that Sergei Yuran bundled over for the equalizer. As soccer-loving prime minister Viktor Chernomyrdin said at Dynamo stadium: 'All is not lost. Hope is the last to die.'

First it was back to the Premiership and it was imperative for Chelsea to win at Villa Park, where Zola had scored both Chelsea's goals in their 2–0 win in the corresponding fixture the previous season. Villa's Steve Staunton said: 'The way Ruud Gullit rotates his squad reminds me of when I was at Liverpool. One international would drop out and another would come in. Zola is a terrific player. Although small, he is extremely strong and has an eye for goals. I voted for him as Player of the Year last season.'

Zola returned from Moscow, where he was not even a substitute, with Chelsea having lost their last two games. Villa's last two matches had ended in impressive draws at Athletic Bilbao and Arsenal.

But Zola was again within sight of his missing form at Villa Park as Chelsea regained their Premiership momentum with another 2–0 win, secured by goals from captain for the day Mark Hughes and late substitute Flo. A missed penalty from Villa's Dwight Yorke helped! Zola was industrious, creating Hughes's goal with an accurate cross, but made way for Flo, who scored with a far-post header with virtually his first touch, his first goal since 9 August. Flo admitted: 'That was a release, a big weight off my shoulders. I have been struggling a bit to find the net, but the boss has been great about it, telling me to relax and not to worry just about scoring goals. All along, his attitude has been that as long as I'm contributing to a winning team, he will not judge me on how many goals I score. But all the same, my goal at Aston Villa was a long time coming – nearly three months – and I can only hope it is the start of a good spell for me.' Gullit stressed: 'We are improving all the time and still have a great chance of being there at the end. It doesn't worry me that we are considered outsiders for the title; that's quite a nice position to be in.'

Flo warned that the return leg of the Cup-Winners' Cup tie would be anything but a formality. Tromso had breezed through their domestic relegation play-off 6–1 on aggregate, and Flo said: 'As we found out, they are a much better team than their place in the Norwegian league table suggests. They have proved they are good enough for their top division, and now they will want to prove they are good enough to topple the Cup-Winners' Cup favourites. Tromso are physically strong, they fight hard, and I think their strategy will be to get men behind the ball and catch us on the counter-attack. When they get their game together, they are a good side, and they have players, like Arst, who are dangerous if we don't watch them carefully.'

Before the game, Gullit was again branded a whinger by Tromso centre-back Steinar Nilsen for using the Arctic blizzard as a 'smoke-screen' for a dismal first leg performance. The Chelsea boss had upset the locals minutes after touching down in Tromso with his reaction to their cloying, muddy pitch – 'It looks like cow****' – which made front-page headlines in Norway. Nilsen, who scored Tromso's first goal, warned: 'I wouldn't like to be in Gullit's shoes if we score first.

We were far from satisfied with his comments after the first leg. He used the snow as a smokescreen for Chelsea's defeat and we will use his words as motivation to pull off an upset. I understand Roberto Di Matteo thought the conditions in Moscow for Italy's World Cup match against Russia were much worse – so where does that leave Gullit's argument? It was so disappointing to hear one of Europe's truly great players moan about our pitch when we moved heaven and earth to make sure the game went ahead. Before the snow fell, we were 2–0 up and it should have been more, so I don't know how Chelsea can complain about the pitch. Conditions were never dangerous and nobody got hurt. Now Chelsea are going to find out we can play on grass, too. We are safe from relegation now, so we are approaching this tie without fear because we have nothing to lose. Thursday night is going to be fun. Chelsea's squad is worth millions, but they will not be comfortable when our underdogs are barking at them.'

'Zola the key to making life too hot for Tromso' was the headline in the *Daily Telegraph* as David Miller suggested it was time for Zola to make his mark on the season. He wrote: 'Chelsea urgently need a performance from Gianfranco Zola more in keeping with the style that made him Footballer of the Year last season. His scoring touch has all but deserted him, yet tonight Chelsea must take an early initiative and he could be the man to secure it.'

In the event, two Italians made a huge impression; there was a Vialli hat-trick and scintillating free-kick from Zola. Grass was more to Chelsea's liking. On the perfect playing surface at Stamford Bridge, Tromso were trounced – sophisticated possession soccer triumphing over the brawn and hump-it-forward style of the Norwegians.

Hat-trick hero Vialli went off just before the end to a standing ovation and a smile and cuddle from Gullit. Ten goals, two hat-tricks and six of his goals in Europe – it was an amazing sequence for a player who had been on the brink of quitting the club.

Still not a permanent fixture in the Premiership starting side, Vialli was proving to be a talisman in the European campaign. Having scored in Bratislava with his bum, he collected another goal against Tromso courtesy of a deflection off the goalkeeper, but his header to complete his hat-trick was vintage Vialli, and by the time Gullit brought him off his personal tally might have surpassed the four he collected at Barnsley. Chelsea might easily have managed double figures.

Vialli had a premonition that he would score a hat-trick. 'Mystic Luca' started off with a header just wide and should have opened the scoring when he shot wide from a Dennis Wise pass. But the goal rout began and ended with Dan Petrescu. After just twelve minutes, Di Matteo's mishit pass came straight back to him and eventually found Wise wide on the right. His cross was met with a glancing header into the corner by the Romanian. Vialli, naturally, grabbed all the head-lines, but Zola was close to returning to his most devastating form. It was from his pass in the twenty-third minute that Vialli struck a shot that bounced off the underside of the keeper's body and crept into the corner.

It was an illusionary moment when Bjorn Johansen gained the benefit of an ineffective Di Matteo challenge – the ball creeping through his legs – and struck a twenty-five yarder into the corner. When Jonny Hansen was shown the yellow card for a foul on Di Matteo five yards outside the area, it was too good a chance for Zola to turn down. He curled a wicked free-kick over the wall and into the corner, his first European goal for Chelsea and his first free-kick success of the season.

It was his third goal of the season overall and his fifteenth in forty-two starts since signing from Parma.

When Hansen handled a Wise shot in the area, the referee showed him a second yellow card and sent him off. Frank Leboeuf kept calm as he waited to take the penalty and slotted it into the corner, finally giving Chelsea a more comfortable lead. Down to ten men, the Norwegians were chasing shadows harder and with less effect. Petrescu set off on a forty-yard run alone through the heart of the defence, but when he was halted, Vialli was on hand to tuck in the rebound from an acute angle. Vialli then rounded the keeper but the angle was too acute, yet he managed to pull it back and it was cleared off the line. He wasn't to be denied his hat-trick; it arrived in the seventy-fourth minute as Chelsea's keep-ball took the play from one flank to another. Vialli then found space to take advantage of Wise's cross.

Finally, from Zola's pass, Petrescu had time to virtually walk the ball in. Chelsea fans enjoyed the night's entertainment, taunting the Norwegian players with 'What's it like to play on grass!' And for their supporters, brave souls who travelled from the edge of the Arctic Circle only to be given a frosty send-off by the fans at Stamford Bridge, it was 'You only sing when it's snowing.'

Chelsea's European ambitions now went into cold storage until March and Gullit's mission was to improve on the team's fourth position in the Premiership. He tipped Vialli for an Italian World Cup recall: 'We had a point to prove – this time you saw the real Chelsea and the real Tromso. Everyone is delighted for Luca. He's made himself a serious candidate again for the Italian national squad because of the way he's been playing lately. Their play-off against Russia in Naples next weekend is such a big game, it would be nice to see a man of his charisma and experience involved. It was important to get this tie out of the way because now we can put Europe to one side until next March and focus entirely on the Premier League and domestic cups.'

Vialli, 'desperate' to score in front of his home fans after eight months hitting the target only on his travels, said: 'I can sympathize with Cesare Maldini because he has so many top-quality strikers to choose from. If he needed my help, of course I would not dream of turning him down. But that's another story. I'm happy as a child because I can't remember the last time I scored a hat-trick in Europe. In fact, I don't think it's ever happened before.'

Dennis Wise admitted Chelsea had been wound up by the provocative comments of Steinar Nilsen and Bjorn Johansen: 'They said a few things after the first leg we weren't too happy about. But just as they know how to play on snow more than we do, we showed we are better on grass than them. Everyone is delighted for Luca – he's come back in the dressing-room afterwards, shaken everyone's hand and said thanks for helping me score the goals.' Tromso coach Haakan Sandberg admitted: 'Was it 7–1? I lost count. But we lost our big chance to knock Chelsea out of Europe in the first leg, when we should have beaten them by two or three clear goals. In the end, Chelsea proved they are better than us.'

Chelsea, having served up their biggest landslide in Europe since they walloped Luxembourg whipping boys Jeunesse 21–0 on aggregate twenty-six years before, were installed 2–1 favourites for the Cup-Winners' Cup by William Hill, who also offered Real Betis, Stuttgart and Vicenza at 7–2.

Vialli's goals in Europe had thrust him back into the forefront of Gullit's plans, but he braced himself for the chop again when West Ham visited the Bridge. Only this time, he was ready for it – unlike his darkest hours the previous season when he was exiled on the bench wondering what he had done to deserve his expulsion. Vialli admitted: 'I did think that my appearance as substitute in the Cup Final at Wembley might be my farewell and that I would be leaving Chelsea in the summer. Although I was very happy at the club, enjoying myself living in London and very happy with my team-mates and the supporters, the most important thing was for me to play in the games. To be honest, I did not see much of a future for myself at Chelsea – but I don't think anyone else wanted me, because my valuation was very low. To use an English cliché, I was sick as a parrot – but now I'm on cloud nine!

'This concept was completely new. I had never experienced it anywhere before in my career. I had always been lucky enough to be a first-choice striker wherever I had played, so this situation was very unusual. I understand that it has to happen sometimes, and it helps if you know the reason you are being left out of the team. If I was the coach, I would always tell the player the reason. But although it's not easy coming in and out of the side, I have no problems with the manager. We had difficulties last season, but it is still possible to be friends in football even if you have problems in the dressing-room. Ruud and I still get on very well because we are both trying to do our jobs and do our best for Chelsea.'

Vialli's four Premiership goals so far had all come at Barnsley and he was indeed back on the bench against the Hammers as Frank Sinclair made his 220th appearance for the Blues – under five different managers – and Zola, remarkably, scored the first free-kick of the Premiership season.

Ex-world heavyweight champion Frank Bruno's guest appearance during the half-time presentations was entirely appropriate as West Ham's Eyal Berkovic and his team-mate John Moncur had actually come to blows. Roberto Di Matteo and Dennis Wise dived in to arbitrate.

Gullit, meanwhile, hauled off Dan Petrescu after only thirty-five minutes to stem the Hammers' early midfield domination. Petrescu tore off his shirt and stalked down the tunnel in high dudgeon, although Gullit sniggered later: 'He will feel better about it when he looks at the league table tomorrow morning and sees where we are.'

Harry Redknapp felt hard done by as West Ham returned home empty-handed despite an enterprising – if unfulfilled – performance on their travels: 'I thought we were in control and Chelsea didn't cause us any problems – that's why they had to make the substitution after barely half an hour.'

Zola punctured their resistance after fifty-six minutes. He burst through the inside-right channel onto Di Matteo's pass and clipped his shot towards the far post, only for Rio Ferdinand's outstretched boot to deflect it cruelly past Craig Forrest on the near post. That was especially tough on England starlet Ferdinand, who had earlier positioned himself immaculately on the line to head another Zola dead-ball special to safety. Only then did Chelsea take command, Di Matteo sliding a left-footer against an upright and Zola lashing a fierce twenty-yarder just over.

Gullit, though, contended: 'When I saw the West Ham players having a go at each other, I thought the tide might be turning in our favour.' Eight minutes from time, Zola delivered the decisive coup after Ian Pearce had been penalized for wrestling Mark Hughes to the ground just outside the box. Just as Ferdinand had been stationed on the line in the first half, John Hartson was now assigned to protect Forrest's right-hand post. But when Hartson changed his mind and drifted into no-man's land, Zola promptly whipped his set-piece speciality through the eye of the needle.

Hartson's goal from the penalty spot reduced the deficit within ninety seconds. But the three points put Chelsea in spitting distance of Manchester United, who crashed at Arsenal.

Unfortunately, Wise was involved in an incident with a West Ham fan who spat in his face as he went down the players' tunnel at the end. Furious Wise turned and appeared to spit back at his assailant. Gullit insisted: 'Maybe that supporter should be called up before the

FA. I don't know what happened, but it is very nasty to spit at anybody. I don't think anything will happen, though.'

The fiercely-contested London derby had been settled by Zola's stunning free-kick from the edge of the box, with Redknapp admitting: 'The little fella was different class. He's a magnificent player. He was the difference between the two teams. During the first half we were always in control and I didn't feel any threat from them. But as soon as he got that free-kick, I knew it would be trouble.

'If only he had switched sides, it might have been a different story.'

Gullit confirmed that Petrescu had been far from happy at being substituted so early: 'During the first half our midfield was a mess. We needed some organizing. I was talking all the time from the sidelines and I had to change it drastically. I had to take Dan off to get us back into the game. It was nothing personal. I had to make a decision for the good of the team. I know he took his shirt off when he was substituted, but I don't have a problem with that. I understand he's not happy because he's an international player. But players have to accept this and if we win, they can't really argue with it. Players with big egos are those who can usually do something extra. You need players like that and it's good to see them not happy at being taken off.'

So, Zola was finally back to his brilliant best. How? Well, apparently it was all down to his old scoring boots! He marked his free-kick winner with a bizarre touchline celebration, racing to the dugout and waving his foot at Gullit as laughing team-mates queued up to kiss his boot.

'Rudi said to me after the Aston Villa game that I wasn't scoring many goals this season because I'd changed my boots,' Zola explained. 'He suggested I used the old ones again and that's what I did in the last two games – and I scored with a free-kick in both. The celebrations were just to show him that I was wearing my old boots.'

Zola was ready to terrorize opposing goalkeepers again with his dead-ball prowess: 'I believe that I am going to score with every free-kick I take. I have been practising them in training every day, every week for an hour or so. And the important thing is that even if I don't score every time, they are always on target now. It is important for me to have a good feeling when I am lining up a shot, and I have that right now.'

Zola put his renewed confidence down to Gullit's decision to pick him for all Chelsea's biggest games while the rest of the squad was constantly being rested: 'We have four strikers at the club but it is my opinion that the coach prefers to play with a big striker and a short one for greater variety of skills. Maybe that's why I play all the games and he changes the other strikers. I am proud of that because it means the coach trusts me. And that is very important for me. I have to be confident to do my job, and I am really happy with the way I am playing. I have been playing well earlier in the season, but I wasn't scoring and that means your performance is not so perfect. Now I am playing well, I am in good form physically and I am also getting goals. And that makes my performance much, much better.'

Zola believed Chelsea were genuine championship contenders despite having lost four Premiership games already. He insisted: 'I think we can do it. The win against West Ham was a very positive thing for us because last season we would only have drawn that game. This time we are winning games even though we are not playing our best form. Manchester United's defeat at Arsenal was also a good result for us, because they are a great team and we have to stay as close as we can to them.'

Confirmation of Zola's regained form came from the media reviews of his performances. Rhys Williams in the London *Evening Standard* wrote: 'Zola was reproducing the form that made him Player of the Year last season. He scampered in and around West Ham's lofty back-line like a squirrel darting around an oak tree.'

Zola wanted news of his return to form to filter back to Cesare Maldini before the vital play-off with Russia: 'It is important to let people in Italy know that I am playing well. Maybe I will send a video to Maldini! I was left in the stand for the last game in Russia and the coach has not seen my good form. Now I will join the squad in better condition and I hope to have a better chance to be involved in the game.'

16

Italy Make It To France

Franco Zola's Italian place was on the line, no longer a favourite of coach Cesare Maldini. Zola had not played in Russia and was not going to win a recall for the second leg in his 'homecoming' to Naples. Zola knew his form with the club would have to become specatcular to win back Maldini's affections after the problems in Rome when the two 'fell-out' over the performance against England. Maldini insisted that he would not seek a 0–0 draw in Naples even though that would be enough to see Italy safely through to the finals; he even suggested his side was incapable of playing the tight defensive soccer which was the hallmark of the great Italian teams of the past. He had been criticized for being too cautious during the group stage, in which Italy drew 0–0 with Poland, Georgia and England – results which pushed them into the play-offs. So now, when some felt he might play for a goalless draw, Maldini said the Italians had to be more adventurous: 'Our 1–1 draw in Moscow was a good result, obviously, but it's not ideal. If you sit back and control the game and then they get a corner ten minutes from the end and score, then you're out of the World Cup. Anyway, we're not capable of playing that sort of game.'

The coach said Lazio striker Pierluigi Casiraghi was still carrying an injury to his left knee and experienced Juventus sweeper Ciro Ferrara was suffering a minor fracture to his nose, but that both men should be fit to play. So Zola, Naples' favourite son, was still not sure of his place in the tense days before the most vital match for Italy in many years.

Maldini said he felt that the Italians, who start their domestic season later than most other Europeans, were starting to get into gear after three consecutive draws since the summer break. 'History would suggest we play better in November than we do in September and October,' he said. 'Psychologically, we're fine. Our preparation will be the same as it is before any game. Let's just go out and play it.

'Zola is in good shape, but Del Piero is in fantastic form,' Maldini said of his two most imaginative players, 'Del Piero has made great strides. Zola is coming off a week with three [club] games, and he played so-so in the third.'

Maldini kept Zola guessing over whether he would return to the line-up. It was a straight choice between Zola and Ravanelli to accompany Casiraghi in attack, with Maldini saying: 'The difference would only be in having that extra bit of power [with Ravanelli], while Zola is that bit more inventive.' Roberto Di Matteo would keep his place after an impressive performance in Moscow, but Attilio Lombardo was ruled out for up to a month after picking up an injury in training. Keen to impress the coach, he tried an elegant flick and strained the muscles in his right thigh! Maldini said: 'We're all disappointed for Lombardo . . . but he was trying to do something which perhaps wasn't really him.'

Former Everton winger Andrei Kanchelskis was also set to miss out for Russia because of an injury picked up in the first leg. But Maldini added: 'From what I understand, they, too, are going to play to score goals, and in place of Kanchelskis they might play someone who has scored a few more goals than him – [Igor] Simutenkov.'

It was Casiraghi who scored the only goal of the game to book Italy's place in the finals. Maldini, who would undoubtedly have lost his job if Italy had failed to qualify for only the second time in their history, said tension had been the main theme of the match. 'The match was terrible from a point of view of nerves, but fortunately the Napoli crowd helped us overcome our fear,' he said. 'We couldn't just sit back and play for a 0–0 draw. We had to go out there and win.'

Di Matteo emphasized the enormity of the occasion: 'Forget about the pressure of an FA Cup Final, it was nothing compared to this. There was so much tension, I feel physically and emotionally drained. I want to sleep for thirty-six hours solid.'

Maldini acknowledged that the Italians had not played to their full potential during a long, hard campaign, and said he would make changes before the World Cup finals: 'We need to change. We need to bring in new players. We want to play at least two friendlies to try out new players.'

Italy's victory was greeted by a volley of firecrackers and a rumbling of drums from a 75,000-strong crowd. The only disappointment for the Naples faithful was Maldini's decision to leave their former idol Zola on the substitutes' bench – perhaps owing to a heavy pitch caused by a week of torrential rain in southern Italy. The crowd, who greeted their side with a message spelt out in fireworks which read 'Italy, we'll take you to France – Naples, the fans' capital', chanted periodically for Zola, but Maldini was evidently not in sentimental mood.

'I'm a little disappointed not to have played, but to compensate for this, at least we've qualified,' Zola said. 'My time will come. A player is not happy when he is not playing, so I am not satisfied with that. But on this occasion it did not matter. All that mattered was that we got to the World Cup.' Zola and Di Matteo paid tribute to their leader on the field, captain Cesare Maldini. 'He is our reference point,' said Zola. 'Irreplaceable' as player and skipper, added Di Matteo.

Di Matteo lapped up Italy's qualification to join England. 'I have a message for the whole of England – we will see you in France,' he said. 'There we want to play you again and then we will see who is the best.'

He knew what would have awaited him and Zola at the Harlington training ground had Italy failed: 'Myself and Gianfranco really took the mick when we beat England, so I know we were both expecting some of the same if we had failed in this play-off. Thankfully that didn't happen.' Zola recounted his conversation with Graeme Le Saux after they returned from the Rome game. Le Saux proudly swapped shirts with him, and Zola recalled: 'He said that he was sorry for us and we would probably take the qualification in the next two games. He was very friendly!' Zola's response? 'Oh, just "Bastard!"'

No mickey-taking from Gullit; he was delighted Italy had made it to France. 'Now we can have some quiet! The World Cup qualifiers are over and I am happy for Di Matteo and Zola that they are going.

I am pleased for the players themselves and I am pleased the qualifying games are over – there will be less players flying around the world now.' Unfortunately, that was not the case as countries wanting to call upon Chelsea's large contingent of foreign stars began making their plans for build-up matches and get togethers.

Gullit was also delighted that Zola was back to his peak form even though he was again left out of the Italian side: 'Franco got his second free-kick goal in a few days and suddenly everyone says he is playing well again. But I thought that he was playing well all the time before. If he isn't scoring, then to the fans maybe he is not playing so well, but we were getting good results and, for the manager, who has to see more, he was playing well. We have a busy few days coming up. Maybe it won't be so quiet after all, but at least we'll all be together.'

Zola wasn't even in the squad as Gullit dispatched the kids to churn out an extra-time win over Southampton in the Coca-Cola Cup to reach the last eight. Teenager Jody Morris broke the Saints' stubborn resistance three minutes from the end of extra-time to put Chelsea, already on the last eight of the Cup-Winners' Cup, into their second quarter-finals. Handicapped by the loss of Petrescu, on international duty, and Vialli suspended, Gullit made nine changes with stars such as Zola, Di Matteo and Leboeuf rested in favour of youngsters Mark Nicholls, Morris and outstanding debutante Nick Crittenden.

Gianfranco Zola celebrated precisely twelve months of Premiership football by describing it as the best year of his life. A few days after a daughter, Joelle, was born to Ruud Gullit and Estelle, they were celebrating a different kind of birthday down at Chelsea's training ground as they prepared for the match at Blackburn Rovers.

'It is impossible to think I could have done so well,' Zola reflected. 'When I came to England, I knew it was at the start of a new adventure and I was very positive, because I felt I could do good things. But I never thought it would go so well for me. I am so happy with the way I've played. My life is perfect.' Now Franco was going back to Ewood Park where it had all started after his arrival from Parma. He wanted to increase his sixteen goals for the club, convinced he could add the Premiership title to the FA Cup and his accolade of Footballer of the Year.

He said: 'I am approaching the next twelve months the way I approached the last twelve. The key to the title is that all the players keep playing as we have been. This time we have proved we have done well also against the smaller clubs. This is another season and Chelsea grew a lot. We have another confidence in ourselves and the team will not want to repeat the mistakes we made last season. It is a good sign, because every time we lose a game we win the next one; this shows Chelsea is a great team.'

But Stamford Bridge old boys Ron Harris and Peter Osgood still doubted whether the current side had defensive abilities or the aggression for an achievement that had proved beyond them in the early seventies. Osgood said: 'They are a great flair side who can score goals, but we've conceded three to Arsenal, four to Liverpool and three at Coventry. You can't go on doing that to win the league.' Hardman Harris added: 'The side we played in, our back four could have a little kick and a dig. Nowadays football is a non-contact sport.'

Zola appeared his usual modest self when he spoke at a press conference about his first year in English football: 'You have to be positive when you start at a new club, but you cannot expect what I have had. It has been a hard year, but the payment for it has been special. We are in a good position in the league and we have to keep going. We know we are a good strong team and that we can win the championship. That is a beautiful feeling, but it's also a dangerous one. We are a target for other sides now. This is a crucial period. The signs are positive, but we cannot get lazy.'

Gullit applauded the way Zola had adapted to a new culture. The player-manager enthused: 'When I bought Franco, I knew what he was capable of. But he was making some big changes in his life, coming from the Latin culture to England, and I couldn't expect he would adapt so quickly. He proved himself right from the start, although I think it helped that there were so many quality players around him.' Zola was just regaining his scoring form, but Gullit must have worried Premiership rivals when he suggested the best was still to come. He explained: 'Franco always gives 100 per cent effort. There isn't anything I can ask him to do extra, except start beating Duncan Ferguson in the air! But he always tries to do things he does well, even better, on his own.'

Zola reciprocated by saying he was happy to play his part in the coach's squad system: 'Maybe four or five years ago it would have been hard for me to accept it, but when I play football I am like a child, and somebody said to me recently that I am not a child any more. Now it is not a problem for me to miss the odd game.'

The celebrations of his first year at Chelsea turned sour with a 1–0 defeat at Blackburn that wrecked the team's chance to move within striking distance of Manchester United. The vital strike came from defender Gary Croft as he cracked in his first Blackburn goal with the venom and accuracy of a seasoned campaigner. Gullit and his players hastily showered and changed for the dash back to the capital. They were on their way to the airport less than thirty minutes after the final whistle – without saying a word to the waiting media.

Zola and Hughes were the first-choice strike partnership, Flo came on as sub, Vialli remained on the bench and the chances went begging. Zola had a free header from two yards out after Wise put over a deliciously inviting cross. Zola took aim and nodded past the post. Then, when his skipper headed down into his path, he uncharacteristically shot wide of Tim Flowers. The Blackburn keeper couldn't believe his luck and admitted: 'Christ Almighty, when I saw Zola up with the ball on his forehead, I thought: "Get your coat on, Tim, and leave." I was fully expecting to see the net bulge and I was delighted to see his header shave the post. The second was knocked down to him and he dragged it wide. When he gets his head down from there, you expect the worst.'

Chelsea had crashed to their fifth Premiership defeat and the title was slipping away. Flowers added: 'They can't afford to be losing more than that. The year we won the championship, our sixth defeat was at Liverpool on the last day of the season. But I still fancy Chelsea's chances. I've watched some of their past players on Sky TV saying they don't. But I disagree. In my mind, any team with firepower like that has got a good chance. They have got good defenders, too, and they will upset one or two of the title favourites.'

Blackburn had risen to second place under Roy Hodgson, a coach with Continental experience. Flowers observed: 'The lads have responded to Roy. He's taken no crap from anyone. He put his foot down from day one. We train morning and afternoon and he's taken the fish and chips off the lunch-time menu. We're eating pasta and all the right food. It's all so professional. We're fit all right after working all day. In fact, the lads were praying for the clocks to go back because at least it would get dark at 3.30pm and we could stop. But he still sends us running in the dark. We've got luminous hats now.'

When Zola made his Chelsea debut, Chelsea were fifth. That was precisely the position a year later. But there had been vast changes. A year earlier the team at Blackburn had been Grodas, Duberry, Burley, Clarke, Petrescu, Zola, Di Matteo, Wise, Minto, Vialli, Hughes. Only Clarke, Petrescu, Di Matteo, Hughes and Zola started a year later. The Chelsea team in a 4–4–2 formation was: De Goey; Sinclair, Leboeuf, Clarke, Babayaro; Petrescu, Newton, Di Matteo, Wise; Hughes, Zola. Vialli was on the bench.

For forty years, Ian Collier has supported the Blues. In an issue of the club's official newspaper *Onside*, he nominated Zola as his No. 1 choice in the 'best ever Chelsea player' category. He wrote: 'I must apologise to Jimmy Greaves, Bobby Tambling, John Hollins, Peter Osgood, Charlie Cooke, Alan Hudson, Ray Wilkins and the rest of his current team-mates, but Franco Zola is the best player I have seen in a Chelsea shirt. I cannot remember seeing any player with better balance, ball control, speed of thought and ability to shoot with both feet. He is the only Chelsea player during my forty years who would get a regular place in a World XI. Apart from Peter Osgood, no newcomer has had such an immediate impact on the team, and the beauty of it is that Franco gives the impression of being modest and down to earth. I only hope that we have the privilege of seeing him play out the full term of his contract.'

Such had been Zola's impact that he was one of the main candidates nominated for European Footballer of the year. Peter Schmeichel, Dennis Bergkamp, Ryan Giggs and Juninho were also shortlisted.

Only three Englishmen – Sir Stanley Matthews (1956), Sir Bobby Charlton (1966) and Kevin Keegan (1978 and 1979) – have ever collected the top individual accolade in European football. David Beckham, Robbie Fowler, Ian Wright and Alan Shearer were the four Englishmen among the fifty nominees.

FA technical consultant Jimmy Armfield said: 'It would be a great boost if we could win, because these awards are very prestigious and we must be in with a chance. To win it you have to beat players such as Sammer, Klinsmann, Djorkaeff and Zidane, so it really would be something if one of our boys could do it. I suppose if Alan Shearer had not got injured and was still scoring, he would have had a bit of a chance.'

Armfield firmly believed the influx of foreign talent into the Premiership had shown the way for England's rising stars: 'The foreign players who have come into our league have set new standards. But our players have lifted themselves and have worked hard at making themselves better. We now have some terrific young players coming through to add to our experienced internationals like Shearer. If Bergkamp won it would be good for Arsenal and the Premier League, but it would not be that big a boost for England,' he said.

17

The First Hat-Trick

Gianfranco bought a new Yamaha piano for his Knightsbridge home, scored the first hat-trick of his career, and was hoping that Chelsea could reach number one in the championship hit-parade. 'Today was special, perhaps the best Chelsea have played since I came here,' he said after the 4–0 win over Derby at the Bridge in late November.

Ruud Gullit refused to discuss Chelsea's title possibilities despite the satisfaction he took from that display, with Zola in sheer majestic form. But the little Italian said: 'I said right from the start of the season that we are one of the four or five teams who can win the championship, and we are now confirming that. We are second in the table and we have played very well to get there, but this is a crucial time.'

Gullit actually described Chelsea's performance as 'perfect'. Coaches throughout the world seek perfection, but few attain it. Chelsea's football was exquisite in its execution – rarely do you see a side control the game so totally that you can count on one hand the number of misplaced passes. Gullit observed: 'In every aspect, it was the perfect game for us. You can't always win a game just by playing as well as we did today, because sometimes you have to work hard. But everything we did today went right and I am very happy.'

Zola was the inspiration with his three goals and revealed that he had supplemented his electric keyboard with a stand-up piano to achieve relaxation at home to counterbalance his frustration at not scoring as many goals as he had wanted. He explained: 'I'm a striker and goals are an important part of a striker's role. When I score, I become more confident in myself. At the beginning of the season I couldn't play any better football because I started the pre-season later, and it is normal you don't play your best football because of that. Then I started to play better but I was not scoring goals and I was trying to cheer myself. First, it is important to play good – and goals are a consequence of that.'

Zola's first hat-trick 'in an official game' was so special that he wouldn't let go of the match ball: 'I waited in the tunnel for the referee, he couldn't escape me. I then took it in the shower and I also kept it when I had a massage. All my team-mates have signed it. My son wanted to play with me and the ball, but I had to tell him I couldn't.'

With his tie askew and a Man of the Match magnum of champagne beside him, Zola was full of smiles as he pointed to the bubbly and said: 'It's too much for me; I don't need it!'

This was the hat-trick game Franco would never forget. Goal number one was a slightly angled twenty-five-yard drive after an excellent pass down the line from Graeme Le Saux, controlled by Mark Hughes and laid off to Roberto Di Matteo, who in turn slid it to his Italian compatriot in the twelfth minute.

Goal number two came in the sixty-seventh minute after a spectacular overhead kick by Hughes was fumbled by keeper Mark Poom. Zola, showing great awareness and determination, reacted quickest to Poom's mistake. His first attempt was saved but he touched in the second rebound.

Goal number three was sheer poetry, with Zola's first-time back-heel flick to Di Matteo being returned with the perfect pass which enabled Franco to slip it past the advancing keeper.

Zola said: 'I scored two with the right and one with the left, and in the first half the keeper made a great save – although the referee didn't think it was a save and gave a goal-kick. I've scored two goals I don't remember how many times, in Italy, especially at Parma. Today was special, maybe the best we've played; everything worked well, defensively, attacking, creating and then scoring four goals – perfect.'

Gullit had made a point of reassuring Zola that he was happy with his performances, and that the goals would come eventually. Gullit revealed: 'I had a talk with Gianfranco recently, when I felt I needed to reassure him about things. People were saying how he wasn't scoring, so I told him he means more to the team than that. I told him I liked how he was creating chances for other people and helping his team-mates to score. I told him I wasn't judging him on his goals – and that seemed to be a relief to him. Now, he is still in excellent form but is also scoring goals as well!'

Zola said: 'When the manager told me I was doing well – even though I wasn't scoring – it made me very proud and happy. Most people judge strikers on their goals and although that is important, I felt I was still playing well. So I was happy the manager appreciated that. He has four strikers, really good strikers doing really well, and we are playing good football and sometimes I didn't. But he said to me, "Don't worry, it is important you do a job even if you don't score." That gave me confidence, more tranquillity, or should I say serenity. But now I think I am getting back to my best. This is the first hat-trick I have scored in my career and I am very happy. I have scored three goals against friends, but this is the first in a competitive match.'

His next statement must have seemed ominous to the rest of the top flight: 'I am getting better than I was last season. I feel I am more consistent than I was and helping the team a lot more. But that was my opinion before this match, so it's not judged on the hat-trick. Now I hope to continue scoring as well as playing well.'

Gullit never had any doubts that Zola was a vital part of his team even when he wasn't scoring goals: 'I'm happy that everybody can score in this team. I felt that Franco had confidence already and that he was confident enough to score goals eventually, but he wanted it desperately because although he knew inside the club how we judged him, outside he was judged on goals. So he was happy to get these goals to relieve the pressure.'

Gullit had even enjoyed watching the Derby game, and added: 'I would have been happy to see it as a spectator. It was good to hear people screaming behind you, "Sexy football!" But the next game could be totally different. You must understand you can't play games

like this all the time, because players are not on top form, there are
injuries or they are not in good shape. Then, sometimes you have to
compensate on other things and find a solution. But I was very happy
today because in every aspect I think we played a perfect game.'

The day belonged to Zola, but he was keen to pass the credit on to
his team-mates. He said: 'It was an excellent performance from everyone in the team and I am very satisfied with the way things went.'

Perhaps the best endorsement came from Derby boss Jim Smith.
After seeing his side mauled, the Bald Eagle confessed: 'We did not
play well – we were soft. It was men against boys. I am disappointed
in us, but I do not want to take anything away from Chelsea. They
were outstanding and they would have beaten anybody playing like
they did here. The front two were absolutely magnificent, Zola and
Hughes were brilliant; they were also very solid at the back, in fact
solid throughout. It could have been eight – we did quite well! I
honestly think they can win the league. They certainly have the squad
and the players to do it ... but they've got to finish in front of
Manchester United. Yet Chelsea could have beaten most teams the
way they played today – very positive, never gave us an inch of room.
They won the battle quite easily.'

But high praise like that was something Gullit dismissed. He
stressed: 'There is still a very long way to go. Obviously, I am happy
with the position we are in, but experience has taught me that you
cannot read into anything at this stage of the season.'

The last time Chelsea won the championship forty-three years ago,
Ted Drake was the manager and Roy Bentley the star, in the days of
Brylcreem and laced-up balls. Now it was sexy football and sweet-
sounding music from the happy feet of Zola. What a contrast it would
be if Chelsea were to be champions again.

With typical humour and yet another display of his white teeth,
Zola said: 'I must go now, because I fear my son will be kicking my
match ball against a wall somewhere. I do not want it damaged. It is
so special to me.'

The resounding victory briefly put Chelsea level on points with
Manchester United, but the champions responded the following day
with an equally emphatic win over title-chasing Blackburn.

Chelsea's demolition of Derby, though, had the pundits drooling.

Alan Hudson in the *Sporting Life* wrote: 'Their passing, movement and ball skills took the game to a level that only Manchester United at their best can match in the Premiership. And at the end of it all was the pocket-sized genius Gianfranco Zola, who scored a thrilling hat-trick and popped up in more scoring positions than I did in my entire career! After a slow start to the season, Zola is on fire and that can only spell good news for manager Ruud Gullit, who must now be harbouring serious thoughts of a place in next season's European Cup, if not as champions then certainly as runners-up.'

Pele came to the Bridge on 3 December, the day before the World Cup draw, to launch after-school classes at Premiership clubs. Graeme Le Saux, Dennis Wise and Zola were there to meet the first pupils. But the following weekend's derby clash at White Hart Lane was also on their minds. It would be a test of Chelsea's staying power, as Zola argued: 'When you reach the top, that is the moment to show you deserve to be top of the league. We will see, and I am looking forward to Saturday when we have to show everybody if we really can win it.' Of next opponents Spurs, Zola added: 'They are a good team in a little trouble but they are improving. Only the best Chelsea will win there.'

To emphasise Chelsea's new status as genuine championship contenders, Zola played a pivotal role in the 6–1 blitz of Tottenham at White Hart Lane, only the second time since 1935 Spurs had conceded so many goals on home territory.

Perfection, Gullit had said after Derby – yet he changed his team again, dropping Hughes down to the bench and bringing in Tore Andre Flo. So what happens? Another hat-trick – this time for the Norwegian who had, like Zola, been patiently waiting to get into his goalscoring rhythm.

Zola began it all with typical ingenuity, wriggling past Ramon Vega and crossing to the near post for Flo to head into the corner. Vega headed an equalizer in the forty-third minute, but in the second half Chelsea turned on the magic. It was too much for Spurs; it would have been too much for anyone bar Manchester United. Again Zola was heavily involved, taking Flo's header in his stride and finding Dan Petrescu, whose cross was headed in by Roberto Di Matteo just after the break.

Chelsea then conjured the goal of the game, Petrescu the goal of the month. Frank Leboeuf launched a sixty-yard pass and the Romanian caught it on the volley: 3–1. Even the hard-to-please Gullit and his entire entourage on the bench applauded that one.

Zola's chipped pass over Scales dropped perfectly for Flo to grab his second, then the little Italian's slide-rule pass created the fifth for substitute Mark Nicholls. Gullit enjoyed that most of all – it was Nicholls's first senior goal for Chelsea.

Finally, the outstanding Leboeuf stepped forward to win possession in defence and a great pass found Flo, who chipped over Ian Walker for his hat-trick.

Christian Gross had to endure the worst nightmare of his coaching career on his grisly White Hart Lane debut. 'I have never lost by this score before as a coach,' he admitted with the angry booing of distraught Spurs fans still ringing in his ears.

Gullit said: 'The title race over? No, the competition is just starting to get interesting. But Spurs did not deserve to be beaten by this score. They were as good as us in the first half. I wasn't too happy with our first-half display, but I saw weaknesses in the Spurs team and I knew how to exploit them. So I got some bottles and showed my players what to do – and they did it.' Chelsea's remarkable record at Spurs continued – they had now won five and drawn four of their last nine league games there.

The chance materialized to join Manchester United at the top of the Premiership, but Leeds were always going to be tough opposition. Zola said on the eve of the game at the Bridge: 'Psychologically it's very important to beat Leeds, because we would go joint top with United. And when someone is first and you are right behind, that gives you even more motivation. United have shown in the Premiership and the Champions' League just what they are capable of achieving. And we have shown we can win things, too – in fact both sides could end up with a few honours this season. But the key thing is to keep it all going, and when you are in front it's very hard – everybody wants to knock you off top spot. If we want to stay at the top we have to keep being consistent, because otherwise we would be satisfied with being a good side, not the best.'

Chelsea had won seven out of their last eight League and Cup matches, hitting the 10 goals against Derby and Spurs with Zola, convinced the team wouldn't crack under the strain of chasing so much silverware. He said: 'It's very important we follow on from last summer's FA Cup Final success, because it's things like that which give you confidence and control within yourself. And when you win a game in the manner we did against Spurs, that gives you great satisfaction and confidence. That means we are strong physically and mentally, and it makes you even stronger. One of the worst things you can do in football is relax, but I believe we have the mental strength to cope. I think the pressure would come if we were near the bottom of the table, but we have everything to play for.'

Gullit again changed a winning side, but there was little room to manoeuvre against Leeds with Mark Hughes suspended. Zola added: 'Sometimes we might not find out the team until ninety minutes before kick-off, and you can end up on the bench. But all the players here accept the situation. It is not a problem for us. We can see it works and the good things that are happening. We have a big squad and can change many players – it gives the chance to rest some. The manager and the company have built this big squad to compete in many competitions. It means sometimes you can be on the bench, but it does not mean you are not good. It is just to give everyone the chance to have a good game, and to give you a little rest that is necessary to be ready for the next game.'

Well, the Leeds match turned out to be one of the big frustrations of the season. George Graham assigned Lucas Radebe to man-mark Zola, and after just six minutes, Radebe kicked the Italian from behind and was booked. The contest was non-existent, it degenerated into a war of attrition until Leeds had both Alf-Inge Haarland and Gary Kelly sent off before half time. Even with a full half against nine men Chelsea failed to break down a stubborn all-out defensive although Flo had a header 'goal' disallowed.

Chelsea embarked on a Christmas and New Year period of wild swings in form and results that left their season in a precarious position.

They were back to their most formidable with a 4–1 win at Sheffield Wednesday with Dan Petrescu opening the scoring against his old club, Vialli getting back among the Premiership goals, plus a penalty from Leboeuf, and a fine finish from Flo.

Dennis Wise explained the reason for his bust-up with team-mate Frank Sinclair after they were involved in a war of words following the build-up which led to Mark Pembridge's twenty-five-yard goal at Hillsborough. That only made the score 3–1 to Chelsea and they almost immediately made it 4–1, but Wise was not happy with his side's defending and made his feelings known. 'It was a sloppy goal,' said Wise. 'I spoke to Frank about it and he didn't take it at all well and what he said to me I didn't take well and that was it. Sloppiness is not tolerated anymore. We want to get as many goals as we can and not concede any. It's not a problem. It's over and done with. We just had an argument on the pitch, and that was it. I love him to bits still. I've always been like that and I'm not going to change. It shows Frank is like that as well, it was him having a go at me as well. It got a reaction out of him because he's got the hump – maybe because he's done something wrong – and then he told me off and said "next time you do something wrong I'll tell you".'

Next was an assignment with old foes Wimbledon on Boxing Day. One of Gullit's first games in charge saw the Dons triumph 4–1 at Stamford Bridge and Wise admitted: 'I think we learnt a lesson from that. It was a day that we didn't play well and they did. We have done quite well in the last few games against them so hopefully we can keep it going and now all the lads know what's coming. We know what they're like and we've got to be up for it, as simple as that. We know how they play and they're capable of beating anyone.'

Gullit gave his players Christmas night at home. Instead of following the stereotyped manager's blueprint and confining his squad to barracks before their Boxing Day match, Gullit agreed to let them remain in domestic bliss. Sinclair said: 'It just goes to show again that Ruud is his own man and doesn't feel he has to copy other managers. Most Premiership players will probably be spending Christmas night locked away in a hotel before their games on Boxing Day. But although we are training on Christmas morning, like we normally would the day before a match, he has allowed us to go home and spend the night with our families. That was a nice surprise for us because, as long as I've been at Chelsea, I can't remember too many Christmas fixtures when we haven't been packed off to a hotel.

Obviously we've got to be sensible about it and repay his trust by laying off the turkey. Players are the same as anyone else: they like to spend time with their families, and this will be my little daughter's first Christmas so it will be nice to be with her.' Gullit gave his players the option of spending Christmas night at home or in a hotel. There was a unanimous vote in favour of the former, and Gullit readily bowed to democracy on the understanding that his players checked in at least two hours before kick-off.

But it was a disappointing Boxing Day draw after taking an early lead with an exhilarating Vialli goal, the Italian turning in from close range a Flo low cross after a neat piece of foot work to beat the defender on the byline.

Zola was left on the bench but came on after an hour to liven up the attack and come closest to a winner. But Gullit's side were held to a draw for the second successive home game, trailing United by seven points with the champions a staggering 6–1 on to retain their title. There was precious little to commend this match, with Wimbledon hardly mustering a decent build-up and Chelsea finding it tough to thread their way through a packed midfield. Leboeuf smashed the ball into the empty dug-out at the final whistle to illustrate the frustrations. Gullit insisted: 'The truth is that outside the club people expect more of us than we already are. That is a compliment to me and my team but we are still taking things step by step. We haven't yet taken that giant step which would put us there. I've been there as a player and I know what has to be done. We are going the right way and we have made an improvement on last year. But we have to be realistic. Everybody complained that our defence was bad. Now our defence is excellent. All the time I've never said we'd be contenders and that's why I am happy the way things are going.'

Frank Sinclair's calamitous back-pass gift-wrapped an equaliser for Michael Hughes. Gullit said: 'It was a very vital moment. We could have been two or three up. We were in control all over. It was a sloppy goal to give away and it affected the players.' To add to the farce skipper Dennis Wise passed the ball out wide to Steve Clarke as he was warming up to come on as substitute!

When an opening presented itself on the edge of the box Zola's shot was deflected wide. Kinnear said: 'Not many teams can afford the luxury of having Zola on the bench and I was surprised when the team sheet came in.'

Chelsea squandered four points in their last two home matches after dropping just three out from their first twenty-one.

Manchester United have that killer instinct that Chelsea are still trying to discover. As Kinnear said: 'Manchester United had £12 million worth of substitutes against us and Chelsea are in that same position. When they scored after about seven minutes I feared the worst. But as the game progressed there was not much difference between us – and we might even have had a chance to nick one on the break.'

There was a glimmer of hope when Manchester United stumbled 3–2 at Coventry, but the next day Chelsea crashed 1–0 at Southampton, much to the displeasure of Gullit, as it left Chelsea seven points adrift of United going into their momentous third round FA Cup tie.

Gullit reacted immediately after a shocking result against the club Chelsea had already beaten twice this season. 'I don't usually get angry but I am tonight.' Kevin Davies's sixteenth minute goal brought Chelsea to their sixth defeat of the season, destroying the chance of taking a second place in the Premiership. Even the bookies were closing the door, upping the odds from 6–1 to 9–1 on Chelsea ripping the title from United.

Gullit refused to mask his disappointment. 'It's a major, major blow to us. We threw it away. It was stupid, suicidal. We spoke about tactics before the match and then the team promptly went out and forgot about them. We must now try and overcome this game, and lick our wounds like a dog that has been beaten. We have now dropped seven points from our last four games and it is such a pity. It means every match now is going to be so vital and it will be difficult because our confidence is a bit damaged.

'I am not the type of manager to force players to cancel a day off and come in and talk about what went wrong, but on this occasion I shall sit on the coach and think about it and make my decision in the morning. I am angry. You prepare teams, you explain the dangers to them and they do the exact opposite.'

Without suspended Dennis Wise and injured Frank Leboeuf, it

called for even more changes than usual. Either Vialli – twelve goals from fourteen games – or Flo would have been odds on playing. Instead, Gullit recalled Mark Hughes following a three match suspension, banking on his love affair of playing against Southampton to play upfront with Zola. Inexplicably, the team that scored ten goals in two away games were sub-standard. Chelsea had more possession, more players of quality but rarely the ability to unlock a team of honest journeymen not afraid to leave their foot in. It wasn't until Gullit shuffled his pack and sent on Flo for Petrescu did Chelsea manage to show true passion. Then Saints keeper Paul Jones was forced into action deflecting shots, or looking in amazement as Chelsea continually flitted away chances into the night air.

Mark Hughes wanted the mouth-watering FA Cup clash against champions Manchester United to be the perfect opportunity to pick themselves up. Hughes was awarded an MBE in the New Year's Honours List, his team-mates bowing in front of him, calling him 'sir' in a light-hearted tribute at the club's training ground.

The Welsh international, who has won four FA Cup winners' medals including Chelsea's triumph last May, is immensely proud of the official recognition for his contribution to the game. 'I won't have any problems in thinking about anything other than the game itself on Sunday. It is the perfect match for us. We were all very disappointed on Monday to lose to Southampton but playing Manchester United is the ideal way to pick ourselves up. I've got very fond memories of my time at United but they know I won't have anything else on my mind apart from beating them. It's a shame that one of us has to go out so early, but if we can beat them we will have knocked out the best team in the competition and we would then fancy our chances. It's a bit like last year when we played Liverpool and hopefully we can get the same result.' Hughes was conscious of the competitive nature of the games between Chelsea and United, yet insisted that there was no bad blood between the two sides, saying: 'We are just two teams striving for success and emotions obviously run high but nothing ever lingers.'

The Welshman retained his modesty despite becoming Mark Hughes MBE. Asked why he felt he had been honoured, he paused, then said: 'I know I'm not everybody's favourite player but hopefully

I've brought pleasure to people during my career. I suppose it's for
longevity as well. But, mainly, I've just been lucky enough to play in
some great teams and this award is very much also a reflection on
those I have played alongside as well as the tremendous support I
have received from my family throughout my career.'

For teams with FA Cup ambitions, Manchester United were the
one to avoid when the third round draw was made. Everybody feared
them. Except Chelsea. Pitting the league champions against the cup
holders at the first hurdle instead of in a dream final, ensured a
thriller. The Londoners have an unrivalled record at Old Trafford,
where they have lost only twice in the past twenty-two years, and in
recent seasons as United have increased their domestic dominance,
Chelsea have been a consistent thorn in their side. In United's
brilliant 1993–94 season they lost just four league games – two of
them to Chelsea. This season they drew 1–1 in the season-opening
Charity Shield, United winning on penalties, and it was 2–2 at Old
Trafford in a premier league meeting in September. Chelsea remembered the two most recent FA Cup meetings; the 1996 semifinal (2–1
to United) and the 1994 final (4–0 to United). Chelsea's best hope
appeared to be a home draw followed by another dose of their
special Old Trafford medicine in the replay.

'It's a massive game,' said Alex Ferguson, 'and in my eleven years
at the club I've had the pleasure, and at times anxiety, of getting a real
hard third round draw. But they don't come bigger or better than this.
It should be terrific. Ruud Gullit has done a fantastic job at Chelsea.
It's fair to say that twelve months ago you couldn't have envisaged
Chelsea as one of our chief rivals for the title. But that is what they
now are. I believe that Chelsea and Liverpool are the two teams who
will push us all the way this season. What Ruud has given Chelsea is
a big-time attitude. They've always been a big club off the pitch but
they've not always had the players to match that ambition on the
pitch. Ruud has bought players with vast international experience,
players who don't freeze on the big occasion. He also has one of the
domestic game's most experienced big-time players in Mark Hughes.
What Ruud has done is mould all these players into a very good
team. They are now genuine challengers for the major trophies and I
can't pay him a bigger compliment than that.'

Zola's admiration for Manchester United was evident of the task facing Chelsea. He said: 'You always hope for an easy draw at this stage. People have said our results against United in the League have been impressive, but that counts for nothing on the day.

'Some people may expect a goal feast, but I think one goal may separate the sides. These games are often like that. A spot of luck or a defensive error creates the only chance of the game. I still feel it will be very entertaining because both sides like to play football. In a way, we're both playing into each other's hands.

'I believe that Manchester United, especially, have moved on from last season; they are improving all the time, which means the rest of us have to improve just to try to keep up with them. In defence, Pallister is so strong, they are flying in midfield, where Scholes and Beckham are so impressive – everyone is better than last year and they focus more than any other team in the Premiership. I marvel at them. I can honestly say United are playing some fantastic, exciting football, some of the best I have ever seen.

'Even for an older player like myself, when you see some of the stuff United and Chelsea have played this season, it gets you so excited. If you are not playing, be it on the bench or say, watching on TV, you just want to go right out there and join in. It can be quite emotional!

'I love football and it's been a real pleasure to have taken part in some of our matches this season – that's the feeling I get when I am on the pitch. Some of our play in some of our games, for instance against Derby and Spurs in the Premiership, has been excellent, and that can and does inspire the younger players. Yes, we are also doing well this season, and we can do better. It's good for football when you have two teams like us creating a good competition in the Premiership – and now in the FA Cup. We have a good respect for them but we do not fear them. Manchester United are setting the standards for all the rest – they are the target for everyone. But we know on our day we are capable of beating anyone and we now know we can win things, as we proved at Wembley last May. It is very important we follow on from that success because it is things like that which give you confidence and control within yourself.'

Chelsea's form dipped, though, with disappointing home draws against nine-man Leeds and then Wimbledon, despite taking the lead. Yet, they were still third in the Premiership, meet First Division Ipswich in the Coca-Cola Cup quarter-finals and were also through to the last eight of the Cup-Winners' Cup. United, knocked out of the Coca-Cola competition by Ipswich, are also through to the last eight in the Champions' League.

Zola said: 'We could both end up winning a few trophies this season. United are the side who have shown the best football in their European matches so far and are probably the favourites to win the Champions' League. They're an awesome side, capable of beating anyone. But the biggest danger is if they become complacent. Last season Juventus went into the European Cup Final feeling they just needed to turn up, and lost out to Borussia Dortmund. Right now, United are where Juventus were twelve months ago. I'm not saying they will become complacent, but the signs are there to be heeded.

'They have got some good young players, they have a lot of power, and that can only help the national side as well. But they have to keep winning and that is very hard because, when you are in front, all the other sides want to knock you off the top – they all want your place.

'The target for Chelsea this year is to win the title, but it is going to be hard for us. We didn't play well over Christmas and now to prepare for a cup tie like this means we have to be extremely focused on one game. The league needs concentration every game and that requires the quality of good footballers and also the qualities of a man.

'We have a very good side here but the hard work has to be done now. There are plenty of games left and who knows what can happen? Your chances can be affected by loss of form, injuries, all sorts of things. But we are better equipped to challenge than we have been previously.'

Zola continues to leave the kind of impression on Chelsea that Eric Cantona had on the youth at United and Jurgen Klinsmann, in his first spell at White Hart Lane, had on the young guns of Tottenham Hotspur – an idol to whom they gravitated. 'I did not know Cantona, but I see the traces of him still at United,' Zola said. 'When a quality foreign player comes to a club, it should have an effect on the young English players. They have someone to confront, to compare with and to follow. When I was a teenager at home, there were players like Maradona, Platini and Zico in *Serie A*. They were an example we tried to copy and it made us more productive as footballers. They put a little more competition into the system and that's good for the level of quality in the game.

'I know I have helped at Chelsea. When I first saw Dennis Wise, he was a good player, but now he has reached a new level, his intelligence has increased and, in my opinion, he is one of the best midfield players I have seen in the last year. He should be in the England squad.' Unfortunately, Wise was suspended for the big cup tie – and it made a far bigger difference than anyone expected.

How Gullit would cope without Wise, and with no recognised alternative with Newton and Poyet injured, was the big talking point. One of the many pundits, Ron Atkinson, felt Vialli should play up front with Hughes, and Zola playing behind them. He argued in his *Sun* column: 'Chelsea may have struggled at Saints, but the one shining light was Zola. He will cause damage to the best team in the world if given space. If United fail to close him down, they really will have problems.'

Despite the difficulty of the draw, Chelsea still had a capacity to lose to the lower teams but beat the best. Cup Final match winner Di Matteo observed: 'We have never lost to Manchester United since I have been here, and we still think we can challenge them for the league. There are so many games yet. I know no team has won losing more than six games but we will fight to the end.' He reluctantly conceded that what sets United apart from the rest of the Premiership is the quality and depth of their squad. 'The main problem for us at the moment is that we have got a few suspensions and injuries and you can't just replace important players like Dennis Wise, Gustavo Poyet and Frank Leboeuf. When everybody is fit we have a strong team.'

What happened at the Bridge as Chelsea opened their defence was one of the most traumatic setbacks of the season. . . . a mind-boggling 5–3 defeat after being five-nil down. If Chelsea were portrayed as the second best team in the land, then God help the rest!

Catapulted out of the FA Cup as spectacularly as they won it. Cosmopolitan Chelsea took twenty-seven years to win the FA Cup again and twenty-seven minutes to throw it away once David Beckham's free kick skidded past goalkeeper Ed de Goey for his second goal, aided by a piece of 'trickery' in the defensive wall with Teddy Sheringham pulling Dan Petrescu away to create the gap for Beckham to aim at.

The in-form Andy Cole had a hand in Beckham's opener and then collected two more goals to bring his relentless run to seventeen in the last sixteen games to forge ahead of Ian Wright in Glenn Hoddle's World Cup goalscorer's pecking order. By the time Sheringham headed the fifth goal in the seventy-fifth minute, the Cup holders were spiralling out of control towards Gullit's heaviest defeat in eighteen months of management.

Gullit was feeling even sicker after making the effort to turn up at Stamford Bridge suffering with a bad dose of flu and was at least cheered by the restoration of pride in an amazing three-goal burst at the end. On came substitute Gianluca Vialli to score twice with his own virtuoso performance in front of goal. Starting with a glorious Graeme Le Saux chip over Schmeichel, it gave Chelsea a modicum of respectability their first-half performance didn't deserve.

Are United invincible? Not quite! Coventry showed a week earlier they can be beaten, but Ferguson's team came damn near close to perfection.

Gullit gambled with Mark Hughes in midfield. He promised in his programme notes that his team would be like a 'wounded animal' after a dip in recent games, but United looked hungrier. By half-time the home side were out, 3–0 down. Gullit sent on Andy Myers for Mark Nicholls, pushed Hughes up front, Zola wide on the left and risked just three at the back. But after forcing a few saves from Schmeichel, United then strode into a 5–0 lead.

In a contest of two attack-minded teams, the Cup holders were put firmly in their place by the champions, a team that refused to be dislodged as number one.

Cocky Ferguson suggested he knew the destruction of the FA Cup holders was on the moment he saw Chelsea's team. When asked where he thought the tie was won, he said: 'Look at the team sheets. I must admit I thought Ruud was going to play only three at the back when I first saw them. But he obviously decided it was win or bust. If you score five away from home it's obviously an emphatic performance – we weren't going to be intimidated or second best.'

Gullit analysed the defeat. 'Too many players were below par and we gave away some sloppy goals. We threw it away ourselves and the players know it. I was sick in bed this morning and I wasn't going to come. I'm glad I did because I was pleased with the way we came back in the second half. We showed some character but before then we were too sloppy. But what we did in the second half after going 5–0 down inspired me.'

Ferguson said: 'I don't think it was a bad thing to lose goals at the end because it can be easy sometimes to get carried away. We were serious, the players were focused and, after losing at Coventry, they were up.'

Although there was some nationwide resentment toward United, it was not the case for Vialli. He was full of admiration for their team. Vialli said: 'I don't think anything will stop them becoming one of the greatest sides Europe has known. They are merciless and have no weaknesses anywhere in the team. I've had a long career and during that time, I had the pleasure of playing in one of the great Juventus sides that won the European Cup in 1995. It has also been a pain to me that I have faced some of the other great sides in the world and I am thinking of AC Milan, who dominated not only Italy but Europe. During their time at the top they were untouchable and when I look at this United side, I see similarities. They are beginning to become on a par with both Juve and Milan. There is no doubt in my mind they will win the European Cup this season. They are young, hungry and work for each other exactly the same as those two great Italian sides did.'

The level of commitment they showed for much of the game was too much for Chelsea to contend with, as Steve Clarke said: 'I have never seen a United side so hungry. They have quality players and so do we but theirs have a real desire. They hunt in packs and when top-class players are working for each other, it unites a team and they become unstoppable. They put us under pressure, hassled us and constantly forced us into mistakes that were punished.'

Ominously, Ferguson said after the game: 'We can get better in terms of being consistent but I saw in the dressing-room before the match that we wanted to win.' Graeme Le Saux believed that the players allowed the tension of the occasion to get to them.

There were also eight bookings, five of them for Chelsea. Leboeuf stored up his anger at Beckham for the next time they meet on the pitch. The two clashed on the pitch then the England international called Leboeuf 'a little baby' on Sky Television. The Frenchman refused to respond to such insults in public; instead he went to the players' bar to challenge him to repeat what he said to him on the pitch. Beckham pulled both his ears outwards to mock the Frenchman's appearance. Gullit instructed his players not to become embroiled in controversy over the defeat or the evident bad feeling between the sides.

It was imperative to restore confidence and, indeed, put the entire season back on track with the Coca-Cola Cup semi-final tie at Ipswich. While Chelsea treated the tournament as a means of involving their entire squad in the early stages, the competition took on new importance, particularly with the football League looking as though they were winning their fight to restore its European place.

A flu-ridden team battled right through extra time, living on their nerves, for another dramatic penalty shoot-out. Gullit came on to play most of the game, despite his heavy bout of flu which had affected a number of players, including Zola.

The Italian sported a new cropped hairstyle, and despite the handicap of his cold, he produced an outstanding display, coming close to a spectacular goal, his volley flying just over.

Ed de Goey saved two penalties and suddenly there was laughter again in the Chelsea dressing room. First Division Ipswich clawed back from 2–0 down to force the game to its nail-biting conclusion. They could have even won it in extra time when, after 113 minutes, substitute Bobby Petta stole in and hit a post. Chelsea can claim equal misfortune when former defender Jason Cundy turned Di Matteo's cross onto a post.

Duberry, Petrescu and Nicholls were rested, while Hughes was left on the substitutes' bench. Top scorer Gianluca Vialli, who came on to rescue pride against United, could have expected a rare full game, but was forced to drop out when a cut on his hand turned septic. Myers, Sinclair, Wise, Lambourde and Granville were charged with the task of restoring respect. Sadly, Myers didn't last long, going down with a twisted knee after twenty minutes and was eventually stretchered off. Gullit, yet to start in the league, finally cast off his tracksuit and slipped into the back four for his first outing since 22 November, also in the Coca-Cola Cup. At least he started there. But as Ipswich pressed and punished errors he ran into all areas until Wise ordered him back into defence. Ipswich, in a rich vein of form, losing only two in eleven games, were watched by former Ipswich and England manager Bobby Robson who flew over from Barcelona to join the 22,500 sell-out crowd.

Chelsea, five times semi-finalists of this competition, unlocked the game with a magnificent fifty yard pass by Leboeuf to Le Saux; with the keeper racing out, his first-touch cross was bravely met by a diving header by Flo squeezing between Mark Venus and Cundy. Gullit creating the second, his pass was pushed on by Flo to Zola, who whipped in a cross that Le Saux stabbed home as the half-time whistle loomed. But seconds into injury time Ipswich raised their battle colours when de Goey palmed out Alex Mathie's shot only for Mauricio Taricco to score. Mathie equalised in the sixty-second minute. Cundy, the former Chelsea player and just back from a two match suspension, collected his ninth booking for a foul on Zola. Hughes replaced Flo for extra time, immediately establishing the attack.

Finally, the penalty drama. . . . Leboeuf put Chelsea ahead (1–0). Scowcroft's shot saved by de Goey (1–0). Zola scored with a powerful strike (2–0). Tanner beat de Goey (2–1). Di Matteo scored (3–1). Taricco shot saved by de Goey (3–1). Hughes sends Chelsea through (4–1).

Gullit was overjoyed. 'To win and try and forget about Manchester United was one thing, to do it against the odds is another. It's made me so proud of my team.' He coughed throughout the after-match interview. He added: 'Don't keep me too long, boys. I want to go home and lay down and feel sorry for myself. Although tonight I won't be able to sleep because of going over this win and the fact I'm feeling very bad. I just hope it doesn't sweep any more through the club otherwise we will be in trouble.'

Gullit led the race to salute his heroes. 'Ed has a habit of making penalty saves. He won us the Umbro Cup in pre-season. He's up there with the best when it comes to saving penalties because he is such a big man and fills the goal. He is up there with Peter Schmeichel when it comes to saving this way.

'It's been hard for us because I've so many players out with flu, at least five and that is why I made so many changes. We had a lot of players ill and tired at the end. We had to battle and that's why I'm so proud of the side.

'I've ordered them all home to bed and to take lots of orange or vitamin tablets to get fit. The ones that are fit will come in tomorrow and have a massage because they must be feeling so tired after the past few days that we've gone through. This result certainly helps erase Sunday's defeat and now perhaps we can go forward again. It was important we won but the way we battled through is good for spirit and morale.'

Ipswich manager George Burley was rightly proud of his team too. 'Someone had to win it and it doesn't worry me deciding ties on penalties. If it had to end this way then so be it, but I couldn't ask for more from my side. Chelsea are an outstanding team with so many great players and for us to take them so close was a magnificent achievement. We beat Manchester United in an earlier tie and now fought hard with Chelsea. I think we can safely say we have done this club proud in this competition. In the end it was down to the people who wanted to take penalties and I would not fault any of my players.'

Arsenal and Chelsea were drawn together to guarantee a finalist from London against a team from the North at Wembley. Arsenal, 2–1 conquerors of West Ham, entertain Chelsea in the first leg. And Arsenal? 'I'm too tired to even think about them at the moment. All I want to do is savour this result and say goodnight, gentlemen,' said Gullit.

Bookmakers William Hill make Liverpool 7–4 favourites for the competition, with Arsenal second best at 9–4. Chelsea 11–4 and Middlesbrough 8–1 outsiders. Liverpool received the semi-final draw they wanted when they avoided their fellow Premiership big guns and were paired with Division One leaders Middlesbrough. Roy Evans' side had the chance of revenge over Boro, who defeated the

Merseysiders 2–1 in the fifth round on their way to last season's final, where they lost after a replay to Leicester. 'It's Boro again for us,' said Evans. 'They beat us in the quarter-finals of this competition last season, so we'll be looking for revenge. They'll be confident because of what they did to us last season. They'll take heart from that. We know it will be tough against them, but we're confident we can do it.'

Both de Goey and Hughes were happy to be going to Highbury for the first match. 'We're very pleased,' said de Goey. 'It's always better to play the second leg at home and we're confident about the game. Losing so badly to Manchester United in the FA Cup wasn't nice and we needed a good result at Ipswich. Now I think the confidence we've lost will start to come back, which is what we need ahead of our next league matches starting with Coventry. But we also know we've a great chance of returning to Wembley and feel we'll be able to do that.' Teetotal de Goey and his wife mix socially with the Bergkamps. They will have plenty to talk about over the next dinner.

When the sides met at Stamford Bridge in September, Nigel Winterburn's late strike sealed a bad-tempered match 3–2 in Arsenal's favour. But Hughes does not think that will matter. 'Playing Arsenal will be a big tie for both clubs. Going to Highbury for the first match could be an advantage, although it's how you play that matters.'

While de Goey was playing down his saves – 'that's the reason I play in goal' – Hughes was a reluctant penalty taker, only the flu virus sweeping through the Chelsea camp had forced his hand. 'I don't usually volunteer for penalties. I missed one in a shoot-out for Manchester United in Europe a few years ago and haven't taken one since. But I looked round at the end of extra time and could see I was almost the only one still standing. I suppose that's when senior players must make it count.'

Of course the big talking point was Zola's haircut! Lebeouf, writing in his *Times* column, told the inside story. 'Light relief at the training ground this week was provided by Gianfranco Zola with his new haircut. I don't know who did it, but some of the lads are convinced that it must have been his wife! I have to say I did not recognise him when I saw him with his shorn head. We are just hoping that it does not have the same effect as it did on Samson!'

Chelsea moved into second position in the Premiership with a 3–1 win over Coventry at the Bridge – the team that had beaten Manchester United and then dumped Liverpool out of the FA Cup. With Blackburn losing at Derby the next day, Chelsea consolidated their position behind United.

The win over Coventry proved vital. On a day when some of the star names, such as Zola, who was still suffering the after effects of flu, failed to show their usual sparkle it was left up to the rest of the team to show a collective fortitude against an in-form Coventry side. Dangerman Darren Huckerby caused panic in the Blues' back line and missed a great chance before the visitors took the lead, John Salako's left wing centre being fired home by Paul Telfer. Gullit put on 20-year-old substitute Mark Nicholls at half time for left back Danny Granville, and entered into the fray himself just before the hour mark, changing the course of the game with Nicholls grabbing a double and Gullit's still mighty presence buying crucial space for his fellow attackers. Nicholls headed in the equaliser from Le Saux's 66 minute cross, and a second from the same player's pass four minutes later.

Di Matteo, Nicholls and then Hughes – with a wonderful dummy – all combined for the Italian to finish with a right foot rocket with 12 minutes left to seal the points.

Clarke, who at Ipswich became only the eighth Chelsea player to achieve 400 games since arriving in January 1987 from St Mirren said: 'We had a little stutter over Christmas. But this was a very, very important game for us because if we had lost we'd have been 10 points behind Manchester United, and in my opinion that would have been too much.'

However, a dismayed Gullit was soon condemning his players for 'sloppy and childish play' as they tossed away both the lead and complete control of yet another game they were expected to win in order to keep the pressure on Manchester United. Instead, Chelsea crashed 3–1 at Everton in the Sky-televised game, with Zola absent with a stomach bug, and Wise and Di Matteo also out.

Even Gullit admitted, 'Everton deserved to win it. In the first half we controlled it and played some good football but then gave away a sloppy goal. What really irritated me was the way we kept giving the ball away in the second half. We did it so often that it made Everton confident and they started to play better. And their last two goals were so bad I don't even want to mention them.'

Chelsea were left seven points adrift of Manchester United and Gullit conceded: 'Of course we were looking to close the gap and even with the players we had missing we had enough out there on the pitch to have won it. There's a lot of points between us and we don't deserve to be up there if we keep playing like that. I told my players they didn't deserve to be in second place after the way they gave away the game, the big clubs don't do this because they stay solid.'

Gullit was also worried that the World Cup could cost Chelsea any lingering hope of the title as their foreign legion was about to head off all around world for friendlies in the build-up to France 98. The Blues stood to lose as many as eight players at various times with a spate of warm-up friendlies and specially organised training camps for the Dutch and Italian national teams. Chelsea would be harder hit than any of the other title contenders, particularly leaders Manchester United. 'It will be a disadvantage and it can sometimes change a season from a good one to a bad one,' Gullit said. 'It is very important to us and our challenge to hold on to our players. They earn their money here and it is important that they do well for this club. Their priorities must be here, but if FIFA tell us they have to go for friendly games, I guess there is not a lot I can do.'

With Dan Petrescu linking up with Romania, Frank Leboeuf with France, Zola and Di Matteo with Italy, Flo and Grodas in the Norwegian squad, Sinclair was expected to make his debut for Jamaica against Brazil in the Concacaf Gold Cup, and Babayaro with Nigeria. Sinclair would be away for a fortnight in Miami, although he persuaded Jamaican officials to let him miss a friendly with Sweden to play against Arsenal in the first leg. Sinclair said: 'It's a once in a lifetime opportunity to play in the World Cup, but I've got to be sensible about it. We're trying to pick the right games in the build-up to France. Ruud is worried about losing international players, but he's been good about it, because he's been there and knows what it means to play for your country.'

Zola was omitted from the Italian squad for the friendly against Slovakia. Cesare Maldini spoke to Zola to explain his decision before announcing his squad. It was, at least, good news for Chelsea because it freed Zola to play in the semi-final first leg against Arsenal. But Roberto Di Matteo was selected.

For Zola it was a huge blow to be omitted for the friendly in Catania, Sicily for the first time since establishing his place in the squad. He knew he had to improve his form at the club to force his way back. Maldini stuck to his word to introduce fresh talent. Immediately after Italy qualified, Maldini promised to use the pre-France friendlies to experiment. His area of greatest concern was his midfield. 'In particular, I'm interested in finding possible midfield substitutes because this is the area in which we are short of players, at least in terms of quantity if not quality.' In attack, Maldini fielded a new combination in Fabrizio Ravanelli and Alessandro Del Piero. Maldini rested both Zola and Christian Vieri while Pierluigi Casiraghi was injured.

Zola determined to put behind him the personal anguish of the 1994 finals in the United States, when, as a bit-part player, he was sent off five minutes after coming on against Nigeria and spent the tournament in deep frustration that Italy could reach the final yet be condemned as negative.

When Zola watched the World Cup draw at home, it would not have crossed his mind that his place in the Finals would be in jeopardy. He said: 'I'm happy with the result, Chile, Cameroon and Austria. But when a team qualifies for the World Cup you know that they must have quality, so we know we will have to play our best to beat the teams in our group.'

Zola was sure that Italy will be a vastly different proposition to the team that were held by England in Rome. 'You can't say for sure now but I think it will be a better team than the one which played England in Rome. There was a lot pressure on us when we played that match in Italy and it was really hard to play a good game. The important thing in Rome was the result and when you play only for the result it is hard to produce good football.'

Zola's performance in Rome was a far cry from his devastating match winning display at Wembley. 'When you play in such a big game and score the winner then it is good for your confidence. It gives you trust in your own abilities and I was in good shape at that time. But the problem is that when you play a qualifying competition for a World Cup, you play matches over a long period. There is eight months between the first game and the last game and form can change in that time. It happened to me and unfortunately when I started this season I was not in perfect condition and it created problems for me. I started the season later than everybody else. Because of Le Tournoi in France during the summer, I started pre-season training later than the other players which meant that I only had 15 days of pre-season training in total. I couldn't train hard so it was difficult for me to find the correct form. When you have to find your form while you are already playing in the team it's hard because there is so much pressure and it makes the situation difficult. But after a while my form started improving, although I was still not scoring goals.'

But it gives him just as much pleasure to make goals for others. 'Oh yeah, because when you create an opportunity for someone else to score it's a great satisfaction. Even though you didn't score yourself, it's the same feeling because you have made the opportunity for a team-mate. It's a good feeling, sometimes it is better. When we played at Tottenham and we scored six I wasn't among the scorers, but I was very happy because I had played some good balls for the others to score. That made me very happy.'

He wants to be in peak condition, naturally, come the tournament in France. 'I hope so. I am really looking forward to the summer in France because the last World Cup was not so good for me. I got sent off and I found it traumatic. France is a real target and I am very focused on it. It will also probably be my last tournament playing in the national team, so it is very, very important to me.'

Zola feels that his affinity with English football can be traced to his island roots. A proud Sardinian, he has had to fight all the way, overcoming his physical frailties to become one of his country's finest performers. He was not big and he was not strong, so he worked on improving those elements of his game that would hold him back. 'I wasn't good at heading the ball, so I improved my skills to get faster and stronger in the legs. When you work hard for something and earn your reward, it is a great satisfaction. Every time I have had a bad moment – and that's normal when you are fighting obstacles in your life – I look back on what I have done in the past and that gives me more power, strength and satisfaction.

'I have set my heart on playing for Italy next summer; what happened the last time hurt me deeply. Only this summer can I fully recover from it.'

Zola believes England will be a force in the World Cup. 'These are very, very positive times for football here, not just one player or one club in particular but for every English player, you can see it in the way they are performing, with a belief in them. A team that has such confidence and power can be sustained in a championship to achieve anything it wants. It was an incredible recovery by England after we had beaten them at Wembley, I really didn't think they could do that. When a team shows itself to be so strong, you have to say well done and congratulate them.'

Any lingering doubts about Zola's commitment to Chelsea were finally dispelled at the beginning of February 1998 with an announcement from the club that delighted their fans and emphasised the growing belief that Gullit was building a formidable squad.

Zola and Di Matteo both signed two-year extensions to their contracts. The pair can see out their careers at the club. Zola signed a deal which commits him to the Blues until 2002, taking him to the age of 35, while Di Matteo agreed a similar contract extension to remain at the club until he is 31. Colin Hutchinson said: 'Gianfranco has demonstrated very forcefully that he is going to spend the rest of his career at Chelsea. He and his family have settled very well in England, they love London and he is in love with Chelsea. We have heard a lot about foreigners being mercenaries, coming here for a quick smash-and-grab, taking the money and then getting out. This obviously proves Zola and Di Matteo are part of the English game and want to play in England and put down some roots in England.'

18

Gullit Sacked

Ruud Gullit 'lost the plot', according to my sources inside the Bridge, when he left out Zola and Wise at Goodison Park and the side crashed 3–1 within striking distance of the Premiership summit. That was one of the reasons the club surprisingly kicked out Gullit after contract talks stalled and then burst into open conflict over his initial wage demand of £2 million a year.

Two defeats by Arsenal further convinced some people inside the club that Gullit was losing his way. After the first leg of the Coca-Cola Cup semi-final at Highbury, which Chelsea lost more emphatically than the final score of 2–1 suggested, there was a players' meeting. Although Gullit approved of such a gathering of his senior players, he was not notified about it in advance. The players' unrest at team selection filtered through to the boardroom giving subsequent credence to Gullit's claims that there was a hidden agenda to his dismissal, that it was not all about a contract dispute. In fact I was told that there were some who wished they had acted earlier ... 'then perhaps we might be playing Barnsley in the FA Cup' instead of suffering such an exit at the hands of Manchester United.

Gullit was axed with the team still second in the Premiership, in the quarter-finals of the Cup-Winners' Cup and within a game of Wembley, but results had dipped and the snipers were undermining his stature inside the club. Days off for his Dutch FA coaching course, commercial assignments, his own fashion label Ruud Wear, the pizza ads, a BBC contract alongside Des Lynam, all raised question marks against his commitment to the cause. Comparisons were made with Alex Ferguson, who never takes a break, and Gerry Francis, who took a fax machine with him on his honeymoon during the close season. Gullit adopted a far more laid-back approach. He was different – a complete contrast to the archetypal British boss. When the players completed their post-FA Cup triumph tour of the Far East at the end of May, Gullit asked when pre-season started. 'July 8,' he was informed. 'See you then,' was his response. The club hierarchy would later use that as an example of Gullit's 'time share' principle – splitting his time between football and his private life and off-field activities.

However, Chelsea had just won the FA Cup, their first trophy in more than a quarter of a century. No-one quibbled then, did they? As Ken Bates concentrated on the Chelsea Village project, acquiring a £75 million Euroloan that required an annual £1.5 million interest repayment, Gullit was left to get on with becoming even more successful. But eyebrows were raised by the 5–3 FA Cup exit at the hands of Manchester United, followed by the omission of both Zola and Wise at Everton when some considered they were ready to play and desperate to do so; left out because they were unable to train. Gullit did not think they were ready – and he picked the team.

The point of no return arrived on two fronts. The club intercepted by accident a fax to Gullit from Nike making him yet another commercial offer; not that he would have accepted it, having already made up his mind to cut back on that side of things in order to concentrate on the team. But it was the fact that offers were flooding in that aggravated an already delicate situation. Then came Gullit's failure in the Coca-Cola Cup against Arsenal, when only a late Mark Hughes goal rescued Chelsea from what threatened to be a mauling. On top of that there was the question of his wage demands. It was time for him to go, and only one man would have pulled the final trigger – Bates.

Gullit, of course, was in fact totally committed to Chelsea, refusing to listen to possible offers from abroad to leave the Bridge. But the Continental system he insisted upon when he took the coaching post, the innovation widely applauded and accepted, suddenly became the main weapon against him. Because he concentrated solely on the team, and was still a player, he was not driving up and down the motorway looking at Third Division players, nor was he scouting abroad. Instead he used his wide range of contacts to attract top-class players to the Bridge.

He did stall on talks about his new contract but made it clear in the media, whenever asked by journalists, that there would be no problem, he wanted to stay. He had decided to sign for a further two years but when it came down to talks, Gullit's asking price and the amount at which Chelsea now valued his services – as a manager only – were wide apart. However, had they really wanted him to stay, the club would have negotiated.

But no longer was Gullit's way apparently good enough. He was under scrutiny, his team selections queried where once they were hailed for bringing back the glory days. Perhaps there was a touch of panic, a sense that the good times could be even better if Gullit was replaced. And did he do all that much in any case, or did Graham Rix run the team with Gullit just the figurehead?

The loss of faith in Gullit within the boardroom was reinforced on that Sunday afternoon at Goodison. Gullit announced that Zola had a stomach bug and Wise a toe injury, and my Chelsea insider told me that it was the beginning of the end when the manager dispatched two such influential players to the stand, not even keeping them in reserve on the bench.

Zola, I am reliably informed, was totally mystified by the explanation given by the manager that he had a stomach bug. He hotly denied it was true; Gullit insists that it was. Maybe Gullit was trying to protect Zola from the inevitable speculation that would have followed if he had said that his Footballer of the Year had simply been omitted from the team. But if that was the intention it backfired – the Italian media had been given Zola's side of the story and his absence became a major talking point. Zola, I am told, would rather have been dropped without being protected in any way. He would have accepted being left out on current form, but was surprised that he wasn't even considered as one of the substitutes; they were Vialli, Gullit, Paul Hughes, Nicholls and Hitchcock.

Niggling grievances were building up behind the scenes. Gullit's belief that the rapid development of Chelsea Village had come about because of his success on the pitch irritated Bates; the manager's idiosyncratic team selections alienated a section of the dressing-room; and Gullit's off-the-field activities increased the feeling that he did not pull his formidable weight in terms of hours committed to the job.

All of this, of course, would have been shrugged off had Chelsea recovered their form. But events on the pitch now also contrived to alienate Gullit from the board. Chelsea were hoping that joyful cup memories of Highbury would inspire Zola to break the worst goal drought in his Stamford Bridge career. Just two months earlier, after that scintillating hat-trick against Derby, he had seemed at the peak of his powers. Since then, his game had gone off the boil – in eight appearances following that hat-trick, the little Sardinian failed to score and his normal charming grin was wiped away by the frustration of being left out of Italy's squad for the World Cup warm-up match against Slovakia in January. So he had a point to prove to coach Cesare Maldini, as well as the chance to put the smile back on Gullit's face, when the Blues travelled across London to face Arsenal in their Coca-Cola Cup semi-final first leg. Gullit, who had clearly placed the competition firmly at the bottom of his priorities back in August, was now aware of how much, suddenly, it meant. 'This is very important for us,' he said. 'We all know what it means for us to go through and get the chance to play at Wembley in a final again.'

International calls deprived Chelsea of Di Matteo and Leboeuf, and the Frenchman's absence tempted Gullit to start himself in defence in a game which would be the first of three meetings with the Gunners in the space of less than a month. There was already bad blood between the teams following their Premiership clash at Stamford Bridge in September, when Arsenal won 3–2 after Leboeuf was sent off, so there was an extra edge to the match.

But there was no edge to Chelsea's game – far from it. Arsenal boss Arsene Wenger was left cursing his side's luck after Chelsea escaped a hiding with just a narrow 2–1 defeat in a red-blooded tie. Gullit agreed that his side 'got out of jail' when substitute Mark Hughes headed the precious away goal they barely deserved. With Wise still out injured, a shambles of a performance was rescued by the decision to send on the rampaging Hughes in place of Flo in the sixty-fifth minute, with Chelsea 2–0 down. Hughes had only been on the field for five minutes when he pulled a vital goal back. Until then, only a superlative display by Ed de Goey had kept the tie alive for the second leg. Wenger said: 'We are going to Chelsea with some regrets because it is not all over. We should have scored four or five.' Zola had now gone nine games without a goal.

Gullit, for his part, had shown his rustiness when he could only get his dreadlocks to a ball pitched forward from the halfway line, leaving his countryman Marc Overmars unmarked in an empty penalty area. Overmars collected his fifth goal in seven games and Arsenal deserved their half-time lead. Gullit reshuffled his pack at the start of the second half giving Frenchman Laurent Chalvert his debut, taking off Petrescu and switching roles with Bernard Lambourde, moving himself from defence into central midfield. But before the new formation had a chance to bed in, Overmars pulled the ball back from the byline for Stephen Hughes to finish off from penalty-spot range.

Zola was the most likely candidate to make any impact for Chelsea and from his cross in the fifty-seventh minute Flo headed just wide. Then a teasing cross by Zola to the near post tempted Arsenal keeper Manninger out of his goal and Hughes beat him to the ball for one of his typical headers. Referee Martin Bodenham could have been excused for raising the red card a few times – Gilles Grimandi and Graeme Le Saux clashed in the fifty-third minute after a running feud that lasted most of the match.

Gullit had picked himself for his first start since 19 November, but his appearance in the back four was 'an emergency'. He complained: 'Our whole spine was gone before a ball was kicked. We had Frank Leboeuf sitting on the bench for France and Roberto Di Matteo away with Italy – they were the first players I signed for Chelsea. On top of that, Dennis Wise was not fit, so we were missing too much quality. The only ones who can be disappointed are Arsenal, because if there was ever a chance of beating us well, it should have been tonight. It is not going to get any easier because De Goey goes away with Holland for the second leg and Frank Sinclair will be away with Jamaica.'

Asked if the problem of international call-ups was partly of his own making because of his preference for overseas signings, Gullit snapped back: 'I thought Sinclair was English, then all of a sudden he finds an uncle who went to Jamaica once. Maybe you have to ask English players why they want to play for someone else.' His remarks were more in defence of his buying policy than an attack on Sinclair's chosen international career. The popular full-back refused to engage his manager in a war of words, declining to comment and saying only: 'Whatever he said, he didn't say it to my face.'

Zola was now sporting a rather severe shorter haircut and Ken Bates, in his own inimitable style, provided a very personal solution to his star striker's problems: 'I offered an important piece of advice, I told Zola to let his hair grow back. He looks like Samson shorn of his locks and the sooner we see his flowing head of hair bouncing about as he does his jinking down the field, the better.'

The missing Di Matteo scored the third goal as Italy ground out a 3–0 win over Slovakia in Sicily, while Leboeuf was sent on in the third minute of injury time with France. He was back, just in time, to witness plenty of activity at the training ground prior to the next Premiership game at home to Barnsley. Six senior players were involved in a crisis meeting after an address from Gullit followed by an extra-strenuous training and strategy session at the Bridge. You would have forgiven Gullit for being furious that his players had held a meeting behind his back. Far from it. He was positively purring with delight about their input and revealed after the Barnsley match that it was yet another Continental innovation! He explained: 'This always happens with the Dutch. It is part of their make-up. It happened when I was a Dutch player in the Dutch team. You'd get the senior players together and find out what's on their mind, they would want to know what's going on and there would be arguments and they would listen.

'I didn't even know about it when the players had their meeting after training and I don't know what they were talking about. But I would encourage it. It's good to let it come out – the longer it stays inside, the worse it is. Always in Holland there would be discussions like this and as a coach I believe it's good to have these chats. I am sure they would have been very honest, very critical of themselves.'

The six senior players were Gianluca Vialli, Steve Clark, Eddie Newton, Dennis Wise, Mark Hughes and Graeme Le Saux. 'I'm sure they were critical of me, critical of the staff, critical of everybody,' said Gullit. 'We had to act very quickly after the Arsenal defeat, but as a result of what we have said and done, I feel we can now only get better. I told the players that everyone, including myself, had to look in the mirror to discover the problems and not blame everyone else. I don't know what was said in the players' meeting but I'm sure the spirit we saw on the pitch against Barnsley came as a result of it.'

The outcome was a highly motivated team performance, not spectacular but a solid 2–0 win over the bottom club. Despite having created Hughes's goal at Highbury, Zola was left on the bench and never made a contribution – apart from showing self-discipline with a half-hour lone training session after the game. With Manchester United losing at Old Trafford to Leicester, the title race suddenly opened up again, with Chelsea back in second thanks to Liverpool finishing goalless with Blackburn at Anfield. Gullit enthused: 'Everyone has been saying it's impossible for anyone to overtake United but I don't believe that. You have to battle to win titles and we are now ready to do that. I am delighted with the reaction in the club following our defeat against Arsenal.'

Gullit's own personal response to the Arsenal defeat was to drop himself not only from the team but also from the bench. His message to the rest of the team was double-edged: 'I told the players, "You are in the Coca-Cola Cup and can go to the final. You're in the Cup-Winners' Cup and you are still there in the championship – don't throw it all away. Look where you are. This is the moment, you can't let it slip away." ' There was a tactical reshaping with three at the back but the day before the game Gullit also sensed a change in attitude, a newly motivated set of players: 'I knew that as soon as I looked the players in the eye. I could see a glint, a sparkle there. I knew there would be a different attitude in this game. I saw that they were eager and everyone was buzzing.

'This for me is the most interesting and important stage of my managerial career,' he went on. 'I've always said the first year is the easiest because nobody knows what you can achieve and the second year is always the hardest because you are under more pressure as people expect a lot more.' Asked about the soul-searching and hard talking that had gone on, Gullit added: 'Discussion like this is democratic and it has to be like that. I want players to take on their responsibilities. I'm here standing on the sidelines, but the players are out there to perform and I want them to show responsibility. The most interesting part for me is to do with all these different characters, and I want them to look inside themselves.'

To arrest the slide, Gullit called upon one of those characters, Gianluca Vialli, who had been kicking his heels on the bench but was still top goalscorer. Vialli opened the scoring with his fifteenth goal of the season and his glorious pass to Petrescu paved the way for the second, scored by Mark Hughes. Wise also returned to the team in Gullit's shake-up and both he and Vialli made a huge impact. At an impromptu talk-in after the match, Wise looked embarrassed when he was asked whether the players had talked about Gullit in their meeting: 'Oh, good question.' Vialli smiled as Wise added: 'I don't want to answer that one. We discussed certain things, we had a little chat and we came out fine. Everyone makes mistakes – but I'm not saying the management had made them. It was important that we didn't waste what we've done in the past few months, not let things slip, because we still have a chance to achieve something. We've been guilty of giving away sloppy goals but we are still in with a chance, even though we've had that bad patch. Let's hope it's gone.'

Vialli had made the most powerful case for staying in the side and now it was his turn to sympathize with the benched Zola. Vialli said: 'I dare you to find anybody who would be happy sitting on the bench. Gianfranco would like to play but he encouraged me before the game and he was very happy at the end of the match because of our performance. For him the team comes first.' For Vialli a meeting of the players was not much of a big deal, as he explained: 'In Italy it happens quite often, players like to have a chat and speak with each other heart to heart to sort things out instead of keeping everything inside.'

Gullit was turning his back on lucrative commercial deals to concentrate on putting Chelsea back on track. His adviser Phil Smith revealed: 'Ruud wants to be absolutely focused on his football and there is no point telling his players that they must be focused if he doesn't heed his own advice. It is important for him that he practises what he preaches. This is a crucial time of the season and he has started playing again whereas he wasn't before. He is a high-profile personality and we have received no shortage of offers. Being high-profile can sometimes be a help with commercial enterprises, sometimes it can be a hindrance. Although Ruud has been criticized in recent weeks it must be stressed that he did the shoot for the pizza advert in the early part of November, although it has only come on TV recently. He has not been doing anything for the past couple of weeks and he will not take on anything new for the time being.'

Zola was determined to reward the club and their fans, as well as himself, with a return to form: 'I will work harder and harder and do what it takes to return to the Chelsea team and the national side. I went through moments like this last season but I kept my place. Now I have been left out and I want to be back as soon as possible. No player is happy at being substitute. But I accept the decision and will fight to get back in at Chelsea. I'm not playing as well as I played last year, but there is nothing wrong. I am working hard but I am not satisfied with what I am doing. In the last few weeks, I have not played so often. I just need to regain my confidence, which only playing can do. The supporters must not be worried about me.' Losing his place in the Italian national side had been devastating, however, and Zola admitted: 'In Italy, there are those who have already crossed out my name. There are people who think that we don't work as hard in England as players do in *Serie A*. They think the Premiership is a holiday. That is not the case. I want to go to the World Cup and we Sardinians are known for stubbornness and hardheadedness. When we want something, nothing can deter us.'

Chelsea were being constantly linked with Rangers striker Brian Laudrup, whose contract expired in the summer of 1998. The Dane's agent Vincenzo Morabito was reported to have held talks with numerous clubs. Laudrup's choice narrowed down to Chelsea and Ajax. PSV Eindhoven's Jaap Stam was a Blues target, together with another powerful defender, Tabio West. PSV valued Stam at a prohibitive £15 million but Chelsea were also tipped to win the chase to buy talented Finnish international winger Joonas Kolkka, whose contract with Dutch First Division outfit Willem II expired at the end of the season; Kolkka indicated his heart was set on joining the charismatic Gullit.

Zola was desperate to get back in the side, but had to be content with a late appearance as substitute in the next league fixture, away at Arsenal. On the bench for the second game running, he said before the match at Highbury: 'In the last four weeks I have not played much. It is not easy to find your form when you are struggling, when you are not playing. I have had moments before like this in Italy, but I was playing games then. I could solve my problems on the pitch. I am training well and I can honestly say that I am OK. It is normal to have problems like this. Every player has them. You cannot have a season where you are on top all of the time. But you have to have confidence in your game. In the past I have sorted myself out by working at my game and playing.' Vialli agreed: 'Gianfranco is going through the same problem I had last year. You have to learn to accept it. Maybe I will have some words of advice for him.' Zola admitted that the Arsenal game was one Chelsea had to win: 'If you had asked me four weeks ago if I thought we were in good shape for the championship, I would have said yes. But it has changed, we just lack a little bit of confidence. We have to get it back if we are going to have any chance.'

But Arsenal defeated Chelsea for the third time, staking their own claim to join the scramble for the title. After another slip by Manchester United, Chelsea came to Highbury with the prospect of moving within two points of the leaders with the champions still to visit Stamford Bridge. Vialli retained his place in attack, but at the other end a slip by Leboeuf as early as the fourth minute let in Nicolas Anelka and Stephen Hughes followed up to score. The young Arsenal midfielder scored again with a header just before half-time, but in between Chelsea felt Steve Bould should have been sent off for hauling back Vialli who was clear on goal. Smarting after the 2–0 defeat, Gullit was furious at referee Dermot Gallagher's decision to show only a yellow card to Bould. 'He has to be sent off for such a thing,' Gullit fumed. 'That is the rule, there is nothing else for it. I'm curious as to what would have happened if he'd given such a decision in the Nou Camp stadium at Barcelona. He'd never get out. He is a top referee, but he decided to play his own game here.

'Obviously, the result was influenced by the fact that he didn't send him off. We'd have been playing against ten men after that. I even turned to our bench and to the fourth official, (Peter Jones), and said: "I bet he doesn't show him a red card." It's just a feeling you get. It disappoints me, but there is nothing you can do. What also interests me is that in the last fifteen minutes he gave every decision our way. It's as if he was trying to make it up to us. But I don't want any favours. I just want him to practise the rules. And I hope something similar doesn't happen when we play Arsenal in the Coca-Cola Cup semi-final second leg on February 18.' Gallagher said Bould didn't go because another defender, Gilles Grimandi, was handily placed to cut out Vialli's hopes of scoring.

Defiant Vialli wanted the team to 'remain confident' despite having lost three of the last four matches. He said: 'We must be confident in our game and stick together at the moment. We must pull together and look to the future. Things will get better and we can still win something this year. We are in the semi-finals of the Coca-Cola Cup, quarter-finals of the European Cup-Winners' Cup and second in the Premiership. I think we can do something this season. The secret is to just carry on playing football and remain confident.'

Incredibly, Vialli would now be handed the responsibility of ensuring that confidence was restored. Four days later, Chelsea relieved Gullit of his duties and appointed Vialli as their new player-manager. Ostensibly the reason was a breakdown of contract talks, Chelsea insisting that they were unable to match Gullit's cash demands for a new contract. But as events unfolded it became a case of claim and counter-claim, of sinister accusations . . . and much to Zola's surprise and anger, it even involved him.

The world began to discover the remarkable behind-the-scenes events once Chelsea issued a statement around midday on Thursday 12 February. In it, managing director Colin Hutchinson said: 'Once it was clear Ruud would not be with us next season, we had to act swiftly. We have decided to make a clean break immediately and Gianluca Vialli is the new player-manager of Chelsea with immediate effect. While we were prepared to give Ruud a contract which we believe would have made him the best paid manager in the

Premiership, we were not able to meet what he wanted and expected. We simply could not afford what he was asking. Ruud was told that unfortunately the gap was too wide to allow further meaningful negotiations and that we would need to actively pursue lining up a replacement. Gianluca was offered the position of player-manager last night and took all of five minutes to accept.'

The uncertainty over Gullit's future had been dragging on for several months, with the club trying to persuade him to extend his contract, which was due to expire on 30 June. Hutchinson said Vialli had already been earmarked as a future replacement for Gullit but his chance had come much sooner than expected. He went on: 'Ruud and I met last Thursday. During a forty-minute meeting it was established that Ruud was prepared to extend by only two years. For our part we indicated that we wished the new contract be as a manager only.

'We believe Gianluca Vialli is destined to become an outstanding coach. Over the last eighteen months we have had the opportunity to get to know him and his deep thinking about football. We had him marked up as a future "possible". His chance, because of circumstances, is to come earlier than expected and at Chelsea. He was surprised and flattered we should consider him as successor to Ruud.'

Chelsea's deal with Vialli would be until June 1999, and would then continue for two more years with the emphasis on managing, although he would still be registered as a player. Vialli also told Chelsea he wanted to retain coach Graham Rix and assistant manager Gwyn Williams. But it was the immediate firing of Gullit, not the hiring of Vialli, that was going to be the main talking point. Hutchinson explained the club's thinking: 'We could not have a situation of Ruud bringing in players his successor might not want. The other impossible situation we have had to face up to is that it would not be fair on Ruud and Gianluca, or the players, for Ruud to continue as manager knowing that within weeks one of his players would take over.

'Ruud Gullit has been relieved of his duties but will continue to be paid under the terms of his contract until 30 June 1998. We have made tremendous progress under Ruud and thank him for his contribution to Chelsea. His place in club history is assured. We wish him well for the future.'

Reactions poured in. Chairman of the Football Task Force and Chelsea supporter David Mellor claimed he was not surprised by Gullit's departure, saying: 'You don't have to be Sherlock Holmes to realize that Ruud was riding his luck a bit, the way the team was play-ing, to insist on a player's contract as well as a manager's. He was rely-ing on the fact that he was irreplaceable, but the graveyards of the world are full of irreplaceable people. And I think there was a rest-lessness with Ruud's management style among the players – the chopping and changing, which was fine if the team were sparking on all cylinders. Nobody was pleased to lose three successive matches to Arsenal, it just rubbed salt in the wounds. If Ruud had said his play-ing days were over and settled for what for most people would be a king's ransom, he would have been all right. But playing a hand of cards which didn't have all the aces it used to have, as he did, made this almost inevitable.'

James Edwards, editor of the *Chelsea Independent* fanzine, disagreed: 'As far as I'm concerned we should pay Ruud as much as he wants. He is the best manager we have had around here for a good decade or so. I'm quite amazed by it.'

Former Chelsea favourite Peter Osgood weighed in with some harsh words for Gullit: 'I don't think Ruud was interested in manag-ing this club. He is arrogant man. Vialli is in a different class.'

Osgood's view was typical of the anti-Gullit feeling that had permeated the boardroom. The Dutchman's refusal to socialize or even acknowledge those on the periphery of the club brought resentment. Worse still, his inclination even to keep the chairman at arm's length would not have won him any brownie points. Ken Bates is omnipotent at the Bridge, and when Gullit declined an invitation from the chairman's office to attend a charity bash Bates had helped to organize, it wasn't the most diplomatic decision – and as it turned out would have only helped to sour relations between the men that mattered most at the club.

As news of Gullit's departure spread, Chelsea fans congregated around Stamford Bridge. Within an hour of the announcement about a dozen were gathered at the stadium gates. The mood was one of shock and surprise rather than heartbreak, and many fans were convinced the team could continue its challenge for glory under new management. Lifelong supporter John Marijetic spoke for many when he said: 'The ground is still here and the club is still here and the supporters will be here for ever. I've been supporting Chelsea since 1962 and I've been through so many managers. The club just keeps going on.' Interestingly, season-ticket holder Tim Veck said: 'For the last three or four weeks this story has been doing the rounds among the crowd, so it doesn't come as much of a surprise. Gullit was a brilliant coach and a brilliant manager, but I think you don't mess about with Ken Bates. If Ken wants something, he gets it, and I trust his judgement on this. It is a bit disappointing but it won't hold us back. We will definitely be in Europe again next year.' At Chelsea's massive megastore, Ruud Gullit shirts, posters, photographs, figurines and even underwear were still on sale.

As Bates and Hutchinson unveiled Vialli as the new coach at the hastily arranged press conference at the Bridge, I left the *Daily Mirror* offices at Canary Wharf to make the hour-long dash to Gullit's flat in Cadogan Square. It wasn't difficult to spot his flat – there were a dozen Fleet Street photographers camped outside. I pressed the Intercom button and Ruud let me in. It was my first visit to Ruud's flat – his privacy is so important to him that previously when we met he had always made the short journey down the King's Road to my flat in Chelsea.

Inside the plush white-walled £1 million pad, rented courtesy of the club, were Jon Smith and his brother Phil, Gullit's UK representatives from First Artist Corporation – who, ironically, also represented Zola. They were preparing a press statement and as a longtime friend of the brothers, I had been asked round as the one soccer journalist trusted by Ruud to help with the statement.

Over a cool glass of apple juice, Ruud confided to me his innermost feelings. He was devastated, dejected. Looking into his eyes, you could see the hurt. Jon and Phil monitored the constant stream of calls on their mobile phones. Ruud, too, had to break off to answer his mobile, as he tried to explain the day's events to his small group of close friends and family. I had been recognized entering the exclusive block of flats and before Ruud took a call on his intercom from someone asking for me. I told Ruud to ignore it as we resumed our conversation.

Ruud was preparing for a meeting that evening at the Conrad Hotel with Ken Bates. He was agitated, rising from his seat to pace around deep in thought.

Ruud discussed at length with me many of the points he would make at his scheduled press conference the next morning, as well as the forthcoming meeting with Ken Bates. Now he wanted to leave his flat without being harrassed by the photographers, but his plan to leave with the Smiths via the back exit was hampered because the door was locked. Unable to get any reception on his mobile from the entrance hall, Ruud returned to his flat to call the porter to come to the rescue. The three of them left the flat by the rear, as I walked out the front. 'Where's Ruud?' asked one of the photographers. I replied: 'He's on his way out.' Well, he *was* on his way out, but what could I say? My loyalties were with Ruud at that point.

Over at the Conrad, the smart up-market hotel in Chelsea Harbour which has been the venue of a number of dinner dates I've shared with Bates, it would prove to be a momentous meeting. Gullit told Bates precisely what was on his mind. The two of them had not had a cross word until then. But now the chairman was confronted with an angry former employee. It was a different side to Gullit, according to Bates, who confided in me the tone of the meeting, though declining to divulge the subject matter of their conversation. Bates told me: 'We shook hands and I told him we might meet up again sometime in the future, and it would be best if we parted friends. He smiled and accepted it. As he left, he stopped to sign quite a few autographs.'

Bates had so far opted not to go public with his own comments, preferring to leave all the talking to Hutchinson.

Next morning Gullit was an enticing mixture of the emotional and angry as he spent two hours conducting seemingly endless interviews at the International Sportsman Club, formerly called Scribes West when it was the haunt of its then owner Terry Venables. It was not the first time, then, that sackings and conspiracies had been the topic of conversation in this particular corner of West London.

Gullit alleged that there had been a conspiracy to get him out, accusing club officials of plotting behind his back and telling 'incredible lies'. He refuted claims that he was greedy and insisted that the club had used his pay demands 'as a big stick to beat me with'. He was adamant that he had never been made an offer to stay and said that he had not stormed out halfway through a meeting on the day of his sacking.

In the opposite corner, the Chelsea board insisted that Gullit had asked for a new contract worth £2 million *after tax* – the equivalent of a £3.7 million a year deal – and that Gullit *was* offered a new deal, worth £1 million a year *before tax*, which he turned down flat.

The Hutchinson and Bates view was that contract talks had broken down because the 'gap' between the two sides was unbridgeable. Gullit dismissed that view: 'I asked for £2 million a year, but that was only what I'd asked for when I first spoke to the club, to Hutchinson and Glenn Hoddle, in Milan three years ago. I told the media and gave my word to Chelsea that I would stay, so my negotiating position was already weak. At the meeting in Milan, Hoddle and Hutchinson went out of the room for 15 minutes, came back and made me another offer. I accepted that offer, and expected that a similar thing would happen here. That is what negotiating is all about, coming to a compromise.'

Hours later, Hutchinson responded to Gullit's accusations only on Chelsea Clubcall: 'He has said that we didn't make him an offer; perhaps he misunderstood, but I repeated the offer to him. It was £1 million per year gross and I said, "would you accept that?" He flatly said no.' At the press conference, Gullit had conceded that he did indeed ask for £2 million. But Hutchinson responded: 'Ruud is the master of the media and he very craftily said he asked for £2 million. He did ask for £2 million. I said, "gross?" He replied, "Netto, I always talk in 'nettos'." That would have been a big commitment to the club – £2 million in his hand when you add on the tax and make it gross comes to £3,720,000.' Hutchinson also talked about Gullit's bonuses, his car and his accommodation – as he put it, 'related contributions'.

Hutchinson admitted: 'We always knew there would be a problem when he would have to drop his salary when he reached a different stage and became a manager only. I don't know what Alex Ferguson earns but it is reasonable to suggest the managers in this country earn between £300,000 and £350,000 to £400,000, while players earn around £750,000 and some of the top earn £1 million. Ruud wanted £2 million net.'

Gullit, of course, claimed he never expected to receive that and that his demand was purely a negotiating ploy. But the Dutchman was also angry about something else. He said he'd only found out that he'd been fired via calls from reporters and Teletext. He only got confirmation when Bates handed him a letter at 6.30pm on Thursday at the Conrad Hotel.

He said he only sensed the ground was about to move from under him following a meeting with Hutchinson on Thursday the previous week, when, according to Gullit, 'At the beginning there was a really good atmosphere. But at the end it was a little bit strange. I said I wanted to stay for the next two years, but they didn't tell me what *they* wanted. I came out feeling they already had a different agenda. Something was not right.'

Gullit reacted badly to the interpretation that 'negotiations' had been 'on-going' since October. 'It's total, incredible lies,' he said. 'The negotiations have never happened.'

For the six days after his meeting with Hutchinson, Gullit heard nothing more and he became suspicious when he heard that Vialli and Zola had met his transfer target Brian Laudrup. Gullit explained: 'They didn't offer me anything, didn't make me that new offer, and didn't speak to me about it for a week, not a word. That made me suspicious. Then I found out about Laudrup and asked myself, "What's going on?" ' He suspected a hidden agenda, a conspiracy.

Gullit thought he had been fobbed off with a story that Laudrup couldn't travel to keep his Monday appointment because his wife Mette was ill. So he contacted the player and his agent to discover what had happened. Gullit said: 'I know from the player that he was surprised, because he was supposed to meet me. I have heard that Laudrup asked where I was – and they said I had other important things to do. I didn't say they were involved in negotiations. I don't know what they talked about. It seems odd to me that he couldn't come because his wife was ill – he could still come for talks alone. It's strange to me that he met Luca and Zola. It's been confirmed to me that it happened. I am confused.'

Laudrup did eventually make the journey on Wednesday and was picked up at the airport by Gwyn Williams. Zola and Vialli met Laudrup at La Famiglia just off the King's Road, one of Bates's favourite restaurants. Zola didn't stay for long, just 15 minutes. His mission was to 'sell' the club to the Dane by informing him how a foreign star like himself had settled into London so easily and that his children had adapted to a perfect school; the priority for the Laudrups was the schooling for their two children.

Zola had a tight schedule that day. He then caught up with Di Matteo and Attilio Lombardo of Crystal Palace with Cesare Maldini for a 6 pm appointment at the Meridien Hotel in Piccadilly, where the Italian national coach dropped off his overnight bag before they were all driven to Wembley to spy on World Cup opponents Chile. They sat together to the right of the Royal Box, leaving five minutes before the end to beat the traffic and make it to Di Matteo's newly opened Fulham Road restaurant La Perla, arriving at around 10.15 and staying until just after midnight. That same evening, Vialli met with Hutchinson to discuss the final details of the coaching coup. Hutchinson and Vialli had built up an excellent rapport after enjoying a lunch together while in Thailand on the end-of-season tour.

Zola, though, had no idea of events behind the scenes. Hutchinson countered Gullit's claims about the get-together with Laudrup: 'There was nothing secret about the meeting. I understand that Ruud is disappointed, hurt and angry, but this is the most unfortunate and unfair part of what has gone on. The Laudrup family, Zola and Vialli, to a lesser extent, are innocent parties.'

Hutchinson explained how Chelsea had targeted Laudrup. The initial approach came from Gullit, the normal procedure, and Ruud had several telephone conversations with the exciting forward, but those would have been about talking tactics. 'Laudrup was due to come to London on Monday to look at houses and Ruud was aware of this,' Hutchinson said. 'On Monday, Ruud was also told that Brian could not come because his wife was ill and he confirmed this with me. Laudrup came on Wednesday, not for negotiations as these were completed three weeks ago. Ruud was aware that we had made Laudrup our best offer. The Laudrup family are very close and they wanted to come to London to look at houses, schools and the area, and Ruud knew this.'

Hutchinson emphasized that Zola's role was purely to illustrate to Laudrup how Chelsea's foreigners had settled in London: 'For Ruud to drag the Laudrups into the situation ... I feel sorry for the Laudrups, who behaved impeccably. They just came down to London to see if it was a place where they could live. There was nothing sinister, no business was discussed. While Brian was down here he met two of our players who have settled in London because he was thinking of moving to the same area where Luca and Gianfranco live. Zola has put his roots down here. Mrs Zola met Mrs Laudrup about how their children have settled in. If there was a conspiracy, we would not have had our meetings in public. We had a meal and Gianfranco popped in before he went off to Wembley to meet Maldini. The enthusiasm of Gianfranco in his meeting with Brian did more in five minutes than Ruud and I could do talking to him for an hour. Vialli talked to the Laudrups purely as a player.'

Zola angrily hit out at claims that he was involved in a plot. He had no knowledge that his meeting with Laudrup was without the knowledge of Gullit or that the manager would be sacked the next day. Zola said: 'Gullit knew well that I only saw Laudrup for no more than ten minutes in a restaurant near Stamford Bridge because I was asked by Colin Hutchinson to explain to Laudrup how comfortable it is to sort out things for your family in London; in particular I told him about the excellent school my children go to and that was it. Like everybody else, I learnt of Vialli's appointment last Thursday afternoon.'

Zola's representative Phil Smith at First Artist, who also represents Gullit, tried to 'defuse' the situation in a radio interview with Brian Alexander on Radio 5 Live. Smith told listeners: 'Zola is disgusted that he has been brought into this situation. He's not angry with Ruud, he's disgusted that Chelsea have brought him into this.' Zola was worried that it was suggested that he was angry with the club for being implicated in a sordid episode when he had made no such attack on Chelsea. Phil Smith told me: 'I'm sorry, but in my view Chelsea had used Zola and I was just trying to protect him.' However, later in the day the Smiths issued a statement that Zola had become innocently embroiled. In truth he had done little more than an important fifteen-minute PR job on behalf of the club without prior knowledge that Gullit was about to be sacked. Zola wanted to stress that he was not unhappy with the club: 'I don't want the club to be tainted by reports that indicate my displeasure.' Phil Smith reinforced that view: 'Gianfranco has no problem with Chelsea. He was asked by his employers to help by seeing Laudrup and that's what he did.' There were plenty of apologies and putting the record straight. Laudrup rang Gullit in Amsterdam to clarify the situation and Zola also rang his former coach.

Zola stressed that the elevation to 'boss' of his Italian friend Vialli wouldn't guarantee him his place, though clearly Vialli's appointment would mean an initial run in the side again. Yet Zola argued: 'It is not the manager who guarantees that you will be in the side – it is you yourself. You have to be in the side with your performances.' Zola was anxious to win back his World Cup place but added: 'Between now and June, anything can happen.'

The debate over Gullit's departure became the biggest soccer story of the season. Gullit never wanted to leave Chelsea. His passion and commitment to the club was unflinching. How do I know? Well, when all the speculation about his future was the subject of constant back page headlines, it just made him laugh: 'Hey, I'm staying, don't worry.' As he sat on the couch in my Chelsea flat, relaxed, expansive, and expressive each Friday evening, as we talked for hours as I wrote his autobiography, his love affair with the London club shone through. The FA Cup was the start, not the end. For anyone who moaned about three defeats by Arsenal, he would shrug his shoulders and smile knowingly about those with short memories. His quest was to bring the trophy with 'big ears' – as he affectionately calls the ultimate European trophy he won as a player – to the Bridge – the European Cup.

Now that dream was over, crushed beneath the lust for glory, power and cash. He came to the club on a free transfer, and subsequently was highly paid, a £1.25 million a year contract. Colin Hutchinson recalled how Gullit never asked for his pay cheque for the first three months and he kept it in his drawer. Gullit then took over from Glenn Hoddle without asking for any more money to do the extra work. 'Just pay me the same amount and spend the money on new players,' was his response; they simply agreed on bigger bonuses for success.

When he left, the club's point of view was that he was still on a player's contract, yet fading out as a player. But Gullit wasn't quite finished, and Gullit even at thirty-five was better than some players half his age you could mention. One appearance from Gullit, if he regained full fitness, was worth half of dozen of mediocrity.

But when it comes to a stand-off at Chelsea, there will be only one winner – Ken Bates. Matthew Harding discovered that. No-one takes on Bates at Chelsea and wins. Not that he and Gullit were in conflict. They actually got on very well, with plenty of kind words so far from Gullit in his autobiography for the controversial, sometimes irascible chairman.

Bates had waited fifteen years for Chelsea to blossom, both off and on the field, and he was the man responsible for the emergence of a sleeping giant. At least, so he thought. Many, however, put the transformation down to the charismatic character at the Bridge, not the controversial one. Gullit had become the main man. His image adorned the lucrative new megastore, his Ruud Wear was on sale within. But there were always the snipers. Arrogant, said those who didn't really know him. Aloof, said those he didn't have time for. Lazy, suggested those who were jealous of his success. Some of the criticism hurt, Gullit confided to me, particularly when it became personal. But he had learned to accept the bad with the good when he was the centre of attention and analysis in equal proportion in Italy. When it was said that he wasn't as dedicated as Alex Ferguson, he made an effort to change. Out went half a dozen lucrative commercial deals set up on the back of his pizza ad. He trained harder, slept less after the birth of baby daughter Joelle, and worried more after defeats. But knowing Ruud as I do, he won't be hiding or sulking.

He's seen it all and done it all before. He has come through far worse than what happened at Chelsea – and on a vastly bigger scale. He walked out of the Dutch World Cup camp two weeks before the World Cup finals in America. He has fallen out with his coaches when he was the star player, just as Luca Vialli resented being on the bench under him. Gullit could handle it because on the training ground he could still hit the ball sweetly over sixty yards out of defence, he could still play in midfield, and could turn his hand to a run down the wing or a stint in attack. This, after all, is the man who in his prime was the World's greatest player. Bigger than Vialli or indeed any of the other foreign imports assembled in the Premiership. 'Sexy football' was only part of it. He was the first foreign coach to win a trophy in English football, the first black manager to be successful; he became a cult figure, an icon. Only Bates would have dared cut him down to size. Whether the club would survive the upheaval, only time would tell.

Vialli inherited a backroom staff that Gullit now believes was disloyal. Gullit vowed to take his own men to his next job in management, hinting that he had been let down by the men he trusted. It was said that Rix did all the work on the training pitch. However, that is much the same as Brian Kidd does for Alex Ferguson. Gullit's answer to anyone who suggested that he was little more than a part-time manager: 'Look at my record.'

Rix was another key personality in the so-called conspiracy to oust Gullit. The former Arsenal and England star had plenty to say only a couple of days later in two Sunday papers. He insisted that he was more shocked than anyone when Gullit was sacked; he was angry to hear that, in some quarters, he was being blamed for Gullit's demise, as the manager pointed an accusing finger at his backroom staff for keeping him in the dark in the Laudrup affair.

Rix told the *Sunday Mirror* he had the utmost respect for his boss but needed to use all his experience to help Gullit make the transition from player to manager, especially when Gullit's team selections left no-one safe from the bench: 'I would try to advise Ruud and sometimes he listened – but sometimes he had already made his mind up. I'd see a practice situation where certain players were not involved with the first team and could see their heads begin to drop. I would pull Rudi and tell him if he was not going to play someone like Mark Hughes, he must not leave it to the last minute to inform him. I said he should treat the player with a little more respect, take him to one side and explain why. Initially his view was, "Why should I? I pick my team." But he later realized he got their respect by telling them what he was doing. It doesn't matter how good you are as a manager or a coach, if the players don't want to perform for you, you've got no chance.'

Gullit also showed Rix how impetuous he could be by wanting to change his line-up just minutes into a game. 'He would say: "We can't have this, I've got to change it" – and that might be five or ten minutes into a match. I'd say: "No, Ruud – you have to think what it might do to the kid if he is taken off after ten minutes." He cooled down a bit. I think it was improving all the time.'

Rix was happy to sit in the background puffing on his cigar until he felt he was needed. Often he would be seen whispering a few well-chosen words in Gullit's ear. And more often than not, Gullit took notice. Rix recalled how Chelsea were losing 3–1 at Coventry in the Premiership, days before meeting Wimbledon in the FA Cup semi-final, and he told Gullit: 'We can't play this way against Wimbledon – we must play with a flat back four.' That's exactly what Chelsea did – and the Dons were given a 3–0 hiding. 'We were pretty much on the same wavelength. But all these good players came to Chelsea because of Ruud Gullit – not because of Graham Rix.'

Rix might have been circumspect in his analysis of Gullit in that interview but he was highly critical in the *News of the World*. Gullit said that he was shocked and saddened that neither Rix nor Gwyn Williams had rung him after his sacking: 'Nearly all the players telephoned. Most did not know what to say, they were too shocked. But Graham Rix and Gwyn Williams, my right-hand men, did not ring. That was strange.' Gullit commented at his press conference that 'the only thing Graham Rix did was referee practice matches in which I played; he did not take training, I did the coaching, I decided what we did, the way we played, even if I was on the field. I laid out my plans.' The next day in an interview with Des Lynam in Amsterdam, Gullit said he knew who had picked up Laudrup for the controversial meeting and his look into the camera said it all. He didn't name him. But Gullit knows it was Gwyn Williams.

Gullit's view of Rix's worth was not shared by Rix himself, who suggested that the laid-back Dutchman was beginning to buckle under the strain. Rix saw the signs at half-time during Chelsea's 2–0 Premiership defeat by Arsenal: 'We were two goals down and Ruud was on his own in the showers. I walked in and he was hitting his fist against his forehead over and over again. In his other hand he had a piece of paper with the team he wanted for the second half. I looked at it and there were only two defenders. I couldn't believe it and told him, "You can't do that. There's no backbone to the team." I quickly scribbled out what I thought the team should be. I said to him, "I'm going to leave you alone for thirty seconds to get yourself together." When I came back he had written up my team and was ready to tell the players about the changes. It was clear to me things weren't going as well as his cool exterior suggested. The guy was really struggling. I was desperate for him to ask me for help but he never asked, it was heartbreaking. I worked with Ruud for eighteen months and I can honestly say I never knew the guy. I think deep down Rudi is quite insecure and the cool thing is just a front.' When I asked Gullit for his reaction, he just smiled . . . Clearly he was not going to respond to events he feels were completely distorted.

Rix maintained he was shocked by Gullit's sacking but added: 'It's probably for the best because we've gone badly off the rails in recent weeks and I'm not sure Ruud could have halted the slide.' That was perhaps the most damning comment. When Hutchinson was questioned by Gary Lineker on Football Focus, the same message slipped out. 'He's lost it,' said Hutchinson. Clearly, the board felt it was time to act and results would improve.

Rix couldn't forgive or forget that Gullit denied him the chance to team up with England coach Glenn Hoddle's staff as a part-timer. 'Glenn wanted me to work with the players when there was an international. Like me, the club saw the advantage of the offer but Ruud refused to let me go. I fought my corner and said Chelsea had so many international players there was very little for me to do when the World Cup matches came around. I'd be left with a handful of players and end up just refereeing meaningless practice matches. But Ruud said no and I had to accept it. He said I had a job to do at Chelsea and I must do it. I was bitterly disappointed and it still hurts.'

Rix was confident of establishing a better relationship with new boss Vialli. 'After the news broke I went to see Luca in the dressing-room. I wished him all the best and his first words to me were,

"Graham, I need your help." It was amazing. I had waited eighteen months for Ruud to say that to me.' Vialli spent his first night in charge over dinner at Langan's Mayfair restaurant with Rix.

Mark Hughes dismissed the notion being spread around that player power had some sort of role in the ousting of Gullit. In an in-depth *Sunday Mirror* interview, he said: 'I am extremely sorry that Ruud has left Chelsea. He was excellent for the club and made a lot of people happy with the way we played. In fact he was one of the main reasons I joined Chelsea in the first place. When Glenn Hoddle told me Ruud was to arrive, I couldn't wait to sign.' As for the player power: 'All because we had a team meeting without him – even though talking together was something Ruud always encouraged. There must have been five or six occasions when Ruud called senior players to have their say.

'At this particular time none of us was happy about the way we had lost to Arsenal in the first leg of the Coca-Cola Cup semi-final. Ruud asked us to see him. There was myself, Dennis Wise, Steve Clarke, Eddie Newton and Luca Vialli. Ruud started with Dennis as captain and we were all allowed to have our say. I simply made the point that we had to look at ourselves and not start hiding behind injuries or other changes to the team. Dennis suggested we leave Ruud and talk to the rest of the lads. Our feeling was that younger players some-times clam up in the presence of the boss, but there was no question of going behind Ruud's back. He was next door only twenty yards away and was very happy with what was going on. The bottom line was we realized there had been a slip in form and we didn't want it to get out of hand. Ruud simply asked us: "How did it go?" – and we told him we thought it would help. We went out to play against Barnsley and Ruud told us he wouldn't need to do a team talk because he sensed that we were ready to sparkle again. Our get-together did its job. Ruud knew all about it and no way was it meant to undermine his position.

'I even heard a story that I was part of a deputation going above Ruud's head to see Ken Bates. That is absolute nonsense too. There was no reason to do that. I have played under some great managers like Alex Ferguson, Glenn Hoddle and Terry Venables and I can tell you Ruud belongs firmly in that category. He has a very shrewd football mind and, make no mistake about it, he was the man behind everything that happened in planning and playing our matches. We've heard he left a lot of the training to others like Graham Rix. That's not so. Ruud would tell Graham what he wanted to achieve and Graham would set the session up. Ruud was very much the instigator and was very much aware of what the team needed to work on.

'People say Ruud could be aloof, but I don't know a manager yet who enjoys telling players they are not in the side. Ruud would simply put the team sheet up on match days, but you had a pretty good idea from the way training had gone. If you weren't wearing the right bib, it looked like you might miss out. Ruud told us at the beginning of the season that he was going to rotate the strikers and it's a myth that he made unnecessary changes. He explained he wanted to change the front players each week to keep them fresh, and you can't say it wasn't a success because we are joint top scorers in the Premiership. Of course his relationship with Gianluca Vialli was strained, especially in the first season. I believe it had improved this time around but you certainly wouldn't expect them to be having dinner together now.

'It was a situation that was always brought home to me because I changed for the game right next to Luca. I was putting on my strip to play and he was donning his to sit on the bench. He always wished me good luck and I believe he sincerely meant it. We all have a lot of time for Luca because of the way he handled his situation with dignity, but no one can say what Ruud was doing did not work.

'Ruud came in for some criticism when we were beaten 5–3 by Manchester United in the FA Cup, because I played in midfield and did not do very well. The truth is, though, he was struggling with injuries in that area. He asked me if I could do a job there and I promised him I would. It turned out I wasn't up to it but that wasn't his fault. I know where the blame lies for that move going wrong.

'You judge a manager, too, on the kind of players he brings to the club and Ruud let no one down with men like Vialli, Di Matteo, Poyet, Zola, Leboeuf and Le Saux. He has passed the test as a Premiership manager. There is no doubt about that.

Hughes recalled the FA Cup triumph: 'All the way through our celebrations, Ruud stood back and let the lads take the plaudits. He's not selfish. He's not arrogant – he is simply professional. I will always consider it a huge shame that the relationship between him and the club grew so sour.'

Gullit spent the weekend in Amsterdam with Estelle and baby Joelle. He relaxed at the Dutch First Division match between Sparta Rotterdam and Heerenveen, with speculation linking him with Feyenoord. But he said: 'It's too early for me to make any decision about my future. I'm just going to sit back and see what is on offer.' He just smiled at claims by Rix that he was on the verge of cracking up in his final days at the Bridge.

Vialli could hardly have a more difficult first match in charge – the Coca-Cola Cup semi-final second leg at Stamford Bridge, with Arsenal 2–1 up from the first match. Frank Leboeuf pleaded with Chelsea fans not to desert the club in their hour of need. 'I have a big message for the fans – don't leave us. We need everyone for our next game against Arsenal. The club has been going very strongly in the last year and we must carry on. I hope everyone will be behind us.'

Vialli's first day in charge was Friday 13th – enough to make him wince when he realized. Rix said: 'Luca is a very amiable sort of guy, very approachable, and he is trying to get that message across – that if the players have a problem, they should come and see him, that we are all in this together. We trained for two hours on Friday and the players really enjoyed it, they were all trying to impress a new manager, albeit a former team-mate. Now we have a few more things to work on before Wednesday's match.'

With implied criticism of Gullit, Vialli spoke of his desire to narrow the gap between his team-mates and the management, to breed an 'open and honest rapport' and to improve communication about decisions. But as he began his first week, he showed his determination to remain 'one of the lads' as he trained alongside the rest of the Chelsea players. Fitness coach Ade Mafe put the first-team squad outfield players through their paces, giving Vialli no special treatment as he jogged and sprinted in the middle of the pack around the training ground near Heathrow Airport and went through stretching exercises like everyone else. As ever, it was Rix who was in charge of the training-session – proving that despite Gullit's departure, there would be continuity.

Around 200 fans were there during half-term week to watch Chelsea's second training session since Vialli became player-manager. Captain Dennis Wise turned to Vialli after he had made a mistake during a game of handball and gleefully shouted, 'That was rubbish, Luca.' His new boss turned and smiled back before sharing a private joke.

Supporter Lee Thompson, 26, who has watched Chelsea train on countless occasions over the past couple of years, said: 'There definitely seemed to be more of a spark among the players. Graham Rix has always been the one in charge during training, so little has changed there. But Gullit often used to stand and watch. Even when he was fit he didn't always train with the players, while Vialli was right in amongst them, laughing and joking.

'Zola had a smile on his face and looked a different player compared to two weeks ago when he was out of the side under Gullit. Everyone has got a chance now to impress the new manager and that can only help.'

Vialli told the players his first job was to sort out their defence. Chelsea's weakness at the back had caused them problems all season. When the players staged their crisis meeting without Gullit, defence was one of the hottest topics. Many felt Gullit had gone wrong switching from a three-man central defence to 4–4–2.

Almost immediately, though, Ken Bates found himself having to reassure Vialli that there wasn't yet another conspiracy at Stamford Bridge, when claims appeared in the *Daily Mail* that Terry Venables or George Graham were being lined up by Chelsea in case Vialli failed. The club contacted Vialli to inform him the speculation was not true. The Chelsea chairman told me: 'Colin Hutchinson spoke to Luca this morning to reassure him. This is a clear attempt to cause trouble in the Chelsea camp on the eve of a very important cup tie. The last time I spoke to Terry Venables was after we had beaten Portsmouth 4–1 in the FA Cup six round last season. I've not seen him or anybody connected to him since. I am not interested in Terry Venables, I have never ever contemplated him as our manager.'

Vialli must have been taken aback but never showed it. Like Gullit, he had ample experience of the Italian media and the relentless speculation and intrigue. 'I'm used to reading silly stories but I cannot think that Chelsea are planning for another change, it would be foolish.'

Bates finally broke cover and publicly admitted what had been going on behind the scenes when he answered questions on the Clubcall line, and of course in his infamous programme notes. He accused Gullit of presiding over a team that underachieved, given the strength of the squad at their disposal, despite being second in the Premiership. Asked about the Blues' rapid ascent to the position of serious title challengers under Gullit, Bates scoffed: 'If you want my honest answer, we're a bit disappointed. With the squad we have, I thought we should have been playing Barnsley in the FA Cup last weekend instead of Manchester United. Maybe we should be five points clear of United in the Premiership instead of five behind them, and I'm not too happy about being a goal down to Arsenal in the Coca-Cola Cup, either. That is a measure of our expectations now. Every supporter should be pleased about that.'

Bates also pointed to the Dutchman's meagre total of 10 starts and 14 substitute appearances in 84 competitive games since he came to the club as a player. 'We felt that he should stop playing. I mean, he wasn't training and therefore wasn't fit to play. We wanted Ruud to stop as a player but quite rightly he told us that was not our decision when to tell him to stop. But equally it was our right not to pay him as a player anymore, particularly when it would be costing us £3.75 million! I'd rather Ruud had stayed. But once we had made our decision it was best to get on with it. You can't cry over spilt milk . . . if indeed any milk was spilt.'

As for the clash of two egos and fears that Gullit was becoming bigger than the chairman, Bates attacked the quality of football writers who he suggested had been 'perpetuating a myth' about that issue. 'The club is too big to be run by one person, even if one person thought he could do it,' he explained.

On his way home from the Bridge, the chairman rang me in the office to chat over the day's events. I told Bates that it was being suggested in *Gazzetta dello Sport* that the club had been thinking about replacing Gullit long before the supposedly fateful meeting with Hutchinson that sparked the contract row. Hutchinson, it was said, had checked out Vialli's managerial credentials with directors at his former club Juventus *ten days* before they fired Gullit. Hutchinson told me: 'Yes, I was in Turin, but as the guest of Juventus to watch their game with Fiorentina, when we talked about many things. The conversation inevitably got round to our Italians and to Luca. Naturally it was a chance to ask about Vialli's managerial potential and everybody told me that Gianluca had all the skills necessary to become an excellent manager.' Hutchinson denied that any decision had been taken in advance to oust Gullit. However, the club must have been thinking about it. Only the timing remained on the agenda.

Before accepting the job, Vialli had contacted friends in Italy including Italian international defender Ciro Ferrara and Juventus manager Marcello Lippi. Again, that suggested that there had been plenty of time for him to consider the offer.

But Vialli revealed in his first pre-match interview that he was approached just three days before Gullit was sacked and accepted the job the night before the axe fell. He stressed: 'No one has stabbed Ruud in the back. I just respond to my own conscience. At the end of the day, you have to look at yourself in the mirror. Only you know if you have done anything wrong or not. It's the way you behave day after day that makes people decide if you are backstabber or not. I can only say that everything done by Colin Hutchinson, the managing director, was correct from my point of view. I knew Mr Hutchinson was going to tell Ruud only the night before it happened. I didn't have time to realize what his feelings would be. Mr Hutchinson didn't want to do anything behind Ruud's back, but he needed to know that I was ready to take over. They only asked me if I was ready twenty-four hours before. Of course I feel sorry for Ruud. We weren't the best of friends and there were problems in our professional relationship. But I really want to wish him all the best.' Yet, by Vialli's own admission he had talks 'three' days earlier!

When club skipper Denis Wise was asked for his reaction to the events of the past week, his initial silence, followed by a drawn-out 'Mmmmm!' spoke as loud as his eventual answer. Wise said: 'We've got to accept it, got to get on with it and get behind Luca because he's the manager now. We like Luca, as we liked Ruud, but we've got to get behind him and stick together as a group of lads. Whatever's gone on has gone on. It's nothing to do with us.'

Vialli had already spoken to each member of the squad individually. Mark Hughes said: 'Luca has a presence about him in the dressing-room. We'll have to wait and see what his style will be, but he's very passionate and emotional about the game, and I'm sure that will come out.' Wise added: 'Luca's always been a bit of a perfectionist in some of the things he does, the way he dresses and presents himself. I'm sure he'll be exactly the same as a manager.'

Vialli's philosophy was simple: 'I want to win games; I want to score goals; I don't care so much about keeping clean sheets. Those are my tactics, I'm not joking. Football shouldn't be too scientific. You want the players to enjoy themselves, but they have to be committed, motivated and determined, to work as a team.'

In response to Fabio Capello's remark that giving him the job was akin to handing a Formula One car to a man without a licence, Vialli, a close friend of Grand Prix driver Jean Alesi, made it clear he did not feel he needed any management L-plates. 'Capello is right,' he said. 'It would never have happened in Italy. There, you are a player or a manager. But I didn't ask for this job. The board thought I was the right person from the way I've behaved and the way I think about football. That means they think I can drive a little bit – and on the left-hand side of the road as well!'

More than 10,000 leaflets were reported to have been printed by an angry supporters' group wanting to thank the Dutchman for his contribution and hammering Bates. There was little sign of any leaflets when I made my short walk to the Bridge, but my *Mirror* colleague John Dillon was on fan patrol. The perfect venue was the Imperial Arms pub, the old haunt of Matthew Harding, now a trendy designer bar rather than the old-fashioned boozer where he supped Guinness before matches. There was only one topic of conversation – Ruud and Luca, Bates and Hutchinson. Peter Osgood and Tommy Baldwin chatted at the bar as fans shook their heads, still confused. 'Vialli? Nice bloke,' said Paul Wills, a regular at Stamford Bridge since 1968. 'Of course, we'll all get behind him. In the end, it's the club and the team that matters. Nothing else. But I genuinely think he might be too nice for the job. It could all go wrong for him very quickly if we lose against Manchester United and get knocked out of the Cup-Winners' Cup by Real Betis. What will Bates do then? Sack him as well?'

Adrian Stelling, a thirty-six-year-old who travels from Leeds for every home match, 'I used to see Matthew Harding in this pub. He had the one thing Bates hasn't got – humility. He'd talk to anyone. Bates seems to take a perverse pleasure in being rude and arrogant towards everyone. I'll tell you the best kind of chairman – it's one no one ever hears from. How many people can tell you who was the Liverpool chairman when they were winning everything in sight in the 1970s and 1980s? The way things have been done have made the club look bad – again. And before anyone gets carried away, we're not really big time yet, are we? We won the FA Cup last season. That's all.'

As the fans made their way to the big game, they found the programme contained the chairman's page as usual, completely dedicated to Gullit's departutre. Bates claimed Gullit and he parted as friends: 'In fact his parting words were, "Please give my love to Suzannah – we must stay friends, this world is a very small one." We didn't see each other much. When we did we had a laugh.' Bates denied a clash of egos: 'I was delighted for all his personal publicity because it promoted Chelsea and made us one of the most high-profile clubs in the world. I certainly did not resent it – he was promoting both the Club and the Village.'

Bates insisted that the real reason for Gullit's dismissal was his desire to remain a player-coach – and that Gullit only had himself to blame for not being told that Vialli was the new coach because he was impatient and stormed away from the meeting with Hutchinson.

Chelsea had been trying to sign Gullit on a three-year coaching contract since October, aware that Hoddle had left the club in the lurch. Bates was not prepared to be caught out again. 'We wanted Ruud to stay as coach and were prepared to pay him more than Alex Ferguson. But money was only discussed recently. When Ruud made it clear that he wanted a package that would cost us £3.7 million plus bonuses, we knew it was the end of the road.

'There you have it. No coupe, no conspiracies, no player revolts, no clash of egos, just an irreconcilable difference of opinions on roles and values. Ruud is part of our history. He led us to the FA Cup and into Europe. He goes with my personal best wishes and as he said, I hope we stay friends.'

In the dressing-room before the kick-off, Vialli cracked open the bubbly. Ruud had some style – Vialli now showed he had it too: 'It's just a superstition I have. I wanted to have a toast and wish good luck to all the players. As we were going out, I wished the players all the best. It was the start of an adventure for me and I think the best way to start any journey is to toast your own success. Dennis Wise said a few words – and nobody understood them!

'You have to work hard in football but also it was important that we had a laugh and the players then went out with real commitment. I couldn't have asked for any more from them.'

The bizarre preparation set the right mood. Fired-up Chelsea won 3-1 on the night to go through to the final 4-3 on aggregate. In an impressive first post-match press conference, Vialli, said: 'The players did a great job and I'm really proud of them. I am envious of Ruud, he was so cool. I don't know how he did it but I must learn. The pressure before the game was huge and it's difficult to handle. I'll have to learn to do that, though. Otherwise I'll end up with a heart attack.'

The only complaint from the players was the quality of the champagne! They finished it off after the match in the dressing-room but Mark Hughes, whose tenth minute opener put Chelsea on the way to glory, admitted: 'You couldn't drink more than one glass – it wasn't very good!' Vialli accepted that, countering: 'I can't afford any better stuff at the moment.'

As Vialli's named echoed around the stadium in triumph, not a voice was raised in protest for Gullit. The fans backed Vialli without reservation. He received a magnificent reception when introduced as the new coach fifteen minutes before the start and the adulation was unreserved as he went off to a standing ovation shortly before the end. The players were pumped up, determined to play for their new manager. While this was essentially the team that Gullit left behind, fine tuning by Vialli tightened the defence and significantly Zola was accommodated in a three-man attack. Gullit never believed that all three forwards could play in the same team, but Vialli picked himself – the sheer pleasure of power – alongside Mark Hughes with Zola rotating on either flank or in deep positions. Not ideal for Zola who prefers to be up front, but better than being on the bench.

They don't call Vialli 'Lucky Luca' for nothing, taking on Arsenal at their weakest without Seaman, Wright, Bould and Keown, with Ray Parlour struggling so badly with his thigh strapped that he failed to finish the first half, Vialli's close friend David Platt coming on as substitute. Nigel Winterburn also hobbled off before the finish and the game was decided in the first ten minutes of the second half. Patrick Vieira was sent off, Di Matteo scored a stunning goal to make it 2-0, then a corner from Zola broke to Dan Petrescu who finished cleverly. Zola had also won and taken the free-kick which led to Chelsea's first goal.

Within a minute of Vialli going off after eighty-two workaholic minutes, a Bergkamp penalty gave Arsenal hope and Adams was flung forward in a frantic bid by the ten men to push the game into extra time. The body language in the Chelsea dug-out illustrated beyond any words how the new regime would operate. Vialli sat down exhausted by his efforts and let Rix carry on the job of dictating from the touch-line, in stark contrast to the way things were under Gullit. Rix waved to the fans chanting his name. He made the decision to bring off Vialli and the new manager felt it was the right one: 'I could not give any more and I know I will have to rely very heavily on Rixie while I am still a player. It will be my decision when I drop out of the side, but he will tell me if he thinks I am taking on too much.'

Everyone was a hero on the night Chelsea reached the League Cup final for the first time since 1972 but it would be sheer nonsense to believe that Vialli had worked some sort of magic in six days in charge. Still, he was on his way to Wembley to face Middlesbrough in an FA Cup final repeat but with one major difference – this time Vialli would surely be leading the attack not sitting on the bench until two minutes from the end.

How could it get much better than this? 'Lifting the trophy is how,' Vialli said, 'but already I have the same sort of feeling now as I had when I won the European Cup with Juventus. It has been an incredible pressure for me this week. I can't handle it the way Ruud did and I've had sleepless nights ever since I took the job. But the players' response was fantastic. I am so proud of them. At the end I couldn't speak the words to properly thank them because I was so exhausted, both physically and mentally.'

Vialli was so nervous you felt he might need a drink to start every game. Champagne, of course. Dennis Wise observed: 'He gets so nervous. He even said it to me before the game, "I'm really nervous." And he said it to me again afterwards. You can sense it with him. He goes so quiet. There was so much expected of him and he was under so much pressure. But he has a lovely presence about him and that's what the players respect. Afterwards, me and Roberto di Matteo were in the bath knackered. He popped his head around the corner and said: "I love you two." That's the way he does things. It's great. He's different. He's a very gentle man. We all love him as a person. And if you've got a lot of respect for someone, you'll work hard for them.'

Vialli took more than an hour to emerge from the dressing-room to speak in the soft, halting English that drips charm and sophistication. It was the same cultured voice he'd used to give the hard word to the players who missed out on the game. Wise said: 'The whole squad was at Stamford Bridge in the morning and Luca apologized to the players who weren't going to be involved. Basically, he said, "Look, lads, I've had to bring everyone in because I need you all to work on the set pieces. Some of you are not going to be involved and won't be going to the hotel. I apologize for bringing you in, but we're all in this together." It's a very awkward thing, but he was honest and truthful. It's his way of doing things.'

And how about champagne before every match? Wise said: 'I wouldn't mind. It was all set out on the table when we came in from the warm-up. It was a lovely gesture and we only had half a glass each. It's a superstition of Luca's. He's got loads of them. I've never known anyone so superstitious. I've watched him having a massage with just his boots on and that seems to be one of his superstitions. But it wasn't as if we were going to get drunk. We only had half a glass each. Still, we had loads more afterwards.'

However, Vialli found enough energy for his favourite past-time . . . a lavish Italian meal at his favourite haunt, San Lorenzo. His players went, too. Di Matteo, Wise, Petrescu, Le Saux and Leboeuf were all snapped outside the venue for the rich and famous in Beauchamp Place.

David Platt masked his disappointment to praise his pal. 'I believe he will make a marvellous manager. He is a big, big man with a passion for the game. I wish him well.'

Gullit sent a message to 'his' players before the semi-final. Some felt immense loyalty toward him, but he told them to go and and play for Vialli and for Chelsea. Gullit still felt part of the Chelsea success story even though he had been exiled to Amsterdam. 'I thanked the players and told them that loyalty in football is Utopia, something that is transient in this sport. Those players I still regard as mine and I want them to be success at Chelsea. That is why I am so happy for them that they won and I want them to continue to do well. Yes, it is true in football: the king is dead, long live the king. I have I experienced that many times myself in my career, and it is no different now.'

Ironically, after all the fuss over money, Gullit stood to pick up a massive bonus if Chelsea won the Coca-Cola Cup, under the terms of his existing contract that Chelsea would continue to honour. But from his Amsterdam home, 'greedy' Gullit was not the least bit concerned about the financial windfall. He told me: 'The bonuses are the dessert – nice to think about that after winning the trophy, because the Cup comes first. You never play for the bonuses as a player, it is always the Cup or the title and then think about the money. The trophies have always been the most important in my career and the money comes with it.'

Chelsea's plans for the following season were already taking shape with speculation that Laudrup, who wanted a cooling-off period after being embroiled in the Gullit conspiracy theory, had decided to sign for and would move to London as soon as his Rangers contract expired on 1 July. He would be the first £75,000-a-week footballer in Britain, with the kind of top-of-the-range playing salary denied to Gullit. Chelsea, in fact, got a bargain because Laudrup, one of the most sought-after forwards in Europe with a value, under contract, in excess of £10 million, was available on a free transfer. Chelsea couldn't afford both Laudrup and Gullit – and they chose the Dane instead of the Dutchman because Gullit was at the end of his playing career at thirty-five while Laudrup is still only twenty-eight. Bates said in his programme notes: 'Did we want a non-playing coach at £3.7 million a year or the opportunity post-Bosman to acquire another two or three world-class players? Colin Hutchinson chose the latter.' (Well, one can imagine that Bates agreed!) The entire package guaranteed Laudrup £50,000-a-week, and with Chelsea sure to be among the clubs fighting for top honours again, he could expect to break through the £75,000-a-week barrier. As Bates pointed out in his contract row with Gullit, there are many inevitable 'peripheries' offered to lure the best to the Bridge; for Laudrup they include a £1.5 million signing-on fee spread over three years of his contract, top-of-the-range car, lavish accommodation in Belgravia, private schooling for his two children and massive bonuses for success. Add that up and it is within range of the £2 million a year 'netto' that Gullit asked for. But it is a player's deal. Post-Bosman, the elite players are becoming multi-millionaires. They will soon be making as much money as their chairman! Chelsea were also in the market for another of Gullit's original transfer targets, Didier Deschamps. Gullit departed convinced that he had left Vialli the material to win the title, but on the same night as the Coca-Cola Cup triumph against Arsenal, Manchester United went further away in the Premiership with a 2-0 win at Aston Villa. A delighted Alex Ferguson took the opportunity to praise Gullit and his achievements at Chelsea: 'I have always found him relaxed and easy to get on with – a good winner and a good loser. He said a few outrageous things in terms of management but he was refreshing and I think he was good for the game. Ruud tried to play the continental way in this country and that requires a delicate touch to operate it successfully. He overplayed his hand at times with varying selections but he was trying to maintain a challenge on every front by keeping a sharp edge to his squad. You could see the reasoning behind the frequent rotation of his strikers. He didn't make as many changes in other positions. Gianluca Vialli and Mark Hughes are well into their thirties and he obviously thought they would be fresher if he didn't play them all the time. But big players have big egos and there were bound to be problems.'

19

'Numero Uno'

Franco Zola has no doubts about the influence of the overseas stars in the Premiership.

Maybe such a view wouldn't be unexpected, after all. But he also puts forward a very powerful argument in favour of the import of expensive foreign stars to English football. 'Players do not just come over here to earn big money before they go back home and retire. Many players who have come over here are not so old and it is wrong to suggest that they are. The stars who are here are players who can offer something to English football.

'I think that some people are worried about the new arrivals hindering the progress of young players in England, but they shouldn't be. If you have good players from abroad, you have good examples to follow. That can only be a good thing and will help young players develop.'

Because of his 'special' relationship with young supporters, Zola gave an insight about the foreign contingent in *Match* magazine, where he nominated three of his Top Ten Foreign Stars from Stamford Bridge – Frank Leboeuf, Roberto Di Matteo and Luca Vialli.

Roberto Di Matteo is an 'Italian' style midfield anchor man. He reads the game with enormous insight and intelligence; the philosophy that a fine interception is as effective as a tough tackle. Not averse to getting stuck in, he can also ankle tap with the best of them, and has picked up a few yellow cards as a consequence.

Roberto was the first current international from Italy to move to the Premiership when he became one of Ruud Gullit's first signings at a Chelsea club record £4.9m from Lazio. There were tears and recriminations when the *Serie A* club sold him. His peculiar brand of midfield player, neat, precise, using up the minimum of effort for the maximum effect, was not appreciated in English football for some time. Roberto also had his problems settling in, with 'cowboy' plumbers making his life a misery when he moved into his Knightsbridge flat, and a couple of colds hampered his progress.

But at Stamford Bridge he became a legend with his goal after forty-seven seconds in the FA Cup Final against Middlesbrough, a flash of skill that makes him a world-class performer as well as a defensive midfield player.

Zola says: 'Di Matteo is a big player. He is one of those footballers who works very hard for the team but can often go without their work being recognised. He is quite a tough midfield player, but he also scores some good goals. He's a very important player for the Italian national team and also for Chelsea.

'Di Matteo has a similar role at Chelsea to the one Roy Keane has at Manchester United, and any United fan will be able to tell you how crucial Keane is to their team. He is one of Chelsea's best stars.'

Leboeuf, a true sweeper in the Continental style, has a pivotal role within the Chelsea team. Zola says: 'Leboeuf is a very good player. Because I am playing with him every week for Chelsea, I get to see Leboeuf in action a lot. I can honestly say he is a great player. He is doing very well in England and many English defenders are learning from the cool and calm way he plays. He has great skill and reads the game very well. Frank Leboeuf is very important to us at the back.'

Zola's admiration for Vialli is undiminished by his problems in his first year, and in fact has been enhanced by Vialli's professional attitude and comeback in his second season. 'Gianluca Vialli is a great, great player. At Chelsea he has had to deal with some problems, and he has not played often, but for me Vialli is an important player. He is very intelligent and he is a great help for the whole team. The fans certainly realise just what a great man he is. All the Chelsea supporters love him. He has a big heart and he is a big figure at our club.'

Sheffield Wednesday have had a torrid season, but for Zola a fellow Italian has been in outstanding form and scored some spectacular goals for the Owls – Benito Carbone. 'Benito is a very good player, but no-one talks about him. He has great, great skills, but he doesn't get the attention he deserves. You don't see many things about him in the newspapers because he is playing for a smaller club, but he is very good. It's not easy to get into the Italy side in his position as there are a lot of challengers, including myself. Also, he is not a striker and he is not a midfielder, he is a player who likes to play between the two. In Italy, there is not much space for a player like him.'

The real big-name strikers are on Zola's list Faustino Asprilla and Dennis Bergkamp.

Asprilla spent three years with Franco in Parma, and the little Italian has had plenty of opportunity to assess his old team-mate's qualities in the Premiership.

It usually takes one world-class striker to recognise another, and Zola has no doubts about the Colombian's colourful talents. He says: 'Asprilla is a player who has great skill. I don't think anybody knows all the skills that Asprilla has.' Newcastle fans know that to be true and were desperately sad when Tino wanted to return to Parma. Zola added: 'He is playing much more consistently and he has shown that he can do great things.'

The majority of Asprilla's explosive tricks are off the cuff, instinctive, and usually unpredictable, so much so that not even his team-mates can 'read' him. Zola added: 'I played with Asprilla for three years when we were at Parma and I really enjoyed the games I played with him. Of course, I never knew what he was going to do next. It is very hard to predict what Asprilla will do when he has the ball, but that makes it hard for defenders to play against him.'

Zola also joins the Bergkamp fan club. 'Dennis Bergkamp is a fantastic player and he has a lot of qualities. I really love to watch him play as he can do so many great things with the ball. He is currently proving to everybody that he is a truly great player, one of the very best. He always makes sure that he has a lot of time on the ball, and he can create openings and score goals from just about any situation and any position.'

Zola's team-mate Tore Andre Flo plundered a hat-trick against Spurs in the Premiership and made his name internationally with two goals against Brazil for Norway. Norway were drawn in the same World Cup group as Brazil and Scotland, and have a profusion of up-and-coming young strikers, Steffan Iversen at Spurs, and Ole Solskjaer at Old Trafford. Solskjaer and Flo are part of successful squads at club level in European football, the ideal way to tune in for the World Cup Finals. Solskjaer is selected as one of Zola's Top Ten foreign imports. Zola says: 'Ole Solskjaer is a very exciting young talent. He is still only twenty-four years old, so no-one can accuse him of coming here to end his career by picking up lots of money. I think his best years are still ahead of him at Man United and yet he is already an accomplished footballer. He has a very good first touch which has helped him to score some excellent goals this season.'

Another Old Trafford giant makes Zola's list. Inevitably the giant Peter Schmeichel, probably even more influential to the success story of Ferguson than Eric Cantona. 'I have picked Schmeichel because he is a very good goalkeeper and he has been very important to Manchester United over the years. Quite simply, they would not have won anything like as many trophies as they have over the past few years without him. I don't know whether he is the best goalkeeper in the world or not because there are many fine keepers, especially in this country and in Italy. But he is definitely one of the best.'

Costa Rican forward Paulo Wanchope has been the surprise of the season; the unpredictable long-legged striker is one of Zola's favourites. 'I have only begun to notice Wanchope this season, but he looks to be a very talented and very exciting player. He has a great deal of skill and he uses it to run at defenders and take them on, so he is always exciting to watch. I know Francesco Baiano from Italy, and he looks to be really enjoying himself playing alongside Paulo. They look a bit like Tino Asprilla and me when we played together at Parma. They are turning Derby into a very strong team and I think Wanchope has a big future. You can never tell what he is going to do next and that can be a very dangerous weapon on the football pitch.' Zola felt quite contented when Wanchope was substitute, Baiano kept quiet too, as Chelsea crushed Derby 4–0 at the Bridge with Zola getting the first hat-trick of his career.

Finally, Zola pays homage to the one time World's No. 1, Ruud
Gullit. 'Gullit is still a very good player. He played for two years in
the Premiership and he did well. Maybe he didn't play his best football, because he came here when he was thirty-two and he's had
many injuries, but he still showed what a great player he is. I think he
played his best football when he was at Milan. I played against him
when he was there and also when he was at Sampdoria.'

Of course, Zola himself is missing from his own list of the Top Ten;
he would not be omitted from anyone else's. The influence of Zola
has been recognised by everyone in the game. Kevin Keegan, in his
role as Fulham's head of operations, wanted to transform his club in
the image of Chelsea. 'It may be a struggle to spot even one Fulham
fan in the street but I believe we can engender the same kind of
enthusiasm at Craven Cottage. Look at our near-neighbours Chelsea.
They should be an inspiration to us. People are flocking there
because of what they're doing out on the pitch with Zola, Di Matteo
and the rest.'

After his first hat-trick of his career in the 4–0 defeat of Derby at
the Bridge, Matt Dickenson wrote in *The Times*, 'Of the high-profile
horde of foreigners to have invaded the FA Carling Premiership in
recent seasons, only Juninho can have come close to inspiring such
genuine and widespread affection as the little Italian. Eric Cantona
was too arrogant, Dennis Bergkamp too aloof. Zola charms all he
meets.' Franco certainly charmed the media. *The Times*' Oliver Holt
wrote of his 'romantic brilliance'. Trevor Brooking pinpoints the
player's confidence. Brooking said, 'He has the belief and confidence
to take on defenders, the art of dribbling has been ignored for too
long. When Zola receives the ball, his first touch is so fine that the
instant control buys him that extra split-second and space to exploit
his skills. He has a superb football brain which selects for him the
most effective pass, often the most simple option. He does not need
to over-elaborate just for the sake of it.'

Graham Rix provided an insight into Zola's professionalism, attitude and commitment, a willingness to practise his skills with junior
players, endlessly wanting to practise to make perfect. 'We've known
from the first day Zola came here what an exceptional talent he has
got. What we didn't realise was what great strength of character he's

got as well. Probably people don't realise, but when he missed the header against Blackburn from three metres, for the rest of that week he practised headers. By himself, after training, simple headers, no-one in the goal, putting them in left, right and centre. It just shows what sort of guy he is. He's Footballer of the Year, everybody's flavour of the month, and yet he knows he's not the best he wants to be. He's still prepared to work really hard for it. He doesn't rest on his laurels. He is a credit to himself.'

It's rare in the modern game to find a player equally at home with either foot. Rix added, 'He has the ability to go forward while changing direction, a skill that others can only dream about. He can beat a player on both sides – he frightens defenders to death. All this and with a smile on his face.'

Rix also spots his enthusiasm for the game, his generosity in wanting to pass on his knowledge and skill. Rix says: 'He has such a positive attitude. He will sign autographs anytime.'

Zola has no aversion to working with the kids at the Bridge. 'When I was a child, small though I was, my father's team let me play. It was such a prize for me to play with them. So now I love to help the youngsters. I pass on the prize. I don't want to be "Billy Bigtime" but if they are interested in what I'm trying to do, I'm happy to help.'

Frank Leboeuf, one of the sophisticates at the Bridge, has a column in *The Times* in which he wrote, 'It seems amazing that people were so quick to criticise Gianfranco Zola and say that he was not the same player as last season. He has shown that he is still the Zola who can turn games with a stroke of genius.'

The English contingent were equally in awe of Zola's talents. Skipper Dennis Wise says: 'I can say with confidence that Franco is the best player I've worked with. You can't afford to give him any space, he'll just say "see you later", and he's gone. Like a magic spinning top, the man is blessed in every way.' Franco just loved to hear such remarks from his skipper. 'Dennis says this? You know what I call him? "Midget"!' With that he laughs out loud.

Few journalists are afforded the privilege of an insight into the Zola family. Suzannah Dwyer is an exception. Partner of the powerful Chelsea chairman Zola calls 'Presidente' and a freelance football writer, Suzannah was commissioned by *Football Monthly* (owned by the Omnipotence of the Bridge himself) for a special for the December 97 issue. At the Zolas' Knightsbridge home, Franca and Franco curl up on a sofa. The Zola children are committed Chelsea fans – Andrea has his own kit and has already accompanied his famous dad in the bewildering world of the after-match press conference, while also being mentioned in dispatches when Zola took his first match ball after his hat-trick against Derby and worried that Andrea wanted to play with it in the local park.

His petite wife frets about her husband whenever he is confronted by one of the intimidatory Premiership defenders like Arsenal's iron man Steve Bould. Are they concerned? 'No,' says Franca decisively, 'no they are not.' Franco laughs, 'You must remember,' he says, 'to me everybody looks like Steve Bould. No, I am not afraid either.' The way he took punishment from Leeds' South African marker Lucas Radebe would bear that out.

But Franca is resigned to the physical dangers associated with his job. She says, 'He does not need to think that I worry. He will play anyway so I do not need to waste my energy this way.'

Zola feels his size can aid his particular skills, as he explains: 'One of the few advantages of my small size is that I have a low centre of gravity, it is not so easy for me to lose balance. I can twist away quickly and stay on my feet. Because I was not so tall, I had to build my physique. I am strong for my size, but I have to work very hard to achieve this. In the past people have said to me I was too small to play football. I prove them wrong, I think.'

More than that, of course. Chelsea stand on the verge of something special, and for Zola the recipe for such phenomenal success in a relatively short space of time is the harmony created by Gullit, whose methods at first created problems, but whose rotation system of a large, talented squad has finally become accepted within the dressing room. Zola says: 'One of the secrets that all the players who come to Chelsea and settle so quickly share is that we have such a wonderful atmosphere at the club. It's easy to tie the players together. I think that when you have a team, the first thing you have to do is build harmony. Then, when you have that, you can reach for great targets. Yes, in our team we have people with generous hearts. We know that we are thirty very good players, so sometimes, at certain times we play or sit on the bench. Of course we all want to play. Every game. But we also want the team to play well, even if we are on the bench. We are a team. We are all working towards a target. This target is achievable if everyone works together. And this is our secret.'

His affinity with the fans is one of his personal 'satisfactions'. He says: 'We, the players, we are living other people's dreams. This is a big responsibility for us all. I recognise that for the Chelsea supporter, my role is so very important. The supporter, he loves so much his team and it is . . . is . . . vital that I do my job well. But I must also be cool and stay balanced in my mind about the game. Before the match, I try to remember how I enjoyed playing as a child and bring that feeling with me to each game. It is important to play with joy. Our main target is to please the supporter. When I play, I am that supporter, playing as he wants me to play, as he dreams me to play. I must give to him his dream so that he feels, at that moment, he is playing. We are all such good spirits at Chelsea, such harmony, I am very happy to be here and be part of the team.'

Zola's popularity is universal among fans in British football. In the first fans' survey conducted by Premier League sponsors Carling, Zola was voted the most popular foreign star playing in the Premiership, second only to Eric Cantona who quit Manchester United at the end of the 96/97 season.

The results:

The top 10 Imports	Per cent of votes
Cantona	26.8
Zola	17.2
Bergkamp	16.6
Schmeichel	9.1
Juninho	7.7
Klinsmann	7.2
Asprilla	4.0
Solskjaer	2.2
Kanchelskis	1.1
Yorke	0.8